100 THINGS
RANGERS FANS
SHOULD KNOW & DO
BEFORE THEY DIE

Rusty Burson

TRIUMPH
BOOKS

Library of Congress has catalogued the previous edition as follows:

Burson, Rusty.
  100 things Rangers fans should know & do before they die / Rusty Burson.
     p. cm.
  ISBN 978-1-60078-642-6
  1. Texas Rangers (Baseball team)—History. 2. Texas Rangers (Baseball team)—Miscellanea. I. Title. II. Title: One hundred things Rangers fans should know and do before they die.
  GV875.T4B87 2011
  796.357'6409764531—dc23
                                        2011049408

This book is available in quantity at special discounts for your group or organization. For further information, contact:
  Triumph Books LLC
  814 North Franklin Street
  Chicago, Illinois 60610
  (312) 337-0747
  www.triumphbooks.com

Printed in U.S.A.
ISBN: 978-1-62937-413-0
Design by Patricia Frey

To my elderly neighbors on King Arthur Court in North Richland Hills who have long since passed away—Mr. Ingram, Mr. Butler, and Mr. Leach. They fostered my love for a great game and some not-so-great Rangers teams. Mr. Ingram talked baseball daily with me; Mr. Leach played catch with me during so many summer days; and Mr. Butler took me to so many Rangers games at old Arlington Stadium that I came to view the old dive as my second summer home. And to my wife, Vannessa, who has allowed me to brainwash our three kids, Payton, Kyleigh, and Summer, making them Rangers superfans. We don't watch all 162 games every year. But we come awfully close.

Contents

Foreword

Like every other Rangers fan, the book I hoped would be published after the conclusion of the 2016 season was one about us bringing home a World Series championship. While that's not in the works for us this particular winter, you can be assured that we will make every effort to see it written in the near future.

Until then, it's great to see books like this one that celebrate the colorful history and commemorate the past and present stars of the Texas Rangers. This was not a franchise that was well-known nationally in the early years in Arlington, but we are very proud that the Rangers have become one of the most successful franchises in MLB, on and off the field.

In 2016, we won our second consecutive American League West title and our seventh in franchise history. There were many great memories and successes, and in the end, many reminders of what we need to do to reach our primary goal—a World Series title for Arlington and the DFW Metroplex.

Our job as a baseball leadership team is to put the club in position to make it into the postseason year in and year out. We do that by prioritizing people first and creating an environment where our players and staff can thrive. We will continue doing that, and continue giving ourselves opportunities in the postseason tournament. Since 2010, we've won four AL West titles and claimed two American League pennants, and have played beyond the 162nd game in six of the seven seasons.

This book celebrates all of those years, as well as the great players, managers, and executives who have contributed to the franchise since first arriving in the Lone Star State in 1972. It also documents some of the leaner years in club history, which makes our recent run of success even more enjoyable for our great and loyal fan base.

Enjoy this stroll down Rangers Memory Lane and know that we will keep pushing to ensure there are more celebratory books about the Texas Rangers in the years to follow.

—Jon Daniels
General Manager, Texas Rangers

Introduction

I don't remember the score. I don't recall the opponent, either. Nor do I remember who pitched for the Rangers or whether the home team won. Considering that it was 1972, my guess is that the Rangers probably did not win, as that woeful bunch lost 100 games even in a shortened season.

But none of that mattered. What mattered was that I was with my dad. At a major league ballgame. And even though the '72 Rangers were awful and the old Arlington Stadium had a distinctively minor league feel to it, I treasured everything about my introduction to the Texas Rangers. I loved the sounds, the smells, the concessions, the manicured field, the Texas-shaped scoreboard and—most of all—being with my dad.

Neither of us knew the difference between a curveball and a fastball at the time, and neither of us could identify a single player in the home dugout. But we both enjoyed the experience enough to return the following year. And the next year. And every other year since then.

Somewhere along the way my dad, Russ Burson, became a much more knowledgeable baseball fan. And his son became a certifiable Rangers junkie.

So many of my childhood memories involve the Rangers. I vividly recall finally talking my mother, Vicki Pekurney, into going to a game several years later…and it hailed on us, but fortunately it was batting helmet–giveaway night, so we had some protection. I recall trying to wear my Jim Sundberg T-shirt—against my mother's wishes and demands—every day in the summer of '77, the season the Rangers won 94 games.

I have many memories of curling up next to my mom and dad's bedroom stereo and listening to virtually *every* game on WBAP with Jon Miller in the '70s and Eric Nadel and Mark Holtz in the '80s.

I planned my summers around Rangers giveaway nights, and bat night was a must on my summer to-do list. God only knows how many times my mom took me to Minyard's to redeem bat-night coupons or how many Rangers logos she sewed onto my T-shirts.

As soon as I could drive, I landed a job…at Arlington Stadium, of course. I worked in the concession stands initially and worked every year until I graduated from college in some capacity at the old Arlington Stadium. During one summer, I even landscaped the front yard of former Rangers manager Bobby Valentine.

I witnessed Nolan Ryan's 5,000th strikeout, and I languished through countless flameouts. I turned my wife, Vannessa Blasingame Burson, into an avid Rangers fan in the early and mid-1990s (we were in attendance for Kenny Rogers' night of perfection), and I had my infant son on my lap in front of the television in 1996 when the Rangers finally made the playoffs…and beat the damned Yankees in the first game of the ALDS.

For 14 years, that was the only playoff game the Rangers had ever won. Until October 2010, the Rangers were the only franchise to have never won a playoff series. But year after year—for 39 seasons—I told anyone who'd listen (mainly my wife, son, and two daughters): "If I could see the Rangers play in the World Series one time…"

Mission accomplished. I witnessed a World Series win in 2010 on my birthday. My wife was by my side, so close to the top of the stadium that we could practically feel the heat of the fireworks when Mitch Moreland roped a three-run homer off Jonathan Sanchez. My teenaged son was in another section of Rangers Ballpark in Arlington with one of my best childhood friends. We may have all shed tears of joy that night.

I paid way too much for tickets located next to the moon, but it was worth every penny. Seeing the Rangers beat the Giants in Game 3 was more of a thrill ride than I'd ever experienced on a roller coaster at nearby Six Flags.

The incomparable thrill of that lone victory in 2010 was followed by the sheer agony of the seven-game World Series defeat in 2011. The 10–9 loss to the Cardinals in Game 6 will torment me forever, causing intermittent queasiness like a recurring illness.

While the heartache of that oh-so-close loss still hasn't faded, neither have the Rangers. Behind fiery manager Jeff Bannister and general manager Jon Daniels, Texas is coming off back-to-back division titles in 2015 and '16. While there is no guarantee of an imminent World Series title in Arlington, I am reassured by the realization that the Rangers—at long last—are relevant regionally, nationally, and even internationally.

They are no longer the not-so-lovable pushovers whose primary purpose was once to entertain local sports fans until the Cowboys' training camp started in July. To fully appreciate the improved national perception, regional appeal, and international reach of the modern-day Rangers, you need to possess an understanding of just how bad and how absolutely irrelevant the Rangers were once perceived…even in the local marketplace.

That's the point of this book: to celebrate the greatest accomplishments, to highlight the most fascinating personalities, and to document the most miserable moments in the history of the franchise. They have all contributed to making the Rangers what they are today. And whether you have been a Rangers lifer like me or you are a recent convert, this tour of the most mesmerizing events in Rangers history will undoubtedly give you a greater appreciation for the recent run to the national spotlight.

In writing and ranking the items in this book, I leaned heavily—either from personal interviews or well-written stories—on the expertise of longtime Rangers experts like beat writers Jim Reeves and T.R. Sullivan; Rangers radio play-by-play voice Eric Nadel; Mr. Ranger Tom Grieve; stadium public address announcer Chuck Morgan; and Mr. Rangers Internet expert, Jamey Newberg. I also dug through volumes of stories in the *Sports Illustrated* Vault, uncovering long-forgotten nuggets and gems from the best and worst of times in Rangers history.

I can't thank all of the contributors enough. This would not be the same without all of their help and outstanding work.

I also thank my neighbors and a whole bunch of other folks for taking me to so many Rangers games long ago. I first dreamed of becoming a sportswriter as I read the daily game stories in the *Fort Worth Star-Telegram* sports section—as a kindergartner.

I grew to love players such as Sundberg, Ryan, Toby Harrah, Buddy Bell, Mickey Rivers, Al Oliver, Pudge Rodriguez, Rusty Greer, Julio Franco, Michael Young, Adrian Beltre, and many others. It would have been much easier to have been a Yankees fan, but I wouldn't change a thing.

The Yankees were winning World Series titles long before I was born. And before my parents were born. If I'd have grown up as a Yankees, Cardinals, or Dodgers fan, I would have never learned so many valuable lessons that the Rangers taught me about patience, perspective, and persistence amid perspiration in the searing summertime heat. Nor would I have learned to appreciate the simple things in life such as merely being in the playoff hunt in September.

Being a Rangers lifer hasn't always been easy. But it has given me many great memories. It has also qualified me to write this book.

Thanks again, Dad, for taking me to that first game so many years ago. Ultimately, this is all a byproduct of that first father-son outing.

1 Salute Tom Vandergriff Whenever Possible

Any list that documents, celebrates, or otherwise pays homage to the history of the Texas Rangers would be woefully incomplete and erroneously deficient without Tommy Joe Vandergriff's name on top of it.

The Rangers would have never relocated from Washington, D.C., and settled in Arlington without Vandergriff's tireless efforts. For that matter, Arlington wouldn't be Arlington—at least not as it is known today—without the leadership and vision of Vandergriff, who died December 30, 2010, at the age of 84.

Vandergriff not only brought big-time baseball to North Texas; he also played major roles in attracting Six Flags Over Texas and a General Motors assembly plant to the city, where he served as mayor for 26 years. His name is synonymous with Arlington's development as a major sports market and with its expansion as one of the 50 most populous cities in the country.

Saluting his statue in Vandergriff Plaza at Globe Life Park in Arlington and telling your children all about this legendary man is practically a duty for all Rangers' fans. Tom's grandfather, a blacksmith named J.T. Vandergriff, first entered the auto industry in 1912 by repairing "horseless carriages." And it was Tom's father, W.T. (Hooker) Vandergriff, who first opened his Chevrolet dealership on the corner of Division and Center Streets in Arlington in 1937 and later added a Buick dealership in town.

Dutifully, Tom Vandergriff returned to Arlington after earning his bachelor's degree at the University of Southern California in 1947 and working in radio in Chicago and Southern California.

He briefly worked in his father's dealerships in the late 1940s. But automotive sales never drove Tom. He had bigger visions in mind.

In 1950, for example, he received a tip that General Motors was looking to build a new assembly plant in the middle of the country. But he didn't think GM would take a phone call from the 24-year-old president of the Arlington Chamber of Commerce. He then decided to run for mayor in 1951…and won. At the time of his election, Arlington had a population of less than 8,000, but a record number of voters (999) cast their ballots for Vandergriff.

Shortly thereafter, General Motors took a phone call from Mayor Vandergriff. He then secured an agreement for the state to build a road, now State Highway 360, to lead to the new assembly plant. The $33 million facility opened in 1953.

Successes like that one, along with the $6 million bond issue he pushed through to form Lake Arlington in 1957, raised

Arlington mayor Tom Vandergriff, left, exchanges congratulations with Washington Senators owner Robert E. Short after it was announced that the Senators would relocate to Arlington for the 1972 season. (AP Images)

Vandergriff's confidence to pursue a personal passion: luring big-league baseball to town.

On October 7, 1959, Arlington voters approved a $9.5 million bond issue to build a stadium, and construction on the original 10,000-seat Turnpike Stadium began in September 1964. But the major league vision was still a long way from coming to fruition. Numerous roadblocks were constantly thrown in Vandergriff's path in the 13 years he actively pursued a team.

Vandergriff was once tossed from a cab because the driver in Washington, D.C., learned who he was and that he intended to meet with Senators majority owner Bob Short to discuss relocation to Texas. Judge Roy Hofheinz, owner of the Houston Astros, also attempted to block the move of a second team to Texas. Even President Richard Nixon once tried to stop the move.

While Vandergriff visited with Short in Washington, D.C., Nixon allegedly sent his son-in-law to Short's offices to encourage the Senators' owner to stay in the nation's capital. During the brief meeting between Short and Nixon's son-in-law, Vandergriff hid in an office closet.

Persistence paid off when, on September 20, 1971, Short received approval from American League owners to move the franchise from Washington, D.C., to Arlington for the 1972 season.

"Simply put, he may have been the greatest man I've ever known," former *Fort Worth Star-Telegram* columnist Jim Reeves wrote on ESPNDallas.com on the day Vandergriff died. "Without Vandergriff, it's hard to conceive what Arlington would be today. There would no General Motors or Six Flags. The Texas Rangers would never have left the nation's capital for a little-known 'hyphen' between Dallas and Fort Worth. And without the Rangers, it's pretty safe to say that the Dallas Cowboys wouldn't have given the city a second glance. Vandergriff made it all happen, sometimes seemingly almost single-handedly.

"He lived long enough to see his beloved Rangers clinch a World Series berth against the hated New York Yankees, and those who saw him there—he watched every home game of the ALDS and American League Championship Series from the city of Arlington's suite at The Ballpark—say the smile never left his face."

Fittingly, the Rangers presented the first American League championship rings in franchise history to the Vandergriff family on March 31, 2011, at the welcome home luncheon—two days before the Texas players, coaches, and support staff received their rings. The Rangers also honored Vandergriff throughout the 2011 season with his picture prominently displayed on the outfield wall in left field.

Bringing Nolan Ryan (the Player) to Arlington

In American history, December 7 is a day that will live in infamy. In Texas Rangers history, it's commemorated far more joyfully.

Exactly 47 years after the Japanese sent shockwaves around the globe by bombing Pearl Harbor—the event that triggered the United States' official involvement in World War II—the Rangers dropped a bombshell of their own in an effort to finally join the World Series foray. On December 7, 1988, the Rangers announced the free-agent signing of pitcher and native Texan Nolan Ryan. The headlines from that announcement didn't jolt the globe, but they rocked the baseball world.

Because of the continuing impact Ryan had on the organization as a player, fan attraction, president, and CEO, that December day in '88 could be considered one of the most momentous in Rangers history.

"Huge," said Tom Grieve, the Rangers' general manager when Ryan signed with Texas. "Nolan brought credibility to our franchise. With Nolan Ryan in a Rangers uniform, the Rangers had arrived as a respected major league franchise. It boosted our exposure in Texas and across the country. The five years he spent as a player for us were invaluable."

While Ryan may have been the most important personnel acquisition in Rangers history, the signing of the strikeout king came as at least somewhat of a surprise nationally because no one initially expected him to leave the Houston Astros, where he'd spent nine exceptional years and was particularly close to his family's hometown in Alvin.

But in what was probably the most regrettable decision in his career as the owner of the Astros, the late John McMullen decided that, at 41, Ryan was too old to earn the millions it would take to re-sign him. Astros fans were livid; Rangers officials leapt into action.

The Rangers weren't necessarily desperate for frontline pitching. Although Texas endured a dreadful '88 season, it was not the pitching staff's fault. Texas' 1988 pitching staff allowed the fewest hits in the American League. But the offense was as stagnant as the Rangers' annual payroll—at $6.5 million, one of the lowest in the majors.

In the fall of '88, Grieve and team president Mike Stone developed plans to upgrade the team's talent and then appealed to majority owner Eddie Chiles and Texas' chief minority owner, Edward Gaylord, for a $4 million increase in the payroll to $10.5 million.

Chiles, who'd owned the Rangers since 1980 and had been looking to sell them, agreed. "If that's what you need, you got it," Chiles said.

Grieve first made a couple of major trades at the winter meetings in Atlanta, bringing Rafael Palmeiro, who finished second in the National League in hitting (.307) in 1988, and starting pitcher Jamie Moyer from the Cubs. He then dealt with the Cleveland

Rangers on the Cover of *Sports Illustrated*

Throughout their history, the Rangers have rarely been considered newsworthy on a national level. As such, the franchise (dating back to the first year in Washington) had been featured on the cover of the nation's most popular sports-related magazine, *Sports Illustrated*, only nine times in its first 51 years (1961–2011).

In comparison, Michael Jordan had appeared on 60 Sports Illustrated covers by 2011, while the Dallas Cowboys had made it onto the *SI* cover 68 times (including regional editions) by the start of 2011 football training camps.

Hopefully, the Rangers are on track to becoming more of a national name under the direction of an ownership team fronted by the legendary Nolan Ryan. That alone should help the Rangers land on the cover of *SI* more frequently in the years ahead, as Ryan already leads the franchise in cover appearances.

Ryan first appeared on the cover of the magazine in a Rangers uniform on the May 1, 1989, edition, accompanying a headline that read: "TEXAS HEAT: The Amazing Nolan Ryan Leads the Red-Hot Rangers."

Ryan was again the cover feature on the April 15, 1991, baseball edition. The headline: "MIRACLE MAN: Ageless Nolan Ryan Launches His 25th Season." Less than a month later, Ryan was again on the cover, although Roger Clemens was the main feature. But in the top corner of the May 13 edition was a small picture of Ryan next to this headline: "UNHITTABLE: Nolan Ryan's Magnificent Seventh."

Technically, the first person in franchise history to ever appear on the cover of *SI* was Ted Williams, on the March 17, 1969, edition next to the headline that read: "Ted Williams Tackles His Problems."

The first person in a Rangers uniform on the cover of *SI* was manager Billy Martin on June 2, 1975. The cover read: "BASEBALL'S FIERY GENIUS." Inside the magazine, in an article written by Frank Deford, Martin, then in his second season with the Rangers, said: "It's been a truthful relationship here with everybody. I have a real foundation here. I think I'll stay here for the rest of my career."

Not quite. He was replaced 95 games into the 1975 season.

The first Rangers player on the SI cover was Bump Wills in March 1977. A little more than 20 years later, Pudge Rodriguez appeared in August 1997, and Josh Hamilton made it onto a June

2008 cover. In the run to the 2011 World Series, Nelson Cruz was an *SI* cover boy on October 24, which also included a front-cover teaser prediction of who would win the Fall Classic.

SI went with Texas in six. So, the noted *SI* cover jinx has officially worked against the Rangers.

Rangers catcher Yorvit Torrealba and Cardinals outfielder Jon Jay were featured on the October 31, 2011, cover under the headline: "Heart and Soul: A great World Series unfolds."

That's it as far as featured covers go, but Billy Martin was photographed for a May 1985 cover at Arlington Stadium...as a Yankees skipper. And the *SI* cover jinx worked to the Rangers' advantage at the start of the 2010 playoffs, when Tampa Bay's David Price appeared on the cover of the October 11, 2010, edition. Price lost both games he pitched in that series.

Indians for second baseman Julio Franco, a .309 hitter over the previous three seasons.

Those two trades made the Rangers better. But when it also became clear that Ryan was available, Grieve went for the biggest move. At least four other teams were also interested in signing Ryan, including the Angels, where he'd starred from 1972 to 1979.

Grieve says 40 percent of the additional budget went toward signing Ryan to a guaranteed $2 million contract for the 1989 season—with an option for an additional year. That instantly made him the highest-paid player in franchise history, and he was worth every penny.

Ryan was an ideal complement to the Rangers' young starters—Bobby Witt, 25, and Kevin Brown, 24, and Moyer, 26. He was also an intriguing contrast to knuckleballer Charlie Hough. Thanks primarily to Ryan, attendance jumped from 1,885,166 in 1988 to 2,101,700 the following year. It was the first time in club history the team drew more than 2 million fans.

"When we signed Nolan Ryan, people said, 'The Rangers are making a public relations statement, they're just trying to sell tickets,'" Grieve told T.R. Sullivan of MLB.com years later. "The reality of the situation is that John Young, our major league scout, said Nolan Ryan was one of the five best pitchers in the National League and could be one of the five best pitchers in the American League. Young said, 'Sign him, put him in the rotation, and we'll be a better team.' That came true, given the way he pitched that first year."

Ryan was 16–10 with a 3.20 ERA in 1989, setting a Rangers record with 301 strikeouts and taking no-hitters into the ninth inning twice.

During his five years with the Rangers, Ryan threw two no-hitters, won his 300th game, and struck out his 5,000th batter. By 1993, Ryan's last year, the Rangers drew slightly more than 2.4 million fans. Undoubtedly, Ryan's five-year tenure in Arlington was a significant factor in the Rangers being able to generate enough public funding for the new Rangers Ballpark in Arlington.

And it wasn't just the Rangers and their fans that benefited from having Ryan in Arlington. He thoroughly enjoyed his tenure with Texas. Even though he spent only five of his 27 total major league seasons with Texas, Ryan wore a Rangers hat into the Baseball Hall of Fame in 1999.

"Those five years I spent with the Rangers were probably the most enjoyable of my career because of the way the fans embraced my family and I," Ryan said. "They really made us welcome."

3 Bringing Nolan Ryan (the Executive) Back to Arlington

When documenting the Rangers' typically tainted and sometimes torturous past or detailing some of the more dreadful and damaging decisions in club history, Dallas–Fort Worth media members and fans often toss Tom Hicks' name onto the grill for a full-scale barbecuing.

Hicks has been roasted, broiled, and burned for years by Rangers followers for everything from the signing of Alex Rodriguez in 2000 to the ballclub's bankruptcy woes a decade later. In 2009 *Sports Illustrated* ranked Hicks as the second-worst owner in baseball (ahead of only Baltimore's Peter Angelos).

While Hicks certainly earned much of the criticism that has followed him, it should be noted that he also was instrumental in one of the most positive decisions in team history. In February 2008 Hicks returned respectability to the Rangers and infused the entire organization with optimism by hiring Nolan Ryan as team president. Ryan, then 61, became the first Hall of Fame player to be named as president of a major league franchise since Christy Mathewson in 1925 with the Boston Braves.

It was a home run move for the Rangers, as Ryan proved to be so much more than a mere figurehead. He's been a mentor, a teacher, and a tone-setter, instilling toughness and increasing expectations throughout the clubhouse and the farm system. By 2010 Ryan's leadership had also proven to be instrumental in taking the Rangers all the way to the World Series. He had also become part of the team's ownership group and had added the title of CEO.

In other words, Hicks deserves a little credit for bringing Ryan back to the fold. If Hicks hadn't made the move in '08, Ryan probably would have eventually landed with the Astros.

"The reason I took this job is that it's a window of opportunity that would probably never present itself again under the guidelines in which I would require, and that would be either with the Houston organization or with the Rangers organization," Ryan said in February 2008, as reported by Alan Eskew of MLB.com. "At my age and this point in my life, it's a good opportunity for me and I always wanted to do something of this nature in baseball.... If we were able to put a winner together and build consistency in this organization, and bring it from where it's been in the last eight to 10 years to being a consistent contender and being in the playoffs that would be very rewarding."

Obviously, Ryan and the Rangers did just that, beginning with the 2010 and '11 postseason runs. One of the primary reasons the team was able to make those runs was the pitching mentality that Ryan has mandated. In 2008 the Rangers scored the most runs in the majors, but they also allowed the most. As a result, Texas finished 21 games out of first.

Following the '08 season, Mike Maddux was hired as the Rangers' new pitching coach, and Ryan began stressing the importance of starting pitchers going deeper into games. Merely throwing 90 pitches or lasting six innings was not sufficient, Ryan told his pitchers. And to handle the Texas heat, they would be required to train harder, emphasizing sprinting over distance running and throwing live batting practice throughout spring training. Pitchers would also perform more long tossing and coaches would pay more attention to the stress of each outing, not simply the number of pitches thrown.

"He really transformed the mind-set of the entire organization's pitching staff," said Rangers radio broadcaster Eric Nadel. "As a player, Nolan was a guy who worked out exceptionally hard and stayed in terrific shape. He made that an expectation from the pitchers, and he instilled in them the belief that they could thrive in the heat and go deeper into ballgames. That mentality has definitely made a difference."

Ryan made a positive and significant difference in many other areas, as well, but the end of his run with the Rangers came to an awkward halt in October 2013, after Texas failed to reach the postseason for the first time since 2009.

On March 1, 2013, Rangers co-chairmen Ray Davis and Bob Simpson announced that Jon Daniels had assumed one of Ryan's titles, president of baseball operations. Ryan later acknowledged that he considered resigning at that point. But the uncomfortable end didn't come until October 17, 2013, at a hastily assembled, 25-minute news conference where Ryan was flanked by Davis and Simpson.

Perhaps the beginning of the end came following the 2012 season when, after an extremely disappointing end to the regular season, the Rangers were beaten in the Wild Card playoff game at home by Baltimore. Following that season, Daniels wanted to fire bench coach Jackie Moore. Ryan, who had hired Moore, did not.

"When Daniels and Ryan couldn't agree, they took the issue to ownership, which sided with Daniels," wrote MLB,com columnist Richard Justice. "Rightly or wrongly, Ryan believed that he was now nothing more than a glorified mascot while Daniels had the real power....Ryan spent most of spring training [in 2013] contemplating leaving the franchise. In the end, he decided to stay for a while longer. Almost no one involved with the Rangers thought the relationship would last. Still, when Ryan announced what the club called a retirement on October 17, 2013, it was stunning."

In a move that was not at all stunning, it was announced in February 2014 that Ryan has decided to join the Houston Astros organization as an executive adviser to his son, Reid, the president of business operations, owner Jim Crane and general manager Jeff Luhnow.

In 2014, the Astros began a major turnaround in the right direction, while the Rangers suffered their worst season since 1985, which led many media members and fans to proclaim that the Rangers had fallen victim to the curse of Nolan Ryan.

Michael Young: The Face of the Franchise

Prior to the 2010–11 seasons, a strong case probably could have been made for Ivan "Pudge" Rodriguez, Juan Gonzalez, Jim Sundberg, Nolan Ryan, and possibly a few of the team's other Hall of Famers in any discussion regarding the MVP in the Rangers' 40-year history in Texas.

There really isn't any doubt now, though. Now that Michael Young, a seven-time All-Star, retired as the franchise leader in games, hits (2,230), at-bats (7,399), runs (1,085), doubles (415), triples (55), totals bases (3,286), multi-hit games (651) and infield hits (209). Now that he played every infield position. Now that he led the two greatest teams in Texas history to their first two American League pennants.

In my book, Young is the all-time MVP of the franchise. Case closed.

No Texas player has ever been more versatile in the field or more consistent at the plate than Young, a line drive–hitting model of dependability for more than a decade. He played second base, shortstop, third base, and first, while also serving as the designated hitter for the first time in 2011, when he tied Boston's Adrian Gonzalez for the most hits in the American League with 213. And he was consistently at his best in clutch situations, driving the ball to the opposite field with the steady productivity of an assembly line.

"He's meant everything to us," Rangers manager Ron Washington said in 2011. "He's the face of the Texas Rangers. He's the one guy you would like to model yourself after. He shows up every day. He's a pro in the way he goes about his business."

Young, who retired at age 37 after playing 12 of his 13 MLB seasons as a Ranger, represents one of the greatest trades Texas ever made and one of the best deals the team never completed.

On July 19, 2000, Rangers general manager Doug Melvin traded pitcher Esteban Loaiza to the Blue Jays for the 23-year-old Young and pitcher Darwin Cubillan. The Blue Jays were 1½ games

The Rangers' all-time leader in games played, hits, doubles, and triples, Michael Young started at second base, shortstop, third base, and designated hitter.
(AP Images)

out of first place, and Loaiza pitched fairly well for Toronto, going 5–7 in 14 starts with a 3.62 ERA. It was not enough to propel Toronto into the playoffs.

Meanwhile, the Rangers sent Young to Double A Tulsa, where they hoped he'd blossom as a solid player. They never imagined he'd become a star.

"We thought he had a chance to be a regular player," said Melvin, who suggested at the time, according to longtime MLB. com correspondent Jamey Newberg, that Young could develop into a Mark Loretta–type. "But we didn't think he'd be an All-Star."

Young proved otherwise. By May 2001, he was in the major leagues for good, serving as the Rangers' second baseman next to shortstop Alex Rodriguez. He hit .300 for the first time in 2003, made his first All-Star team in '04, and led the American League in hitting in '05.

He switched from second base to shortstop in 2004 after the Rangers traded Rodriguez to the Yankees. Four losing seasons followed in the next five years, and the Rangers asked Young to move to third to accommodate rookie Elvis Andrus in 2009. He played well at third for two years, and after playing 1,508 regular-season games without a playoff appearance, Young helped to lead the Rangers past the Rays in the ALDS and past the Yankees in the ALCS to reach the 2010 World Series.

The following off-season was not exactly a victory tour. Texas signed two-time Gold Glove winner Adrian Beltre in January 2011 to play third base, where he won another Gold Glove in 2011. Young said at the time of the trade that he would make the sacrifice to move to DH. But after Texas showed interest in potential DHs Jim Thome and Manny Ramirez before trading for Mike Napoli, a catcher/first baseman/DH, Young said he felt betrayed by general manager Jon Daniels and asked to be traded.

The Rangers tried to oblige. Fortunately for the team, Young's contract, which guaranteed $46 million through 2013, proved to be too much for any serious trade talks.

When Young reported to Arizona for spring training in 2011, he told teammates he wouldn't be a distraction and was focused on preparing for the season. He did just that, and he was easily the most consistent player on the everyday roster in 2011.

Playing 159 games at various positions, Young led the Rangers with a .338 batting average—his career best. He also became the first player in major league history to collect 200 hits in a season while starting at least 30 games at three different positions. Young had such a good year in 2011 that at one point, Napoli ordered a box of T-shirts for his teammates with this message on the back: "Hit like Mike." And after a dismal start to the 2011 postseason, Young still managed to collect 16 hits and 12 RBIs in 17 postseason games.

"Michael is incredible," Beltre said. "He just goes out and does the same things, day after day, year after year."

"He's remained a great player in his transition," Yankees manager Joe Girardi added in 2011. "I think he's appreciated by the people who are in the game, but maybe for all the fans who don't get to see him play a lot, maybe they don't understand how good he really is."

In December 2012, the Rangers dealt Young to Philadelphia for right-handed reliever Josh Lindblom and minor league righty Lisalverto Bonilla. Young split his final season (2013) between the Phillies and Dodgers.

In January 2014, however, Young returned to Arlington, where he stood in front of a gaggle of Rangers personnel—from coaches and front office to clubhouse attendants—and officially ended his playing career.

"My time in Texas is 13 of the best years of my life," Young said at the news conference. "It was my honor to be able to play for them [the fans] on a daily basis. I owe this community everything."

Fortunately for everyone, the Rangers announced in November 2014 that they had finalized a deal to bring Young back to the organization as a special assistant to general manager Jon Daniels. Young has been instrumental in the development of some of the youthful players in the organization, and he played a role in luring free agent outfielder Ian Desmond to sign with Texas for the 2016 season.

On July 30, 2016, Young became the 20th member inducted into the Rangers Hall of Fame. "I blinked and 17 professional seasons kind of flew by and here I am," Young said during the Rangers Hall of Fame Luncheon. "One thing that helps is that I still have the energy and the role in the organization. For me, that makes the time spent with this organization so much more productive. I'm lucky for that."

Rangers' fans were lucky to watch Young for all those seasons. Additionally, Young's impact on the field was equaled by his involvement in the community off the field. He was a two-time Marvin Miller Man of the Year Award winner, and he and his wife serve on the board of directors for the Texas Rangers Baseball Foundation.

"You were always one of my favorite players to watch throughout my career," for Yankees' legend Derek Jeter said of Young during a video tribute during the induction ceremony. "This just goes to show you're one of the greatest to put on a Rangers uniform of all time."

Perhaps even the greatest of all time. Others have produced flashier years in a Texas uniform, but no one has performed multiple roles with more reliability and professionalism than Michael Young...the Rangers' all-time MVP.

5 Remember the 2011 Series Run, Not How It Came Undone

You obviously wouldn't be reading this book if you didn't have a deep connection with the Rangers. And if you care about the Rangers, you will never, ever forget the sheer agony, the absolute anguish, the gut-wrenching, stomach-churning grief, and the head-shaking, sleep-depriving torment of Game 6 of the 2011 World Series.

What if Nelson Cruz had caught David Freese's two-out, two-strike deep fly to right? What if Neftali Feliz would've been given another shot at redemption in the 10th after blowing a save in the ninth? What if Scott Feldman could have finished off Lance "Freaking" Berkman on a 1–2 pitch in the 10th?

Exhale. Deep, calming, cleansing breaths. This memory will cause pain for a long time. Like forever.

Ask Red Sox fans about Game 6 of the 1986 World Series, when they had the Mets on the ropes with a 5–3 lead in the 10th. Ask Giants fans about Game 6 in 2002, when San Francisco led 5–0 over the Angels entering the bottom of the seventh.

Oh, what might have been. As the network television commercials routinely remind us throughout the postseason: legends are born in October. Unfortunately, that's also when gut-shot wounds are administered..

The scars from those penetrating wounds never completely heal. But they are a little easier for those fan bases to stomach now that the Red Sox have won a pair of World Series titles in 2004 and '07 and the Giants claimed the 2010 Fall Classic.

Hopefully, it will one day be that way for the Rangers.

It will never be easy to replay Game 6 of the 2011 World Series in your mind or to re-watch on your television (and rest assured, it

will be replayed over and over again as long as you live). Not when
the Rangers were so close that you could practically taste the ginger
ale bath. Not when they had a three-run lead in the bottom of the
eighth. Not when they were one measly strike away from a World
Series title...twice.

But here's the point to remember: great sports pain often pre-
cedes championship champagne.

There are hundreds of citable examples throughout sports
history to verify that point, but we'll stick to the neighborhood.
The team that now plays across the street from the Rangers in Jerry
World is often labeled as "America's Team." Back in the 1960s,
though, the late Steve Perkins penned a book about the Cowboys
called *Next Year's Champions*.

The book, released in 1969, detailed the heartbreaking championship game losses to the Packers at the end of the 1966 and
'67 seasons, along with the conference championship game loss to
the Browns the following year. The title of the book became the
nickname of the team...until the Cowboys won Super Bowl VI and
forever changed the image of the franchise.

Shortly thereafter, Perkins wrote another book called *Winning
the Big One*, which documented how rewarding it was to win the
1971 title after enduring all the anguish in the late 1960s.

There are no guarantees that the Rangers will ease the pain of
their near-miss in 2011 by repeating the championship feats of the
Cowboys. Or the Red Sox. Or the Giants. Or even Dirk Nowitzki's
Dallas Mavericks, who made the playoffs 10 straight years before
winning it all. The championship window of opportunity was sup-
posedly shut on the Mavs before they finally broke through.

If you choose to look back on the 2011 World Series as part of
the maturation process of the franchise instead of viewing it merely
as the most agonizing end to a season in Rangers history, it makes
it much easier to fully appreciate all that the team accomplished in
a rather remarkable season.

The 2011 Rangers won more regular-season games (96) than any other team in franchise history; they won 12 in a row in July, and with the Angels closing in the American League West standings at the end of August, they went 19–6 in September to blow Los Angeles away and secure the No. 2 playoff seed in the American League; they rebounded from a crushing defeat in the opener of the ALDS to beat the Rays in three consecutive nail-biting wins; they rode Nelson Cruz's bat and the remarkable efforts of the bullpen past Cy Young candidate Justin Verlander and the Tigers in the ALCS; they pushed the 10-time World Series champion Cardinals to the brink of elimination with gutsy comebacks, gritty pitching performances, and Mike Napoli's heroics; and they won more post-season games (10) than any team in franchise history, playing in a Game 7 for the first time ever.

As Jamey Newberg, the longtime daily chronicler of the Rangers wrote so eloquently in his end-of-2011 *Newberg Report:*

"In beating St. Louis three times and lining up at the goal line for a decisive fourth win, the Rangers recorded 107 outs, some in ways I'll never forget, and put themselves in great position to get that 107th and final win of 2011, to finish off the 107th World Series. The inability to get that final strike, that final out, that final win, will unfortunately be what sticks, because the whole point of this game is to win championships. But that doesn't diminish the greatness of the season…. This season might be the hardest I've ever had to say goodbye to, and may always be that, largely because of how it ended, which I don't plan on getting used to, but also because I've never been more fulfilled as a sports fan as I was by the 2011 Texas Rangers."

Indeed, it was better to have loved and lost Game 6 (and Game 7) with this team than to have never fully opened your heart and poured your sports soul into the pulse-quickening, knot-in-your-throat reality that your Rangers were within a whisker—one strike in back-to-back, chest-pounding innings of tension—of being called "world champions."

For now, the label "next year's champions" must suffice. But at least there's a positive precedent for that. Remember the journey, and remember that the Rangers' window is wide open.

6 Sit Down, A-Rod: Closing Game 6 of the 2010 ALCS

From a theatrical standpoint, perhaps the ending of the deciding Game 6 of the 2010 American League Championship Series could have been more fittingly dramatic if the potential winning run had been in scoring position. Or if that runner had been another former Texas Rangers player—like Mark Teixeira—who'd also chosen to leave Arlington.

Even without those added storylines, however, Hollywood would likely have approved of the grand finale of the Cinderella-like tale of how the Rangers won their first-ever American League pennant.

One out away from reaching the organization's first World Series and ending 39 years of frustration in Arlington—50 years overall, including the franchise's origins as the Washington Senators—the Rangers had rookie closer Neftali Feliz on the mound before a towel-waving, combustible crowd of 51,404 inside Rangers Ballpark in Arlington.

Feliz, a composed righty who won 2010 Rookie of the Year honors, was one of the key acquisitions from the 2007 trade that sent Teixeira to Atlanta and energized Texas' farm system with talented prospects. Feliz represented a change in philosophy for the franchise, embodying a wiser financial game plan and Nolan Ryan's commitment to developing pitchers. Perhaps Feliz also signified the end of the decades-long approach of acquiring big bats at the expense of every other aspect of the team.

Stepping into the batter's box for the New York Yankees—the team that had eliminated Texas in all three of its previous playoff forays—was Alex Rodriguez, the symbol of everything that went wrong for the franchise under former owner Tom Hicks. If you were looking to pinpoint one reason above all others that Hicks was broke—the Rangers had been in bankruptcy throughout much of the 2010 season and Texas entered the year with the 27th-lowest payroll in the major leagues—you could start with A-Rod.

It wasn't Rodriguez's fault; he merely signed the ridiculous 10-year, $252 million contract that Hicks presented him in December 2000. Rodriguez was also one of the largest unsecured creditors owed money by the Rangers in the messy bankruptcy case in the summer of 2010 before a group led by Ryan and Chuck Greenberg bought the team from Hicks in an auction. Rodriguez was owed about $25 million in deferred compensation for his three seasons in Texas.

It certainly seemed appropriate that one of the key faces of the new-and-improved Rangers squared off against the undeniable face of the franchise from 2001 to 2003, when Texas went a combined 216–270 and finished a combined 99 games out of first place in the American League West.

New school versus old guard. Flamethrower versus former franchise flame. What irony for the Arlington crowd. How intriguing for the national television audience. What a storyline for the media covering the game.

As a side note, it should probably be pointed out that it was hardly a do-or-die situation for Feliz. The Rangers led 6–1 heading into the top of the ninth, and Feliz had already struck out Curtis Granderson to open the ninth and followed up by inducing

A-Rod's Secretive Signs While with the Rangers

For the most part, Alex Rodriguez was applauded by Texas for everything he did on the field during his three seasons with the Rangers. He produced exceptional numbers, he hustled, and he did all the "little things" to win favor with the fans.

Some of the little things he did without the fans noticing, however, made him far less popular in the clubhouse. In a 2009 *Sports Illustrated* article, some former Rangers players told Selena Roberts that in lopsided losses (and for the Rangers, there were plenty), A-Rod would occasionally violate a sacred clubhouse code by tipping pitches to opposing middle infielders.

"From his shortstop vantage point, he would tip pitches to the batter at the plate in a quid pro quo," Roberts wrote. "It would always be a middle infielder, who could reciprocate."

"It would be a friend of his, a buddy who maybe had gone 0-for-3 and needed a hit," one former player told Roberts. "Alex would see the catcher's signs. He'd signal the pitch to the hitter, do a favor for him. And down the line, Alex would expect the same in return."

Allegedly, Rodriguez would never tip pitches when the game was in doubt, but if it was a blowout, he would deliver signs from shortstop after he had seen what pitch had been called by the Rangers' catcher.

"It wasn't like he did it to throw a game—that wasn't it at all—but he did it to help himself," said a former Ranger. "He didn't care if it killed his own guys. It was about stats for Alex: his."

Rodriguez expected the same gifts in return. If he was hitless near the end of a blowout game, he could look to a buddy in the middle infield for a sign. "Here was the game's best player, and yet he felt he needed this," said another former player.

Robinson Cano, easily New York's most dangerous hitter in the series, into a groundout.

It was obvious, however, that the rookie wanted to end the game against A-Rod. Feliz's first pitch, a ball up high, was a four-seam fastball that was clocked at 100 mph on the radar. He then threw back-to-back 99 mph fastballs, one for a called strike, the next fouled back to the screen.

With the crowd growing more feverish on every pitch, Rodriguez dug in, wiggled his bat, and obviously guessed fastball.

Wrong.

Feliz threw a wicked curve. A-Rod froze. Home-plate umpire Brian Gorman called, "strike three," and pandemonium inside the ballpark ensued.

Red fireworks immediately burst high into the air, as Pat Green's "I Like Texas" blared across the public address system and a dog pile of celebrating Rangers formed in the infield.

"This is going to hurt," Rodriguez told *The New York Times* after the game. "It's going to hurt for a while. And it should."

Meanwhile, on the other side, it will be remembered fittingly and fondly forever more.

Ivan "Pudge" Rodriguez: Teen to Texas Legend

Ivan Rodriguez won a World Series with the Florida Marlins in 2003, appeared in another Fall Classic with the Detroit Tigers in '06, and had—at last count in 2011—played for six different teams since making his major league debut in 1991.

But don't be confused with the journeyman nature of the latter half of his career. Pudge will undoubtedly enter the Baseball Hall of Fame in Cooperstown one day with a *T* on his hat.

From 1993 to 2001, Chuck Norris was the fictional Texas Ranger. Throughout that time period—and even before and after—Pudge was the real one.

The Puerto Rican–born Rodriguez signed with the Rangers when he was 16 years old. He was practically raised in the team's farm system, making his professional debut with the Gastonia

Rangers of the South Atlantic League in 1989. And he made his first start with Texas on June 20, 1991, at the age of 19, catching Kevin Brown in a 7–3 win at Comiskey Park.

For the remainder of that season and the next 11, Rodriguez guided the Rangers to their first three playoff appearances, represented the team in 10 All-Star Games, earned 10 Gold Gloves, picked up six Silver Slugger Awards, and won the 1999 American League MVP. He was a terrific hitter for Texas, hitting .300 or above in eight straight seasons from 1995 to 2002. And he changed the game with his remarkable right arm. Opponents simply chose not to even run against Rodriguez.

"I call it the 'drop anchor effect,'" former Rangers first baseman Will Clark said regarding Rodriguez's canon arm. "Guys get to first, drop anchor, then wait 'til it's safe to go to second."

Along the way, Pudge also became one of the most popular players in team history for reasons beyond just his performance on the field.

Fourteen hours before the trade deadline in 1997, for example, Rodriguez arrived at the office of then–team president Tom Schieffer unannounced and without his agent, Jeffrey Moorad. For more than a year Rodriguez and the Rangers had not been able to agree on a long-term contract. But Rodriguez walked into Schieffer's office that late-July day and announced, as reported by Johnette Howard in a 1997 *Sports Illustrated* article: "I don't want to be traded. I want to stay here. This is eating me up. I want to finish my career here."

He obviously didn't do that, but he did spend the ensuing five seasons in Texas, adding to his Lone Star legacy before signing with the Marlins before the 2003 season. Later in the decade, Rodriguez played for the Tigers, Yankees, and Astros, and as fate would have it, Pudge returned to Arlington for an interleague game on June 17, 2009, to play his record-setting 2,227th game behind the plate. Wearing an Astros uniform, Rodriguez surpassed Hall of Famer

Ivan Rodriguez poses with his Gold Glove Award in October 1996. The Rangers catcher won 10 consecutive Gold Gloves from 1992 to 2001. (AP Images)

Carlton Fisk and moved into first place all-time for the most games caught in the Rangers' 5–4 10-inning win.

In the third inning, a tribute video honoring his accomplishments played on the scoreboard at Rangers Ballpark in Arlington, and throughout the night Rangers fans showered him with ovations.

"It was awesome," said the then-37-year-old Rodriguez. "What happened out there was unbelievable. A standing ovation my first time up, it was awesome. I got some goose bumps when that happened. The video that they did in the third inning was unbelievable.... That's why it's so special for me. I did it in the place I started in 1991, where Bobby Valentine gave me the opportunity to play in the big leagues and be able to play this many years. Eighteen years later, look where I am, still playing ball and breaking Carlton Fisk's record in Arlington. I always said these fans are the best. They always support the Rangers every single day, even if they are doing good or not doing good. It was very special for me to break the record here."

Two months later, hoping to make a push for the 2009 playoffs, the Rangers reacquired Rodriguez in a trade with the Astros. Playing a reserve role for the rest of the '09 season, Rodriguez hit .245 in 28 games, bringing his career appearance total to 1,507 games in a Texas uniform.

"I didn't have the benefit of being here the first time he was here," Rangers general manager Jon Daniels said at the press conference announcing the trade that returned Rodriguez to Texas. "But he was one of the greatest players to ever put on the Rangers uniform and the greatest position player. Next to Nolan Ryan, he's one of the biggest icons we've ever had."

Always will be. No matter how many other uniforms he ultimately wears.

8 Shot of J.D. Helps Rangers Rise in Relevance

In October 2005, then–Rangers owner Tom Hicks became the subject of sarcasm-laced commentaries by media covering the Rangers for yet another baffling decision regarding the future direction of the only team in baseball never to have won a playoff series.

Hicks had just announced he was replacing 57-year-old general manager John Hart with Jon Daniels, who at 28 years and 41 days old became the youngest general manager in major league history.

It appeared that Hicks was simply trying to duplicate Boston's blueprint for overcoming a cursed baseball existence. In 2002 the Red Sox hired 28-year-old, Yale-educated Theo Epstein, who never even played high school baseball, as general manager. A couple years later, Beantown celebrated its first World Series championship in 86 years. Epstein later led the Cubs to their first World Series title since 1908, in 2016.

Daniels seemed like a copycat move on Hicks' part. He was a pencil-necked, Ivy League (Cornell) graduate who hadn't played baseball since eighth grade.

Flash-forward six years to October 2011. The Rangers, with a roster masterfully created by Daniels, were twice within one strike of winning the World Series. With the 13th-highest payroll in the major leagues ($92.1 million), the 2011 Rangers won their second consecutive American League pennant in what was supposed to be the year of the Red Sox. Or maybe the Yankees.

It's been a remarkable ride for Daniels, who also constructed a 2010 World Series participant with a payroll of $55.2 million, which ranked 27th out of the 30 major league teams.

Hicks probably deserves a pat on the back for finding a diamond in Daniels. And Daniels has continued to earn praises and raises for being fearless in pulling the trigger on trades, while still exercising financial responsibility.

In 2015, for example, Ken Davidoff of the *New York Post* rated Daniels as the second-best GM in all of baseball, behind only John Mozeliak of the Cardinals and ahead of Theo Epstein of the Cubs and Brian Sabean of the Giants.

Since the Rangers have been nationally relevant, Daniels has often displayed a golden touch in the off-season and at the trade deadline.. At the 2010 trade deadline, Daniels pulled off a coup by acquiring Cliff Lee from Seattle...the same Lee the Yankees had been certain they would land. Lee was the key to the first World Series appearance, and a tunnel-like, singularly focused vision was critical in building the 2011 American League champs.

The signing of free agent Adrian Beltre was huge in '11, as he won a Gold Glove and the Silver Slugger. Acquiring Mike Napoli was equally big, as the catcher occasionally carried the Rangers' offense. In-season acquisitions of relievers Mike Adams, Koji Uehara, and Michael Gonzalez also transformed a soft bullpen into a strength.

Offseason additions of free agents Yu Darvish and Joe Nathan and trade deadline acquisitions of Ryan Dempster and Geovany Soto helped the Rangers earn the Wild Card in 2012. And one of the best trade deadline days in team history came in 2015.

In an eight-player swap between the Rangers and Phillies, Texas acquired starting pitcher Cole Hamels, reliever Jake Diekman, and cash for left-handed pitcher Matt Harrison, right-handed pitchers Jerad Eickhoff, Alec Ashe,r and Jake Thompson, catcher Jorge Alfaro, and outfielder Nick Williams. In a separate deal, the Rangers acquired right-handed reliever Sam Dyson from the Marlins for catcher Tomas Telis and Cody Edge.

The Rangers were 50–52 at the time of the 2015 trades, seven games back of the Astros in the AL West. They went on to win the division, as Hamels thrived and Dyson became one of the team's best relievers.

At the 2016 deadline, Daniels again worked his magic. He had spent weeks talking to the Rays about their starters, made the necessary calls on the White Sox's Chris Sale and Jose Quintana, and he even pursued pitching rentals on the final day. But when the cost of starting pitching became too much for the Ranges to pay, Daniels shifted gears and improved the offense and the defense at catcher.

Texas landed catcher Jonathan Lucroy, designated hitter Carlos Beltran and reliever Jeremy Jeffress, giving the Rangers a lift. The moves cost the Rangers three of their top five prospects entering the season, according to Baseball America: center fielder Lewis Brinson and right-hander Luis Ortiz went to the Brewers for Lucroy and Jeffress, while righty Dillon Tate to the Yankees in a package for Beltran.

Ultimately, the moves didn't propel the Rangers back to the World Series, but Texas won its seventh AL West title in comfortable fashion, outdistancing the Mariners by nine games.

To fully appreciate Daniels' impact on the Rangers' rise, it's important to examine some of the moves he made long before the team sniffed the postseason. In 2007 he traded Mark Teixeira to Atlanta for, among others, closer Neftali Feliz, starting pitcher Matt Harrison, and shortstop Elvis Andrus. That trade—and several others—bolstered the farm system dramatically. In 2008 the Rangers made the largest one-year jump in the history of *Baseball America's* farm system rankings, improving to fourth after being 28th prior to 2007. One year later, the Rangers' farm system was ranked No. 1.

Other Daniels moves to remember:

- In July 2006 he dealt Francisco Cordero, Laynce Nix, Kevin Mench, and Julian Cordero to Milwaukee for outfielders Carlos Lee and a little-known prospect named Nelson Cruz.
- His first three drafts included Derek Holland, Mitch Moreland, Tommy Hunter, Justin Smoak, Chris Davis, and Julio Borbon.
- In the Rule V draft, he took a chance on an outfielder named Alexi Ogando.
- He traded arguably the top pitching prospect in the organization, Edinson Volquez, for a risky outfielder with a history of drug abuse, Josh Hamilton.
- Prior to the 2010 season, he signed Colby Lewis, a former Rangers pitcher who'd spent two years in Japan.
- During the final month of the 2016 season, Daniels took a chance on outfielder Carlos Gomez, who hit .210 with Houston in 85 games with a 31 percent strikeout rate in 323 plate appearances. The former All-Star outfielder played so poorly with the Astros he was released on August 19. After losing Shin-Soo Choo to a broken forearm, Daniels signed Gomez to a minor league deal the next day. Fifteen days later, Gomez donned a Texas uniform and launched a three-run homer in his first at-bat. He hit .284 in 116 at-bats in 33 games with Texas, becoming the leadoff hitter for the team with the best record in the American League.

All of his moves have not been golden. He shipped Alfonso Soriano to Washington for outfielder Brad Wilkerson, outfielder Terrmel Sledge, and pitcher Armando Galarraga in his first trade. Wilkerson did almost nothing for the Rangers; Sledge was involved in another bad deal; and Galarraga almost threw a perfect game in 2010…for the Tigers. Meanwhile, Soriano in 2006 finished sixth in the MVP balloting with over 40 homers and steals.

While that Daniels deal was a dud, the next one was worse. A month after the Soriano trade, Daniels sent first baseman Adrian Gonzalez to San Diego along with starting pitcher Chris Young and Sledge for starting pitcher Adam Eaton, relief pitcher Akinori Otsuka, and minor leaguer Billy Killian.

Ouch.

Gonzalez went on to become one of the best young hitters in the National League (and later signed a huge deal with the Red Sox), and Young won 33 games over five years for the Padres while compiling a 3.60 ERA. Meanwhile, Eaton went 7–4 with a 5.12 ERA with the '06 Rangers, leaving after the season for Philadelphia. Otsuka pitched well in Texas for two seasons, recording 36 saves, but this was a dismal deal for Texas.

More recently, Daniels pulled off one of the biggest one-for-one baseball trades in recent memory, when the Rangers traded All-Star second baseman Ian Kinsler to Detroit for perennial All-Star first baseman Prince Fielder in November 2013.

Fielder played just 42 games in 2014 before undergoing neck surgery. He was the comeback player of the year in 2015, playing 158 games, hitting .305 with 23 homers and 98 RBIs to help the Rangers win the AL West. But after a miserable start in '16, an emotional Fielder was forced to retire after his second spinal fusion surgery in three years. In comparison, Kinsler was a steady force for the Tigers.

But Daniels remains unafraid to make bold moves. Many of his moves in recent years resulted in the Rangers moving from the basement of the West to the American League penthouse.

The team's 2010 accomplishments resulted in Daniels being selected as Baseball America's Major League Executive of the Year. He is just the second Rangers executive to ever earn the award, following general manager Doug Melvin in 1998.

In other words, this J.D. has given the franchise a powerful shot in the arm.

Winning Games 4 and 5 of the 2011 World Series

After being battered and bludgeoned by the Cardinals, 16–7, in Game 3 on October 22, 2011, at Rangers Ballpark in Arlington, the Rangers faced the grim possibility of again watching a visiting foe wrap up the World Series on Texas' turf.

A year earlier, the Giants finished the Rangers in five games, dog-piling in the middle of the Rangers' infield. And after the debacle of Game 3 in the 2011 World Series gave St. Louis a 2–1 series lead, it wasn't difficult to envision history repeating itself.

St. Louis pounded out 15 hits, and first baseman Albert Pujols hammered three home runs among five hits, while also driving in six runs and amassing 14 total bases.

"He's the best player in the game," Rangers outfielder Nelson Cruz said of Pujols. "If anybody is going to do that, it's him."

One night later, the Rangers desperately needed someone to step forward and save the series from spiraling out of control. A young left-hander who celebrated his 25th birthday earlier in the month did just that.

Before an appreciative crowd of 51,539 at Rangers Ballpark in Arlington, Derek Holland held the potent Cardinals lineup to only two hits over 8⅓ masterful innings, leading the Rangers to a 4–0 victory that evened the World Series at 2–2. To the chagrin of the fans, Neftali Feliz entered the game in the ninth to record the final two outs.

But undoubtedly the night belonged to the "Dutch Oven," who turned in the longest scoreless effort by an American League pitcher in the World Series since Andy Pettitte went 8⅓ scoreless innings in a 1–0 victory over the Braves in 1996. Holland's performance also marked the first time a pitcher has gone at least 8⅓ scoreless innings and allowed two hits or fewer in a World Series game since the Pirates' Nelson Briles in the 1971 World Series.

"I'm just happy that I got to shut down the Cardinals," Holland said. "They were red hot yesterday, obviously. I made my pitches when I needed to and did everything I could to get momentum on my side. I have had my ups and downs, and I felt like I wanted to redeem myself from when I pitched against the Tigers [in the ALCS]."

Holland entered the game with a 5.27 ERA and a .316 opponents' batting average in three starts and one relief appearance in the 2011 postseason. But he was masterful against the Cardinals, retiring 12 of the first 13 batters he faced. Overall, he threw 116 pitches and struck out seven Cardinals batters while walking two. The only St. Louis hitter to collect a hit against him was Lance Berkman, who had a double and a single.

The next day on ESPN 103.3 FM, Rangers pitching legend and former president Nolan Ryan told hosts Randy Galloway, Ian Fitzsimmons, and Matt Mosley that Holland's effort, considering the circumstances, was the most meaningful and impressive pitching performance in team history.

The Rangers' offense had given Holland an early lead against Cardinals starter Edwin Jackson. Elvis Andrus reached on a one-out

Derek Holland delivers a pitch during Game 4 of the 2011 World Series. Holland pitched 8⅓ scoreless innings as the Rangers won to even the series at 2–2. (AP Images)

single in the first inning and scored on Josh Hamilton's double into the right-field corner.

The 1–0 lead stood until the sixth. Jackson was effective all night, but he walked seven batters, which caught up to him in the sixth. The right-hander walked Nelson Cruz and David Murphy with one out, and Cardinals manager Tony La Russa went to the bullpen for Mitchell Boggs. On Boggs' first pitch, Mike Napoli crushed a majestic homer over the left-field wall to give the Rangers a 4–0 lead. It stayed that way.

The win in Game 4 saved the series for the Rangers, while Game 5 gave them a great chance to win it all.

St. Louis built a 2–0 lead in the second off Rangers starter C.J. Wilson, but Texas tied it with solo homers by Mitch Moreland in the third and Adrian Beltre in the sixth off Cardinals ace Chris Carpenter.

With the score still knotted at 2–2 and fans chanting "Na-po-li, Na-po-li," the Rangers' clutch catcher delivered a bases-loaded, line-drive double that scored Michael Young and Nelson Cruz and propelled the Rangers to a 4–2 victory before a feverish crowd of 51,459 fans in the final home game of the year at Rangers Ballpark in Arlington. It marked the first time in franchise history the Rangers had ever held a lead in the World Series, taking a 3–2 advantage back to St. Louis.

10 Simp-Lee Sensational: Winning Game 5 of the 2010 ALDS

Following a Sunday afternoon home loss to the Tampa Bay Rays in Game 4 of the 2010 ALDS—the Rangers' second home playoff setback in as many days—Texas fans shuffled silently and sorrowfully out of the stadium's shadow-covered concourses and into the sun-splashed parking lots, shaking their heads constantly and muttering mostly four-letter curses to themselves.

It was a remarkable reversal of energy and enthusiasm in a span of just over 24 hours. A day earlier—October 9, 2010—red, white, and blue–clad, antlers-toting, claw-gesturing, towel-waving Texas fans had packed Rangers Ballpark in Arlington with a level of combustible anticipation that was comparable to Times Square on New Year's Eve.

Unfortunately for most of the 100,964 fans who filled the ballpark with euphoric hopes over those two days, the Rangers—like the Times Square tradition—dropped the ball.

After winning the opening two games in St. Petersburg, the Rangers returned to Arlington with two chances to win a home playoff game for the first time in history and to finally erase the stigma of being the only major league franchise to have never won a playoff series.

With a 2–1 lead through seven innings of Game 3, the Rangers were six outs away from allowing the hometown fans to celebrate like never before. But then the Rays rallied in Game 3 and dominated Game 4 to take the series back to South Florida for a winner-advance-on Game 5.

Many of the beaten-down, sunburned Rangers fans leaving the stadium on October 10 braced for the worst, as the life seemed to be sucked out of the ballpark. The last two days of despair—not to mention nearly four full decades of plenty of Rangers wretchedness—had many fans prepared for the addition of a new chapter to the franchise's book of heartache.

As the team prepared to leave town for the series finale, however, there was at least one legitimate sliver of hope that these Rangers fans could cling to that no other previous Texas playoff team could offer: an ace in the hole.

The Rangers didn't need Cliff Lee to win the 2010 American League West division title, but they needed their ace in a big way in the Game 5 spotlight.

"No one wanted to admit it, but there was a great deal of pressure riding on Game 5," Rangers radio play-by-play announcer Eric Nadel said. "If they had lost that game—no matter the circumstances—it would have been a case of same ol' Rangers. Lost another playoff series. Still the only franchise to have never won a playoff series. Same ol' song and dance. But the big difference was

Cliff Lee pitches during Game 5 of the 2010 American League Division Series. Lee struck out 11 Tampa Bay Rays, and the Rangers won 5–1 to advance to the ALCS. (AP Images)

that the 2010 team had the playoff-proven Cliff Lee on the mound for Game 5. They needed him to be really good."

Instead, he was simp-Lee spectacular in what may still be—at least at the time of this printing—the single biggest win in Rangers history. There was definitely not going to be a World Series in 2010 without this win, and there may not have been the same carryover in 2011 that carried Texas back to the Fall Classic.

In St. Petersburg, Lee outdueled Rays ace David Price for the second time in the series, recording 11 strikeouts in a complete-game gem. He threw 120 pitches—90 for strikes—and did not issue a walk in recording a 5–1 win.

"When we made the deal for Cliff, it changed everything," Rangers team president Nolan Ryan said, referencing the July 9 trade that brought Lee from Seattle to Texas. "We had that lead horse for our pitching staff. I really think these two teams matched up so well. The difference was Cliff Lee. I've never seen a guy who has the confidence and the ability to throw strikes like he does and never waver. Early in this series, I said I hoped someone would step up. I was thinking in terms of one of our offensive guys—Josh [Hamilton], Vlad [Guerrero], Nelson Cruz. I didn't know it would be Cliff stepping up again like that, but I'm sure glad he did."

The Rangers did receive some nice performances from the offensive cast in Game 5, as Elvis Andrus scored from second in the first inning on a groundout by Hamilton. Cruz and Guerrero also scored from second without the benefit of a base hit, and Ian Kinsler finished off the Rays with a two-run homer in the ninth.

But this game was primarily about Lee's brilliance ending decades of shortfalls and frustrations for the Rangers and their long-suffering fans. In the process of winning Game 5 at Tropicana Field, the Rangers also earned a new distinction while eliminating the stigma of never previously winning a playoff series. In beating the Rays, the Rangers became the first major league team to win a five-game Division or League Championship Series by winning all three games on the road.

11 Rangers Shift Into Cruz Control in 2011 ALCS

After finishing second at the 2009 Home Run Derby behind Milwaukee's Prince Fielder, Nelson Cruz was featured in an MLB 2K10 video game promotion with Oakland pitcher Andrew Bailey. In the humorous spot, Cruz sketched stick-figure pictures of him launching one of Bailey's pitches to the moon with a bat that he referred to as his "boomstick."

The nickname instantly gained regional appeal among Rangers fans. In the 2011 ALCS, the moniker went national, as Cruz proved on a big stage that the boomstick could ignite explosiveness of historic proportions.

The Rangers rode Cruz's bat to their second consecutive American League pennant, defeating the Tigers 4–2 in a classic postseason series filled with extra innings and extra drama. In six games, Cruz blasted six homers to win ALCS MVP honors.

Reggie Jackson (1977) and Chase Utley (2009) hit five homers in the World Series, while Ken Griffey Jr. (1995) and Juan Gonzalez (1996) blasted five apiece in a division series. But no one before Cruz had ever launched six in a single series. And no one had ever delivered as many RBIs in a playoff series as Cruz's 13 against the Tigers.

Of course, no one has ever carried a boomstick quite like Nellie.

"When he gets going, he's as good as any power hitter in the game," Michael Young said during the Detroit series. "He's got that knack for big RBI."

Added Rangers manager Ron Washington: "Yes, it's amazing with him hitting the ball out of the ballpark the way he's doing it [in the ALCS]. But it certainly isn't anything we haven't seen before."

True. Cruz continually proved he was capable of carrying a team on his broad shoulders for short periods of time. He slugged 33 homers in 2009, and despite an injury-riddled 2010 regular season, he caught fire in the postseason. Cruz hit six homers and

Nelson Cruz celebrates after hitting a grand slam to win Game 2 of the 2011 ALDS. Cruz set postseason series records with six home runs and 13 RBIs in the six-game series win over Detroit. (AP Images)

Mashing Mench: The Unlikely Homer Streak in 2006

The 2005 Rangers led both leagues with 260 homers, as nine players produced at least 10 homers and seven of those sluggers clubbed at least 20 dingers. They also led all of baseball in big blasts in 2003, 2002, 2001, and 1993.

So, it's really not surprising that a Rangers player captured national attention in April 2006 for his home run heroics. What was surprising, however, was that the player who powered Texas with a fascinating big-fly stretch was not a household name. Not even in the Metroplex.

From April 21 to 28, Rangers outfielder Kevin Mench hit at least one home run in seven consecutive games, setting a team record and becoming the only right-handed hitter in major league history to accomplish such a feat. His homer-hitting stretch, which included two grand slams, ended one game short of tying the major league record set by Dale Long in 1956 and matched by Don Mattingly in 1987 and Ken Griffey Jr. in 1993. But it was a sensational stretch, nonetheless.

"I've never seen anything like this, this is unbelievable," shortstop Michael Young told MLB.com's T.R. Sullivan on April 28, following Mench's homer in the eighth inning at Cleveland. "Anytime a player gets on a streak like this you're surprised. But Kevin is definitely capable of doing this."

The streak ended in a 7–5 win at Cleveland on April 29. Afterward, Mench didn't seem too dejected, saying, "I didn't care one way or another if it's over. I'm just going about my job. We got a good win tonight."

Interestingly, the Pirates, Dodgers, Royals, and Blue Jays all made inquiries about trading for Mench prior to 2006, but Rangers general manager Jon Daniels believed Mench was on the verge of a breakout season.

Mench rewarded the Rangers with his stretch in April '06. After his first 10 games of the season, Mench was hitting .282 without an RBI. The right fielder then missed five games with a sprained toe, and when he saw a foot specialist he was told to wear a bigger shoe.

Mench had been wearing size 12 since the age of 15, but the foot specialist told him to change to a 12½. The larger shoe fit, and Mench began a terrific tear at the plate. In addition to the home run streak, he collected 10 RBIs and produced a .957 slugging percentage from April 24–30.

Unfortunately, a cool stretch followed. Mench hit only five home runs in the other 80 games he played for the Rangers in 2006, and on July 28, he was part of the trade that sent Francisco Cordero and Laynce Nix to Milwaukee in exchange for Nelson Cruz and Carlos Lee.

In five seasons in Texas, Mench hit .274 with 80 homers and 265 RBIs in 510 games. But it was his stretch in seven of those games that will be remembered for years to come.

delivered 13 extra-base hits during the Rangers' 2010 postseason run, which ended in a five-game loss to the Giants in the World Series.

Entering the 2011 postseason, however, Cruz seemed like an unlikely offensive hero. He hit .190 with one home run and three RBIs in his final 11 regular-season games after returning from a strained left hamstring in mid-September. He then went 1-for-15 with no home runs or RBIs in the Rangers' four-game ALDS win against Tampa Bay.

But once the Rangers reached the ALCS, the Texas offense Cruz-ed to new heights. Hitting in the seven hole, Cruz blasted a solo homer off Tigers ace Justin Verlander in the fourth inning of the series opener for what proved to be the game-winning run.

In the second game, Cruz tied it at 3–3 when he led off the seventh with a solo homer that chased Max Scherzer. Cruz finished the second game with a walk-off grand slam, the first in major league playoff history. He also hit a three-run bomb in the 11th inning of Game 4, after throwing out Miguel Cabrera at the plate to keep the game tied in the bottom of the eighth.

Cruz chased Verlander in Game 5 when he pulled a 100 mph, 0–2 fastball that hit the left-field pole. And he capped off the Rangers' 15–5 win in Game 6 with a two-run shot. Overall, he hit .364 (8-for-22) against the Tigers.

"You just continue to say, 'Wow, this guy is really good,'" David Murphy said. "He had an amazing [ALCS]."

The boomstick cooled considerably in the World Series, as Cruz was 5-for-25 with two homers and three RBIs against the Cardinals. Unfortunately, the most lasting—and haunting—image of Cruz from the 2011 World Series is the play he failed to make in Game 6.

With two outs, two strikes, two Cardinals on base, and the Rangers nursing a two-run lead in the bottom of the ninth, David Freese drove a 98 mph Neftali Feliz fastball to deep right field. Cruz didn't read the ball well off the bat, didn't accurately judge where he was on the field in relationship to the wall, and didn't manage to even get a glove on the ball.

Freese tripled, and both runners came around to score to tie a game the Cardinals won in the 11th. It was not an easy play, but it was the kind of play Cruz has made countless times in his career.

It was an unfortunate ending to a fantastic postseason run. With eight homers in 17 games, Cruz tied Carlos Beltran and Barry Bonds for the most homers in a single postseason. And it's doubtful the Rangers would have reached the 2011 World Series without Cruz's heroic ALCS. Remarkably, Cruz's 14 postseason home runs in 2010–11 already tied him for the ninth-most in major league history.

His road to stardom with Texas was remarkable as well. The Rangers acquired Cruz and Carlos Lee from Milwaukee in a July 2006 trade. Cruz finished that season with the Rangers and then started and ended 2007 in the majors, sandwiched around a stint at Triple A Oklahoma.

At the end of spring training in 2008, however, the Rangers faced a decision between Cruz and Jason Botts regarding the final roster spot. Both young power hitters were out of minor league options, and the Rangers went with Botts, who hit .158 in 15 games and was designated for assignment. Botts played in the Mexican

Pacific League and Japan's Pacific League in '08, but he has not made it back to the big leagues.

Meanwhile, Cruz cleared waivers and was sent outright to Oklahoma City, where he had an MVP season. He hit .342 with 37 home runs and 99 RBIs in 103 games before being called up by the Rangers the final six weeks of the season. He hit .330 with seven homers and 26 RBIs in 31 games, and his boomstick was a mainstay in the Rangers' lineup until he signed with the Orioles in February 2014.

12 Rangers Win 2011 ALDS in "Year of the Napoli"

It may have actually started earlier in Mike Napoli's fourth-inning at-bat against Tampa Bay's James Shields on October 1. But it wasn't audibly detectable throughout Rangers Ballpark in Arlington until Shields fell behind 3–0.

At that point, it seemed like all of the 51,351 fans inside the stadium were chanting: "Na-po-li, Na-po-li, Na-po-li."

The Rangers had already laid an egg the previous day in Game 1 of the 2011 ALDS. Tampa Bay rookie Matt Moore made the Rangers' powerful lineup look meek, as the Rays coasted to a 9–0 victory, the largest shutout loss by an American League team to open the postseason since the Tigers fell to the Cubs 9–0 in Game 1 of the 1945 World Series.

In Game 2 against Shields, an All-Star and one of the hottest pitchers in the American League during the second half of the season, the Rays built a 3–0 lead in the top of the fourth before a worried crowd.

Lose this game, and the Rangers' defense of the 2010 American League pennant could've been short-lived.

Texas desperately needed someone to ignite a fire. Up stepped Napoli, who was stunned initially by the show of support from the chanting fans. He took a strike and swung and missed at Shields' fifth delivery, running the count to 3–2. With each additional pitch, the chant grew stronger as the tension mounted.

The Rangers had cut the lead to 3–1. Bases loaded. Nobody out. Make-or-break moment of the game—maybe the entire series. Shields delivered an 85 mph cutter; Napoli fouled it off, and the crowd volume increased.

Pitches seven and eight were a four-seam fastball and a change-up. Napoli spoiled both. Ninth pitch: 88 mph slider, up in the zone. Napoli crushed it to left.

Two runs scored to tie the game, and the Rangers eventually took a 5–3 lead en route to winning the game, the ALDS, the American League pennant, and pushing the Cardinals to the brink of elimination in the World Series. Beginning with that first night in October, Rangers fans loved chanting Napoli's name.

"It's awesome," Napoli told MLB.com's John Schlegel regarding the chants heard throughout the playoff run. "I love it every time I come up to bat and I hear that. It pumps me up."

Napoli pumped up the Rangers' playoff hopes by hitting .383 with 18 homers and 42 RBIs in the second half of the season, helping the Rangers bury the Angels in the American League West. Then in the ALDS against the Rays, Napoli kicked into an entirely new gear. He had the big hit in Game 2 against Shields and followed that up with even bigger things when the series shifted to St. Petersburg.

With the Rays leading 1–0 in Game 3, Adrian Beltre lined a single to left off David Price to begin the seventh inning. Napoli then fell behind 0–2 and fouled off two pitches before Price evened the count at 2–2. On the seventh pitch of the at-bat, Napoli—choking up on the handle with two strikes—cranked a 94 mph,

Mike Napoli hits a two-run double during Game 5 of the 2011 World Series. The Rangers catcher hit .350 during the World Series with two home runs and 10 RBIs, joining Mickey Mantle as the only two players to produce four multi-RBI games in the same World Series. (AP Images)

two-seam fastball into the left-center field bleachers to give the Rangers their first lead of the game.

"David was still doing a nice job of working through the [inning]," Tampa Bay manager Joe Maddon said. "But this is the year of the Napoli, man."

He added to his heroics later. With the Rangers leading 4–3 in the eighth, Napoli gunned down B.J. Upton attempting to steal second. The Rangers held on to win 4–3.

Beltre (three solo homers) and pitcher Matt Harrison did most of the heavy lifting in the Rangers' 4–3 series-clinching win in Game 4, but it was Napoli who put the team on his shoulders earlier in the series and placed the Rangers in position to beat the Rays for a second consecutive year in the ALCS.

Napoli Would Have Been 2011 World Series MVP

Mike Napoli drove the Rangers to the brink of their first World Series title in 2011. And if Texas would have finished the Cardinals off in Game 6, there's no doubt that Napoli would have been driving away from Busch Stadium on the night of October 27 in a new black Corvette.

Instead, the car and the MVP Award presented by Chevrolet went to St. Louis' David Freese the following night. But until things went terribly south for Texas in the late innings of Game 6, Napoli's name could have been etched into that trophy.

He hit .350 during the World Series with two homers and 10 RBIs. He also joined Mickey Mantle as the only two players to produce four multi-RBI games in the same World Series.

Napoli was so hot in the series that the Cardinals walked him three times in Game 6. When St. Louis did pitch to him, he singled home a run in the fourth to give Texas a 3–2 lead. He rolled his ankle in a gruesome-looking injury at second base later that inning, but he displayed his toughness by staying in that game and playing in the next.

Right from the start of the Fall Classic, Napoli began making a major impact on the series, homering for Texas' only two runs in a 3–2 loss in Game 1. He was 1-for-2 with a pair of RBIs in a blowout loss in Game 3, and he was especially big in the Rangers' 4–0 Game 4 win, blasting a three-run homer and calling a great game for pitcher Derek Holland.

In Game 5 Napoli delivered the game-winning, two-run double in Texas' 4–2 victory, and he also threw out two base runners.

"At this point, I'm not surprised by anything he does," teammate David Murphy said of Napoli after Game 5. "He's Superman right now."

"I think he's probably the best catcher in baseball, in my opinion, all the way around," said Rangers reliever Scott Feldman, as reported by ESPNDallas.com's Richard Durrett. "He's been a huge addition for us."

13 Rangers Win First World Series Game in Arlington

In the grand scheme of things, the Rangers' 4–2 victory in Game 3 of the 2010 World Series at Rangers Ballpark in Arlington didn't alter the direction or influence the ultimate outcome of the 106th Fall Classic. The Giants, who won the first two games of the series at San Francisco's AT&T Park, bounced back from the Game 3 loss and won the next two games to claim a world championship.

But the victory in Game 3 gave Rangers fans bragging rights in their home state. Five years earlier, the Houston Astros became the first team from the Lone Star State ever to reach the World Series but were swept by the Chicago White Sox in the 2005 Fall Classic.

The Rangers avoided that indignity, treating the 52,419 fans who piled into the ballpark on October 30—the largest crowd ever to see a baseball game in Arlington—to one of the most satisfying victories in the history of the franchise.

In terms of sheer, unbridled emotion and pure elation, the atmosphere for Game 3 of the World Series did not equal Game 6 of the American League Championship Series eight days earlier when the Rangers eliminated the Yankees. But it was spectacular nonetheless.

"That was fun," said third baseman Michael Young, who made his major league debut with the Rangers in 2000. "That was great. That was the atmosphere we envisioned for the World Series."

The sold-out crowd arrived early and stayed late, soaking up the atmosphere of late-October baseball and attempting to receive their money's worth for the outrageous ticket prices that many fans paid. According to FanSnap.com, an online ticket comparison-shopping site, the average price Rangers fans were paying for World Series tickets in Arlington prior to Texas winning the pennant was $1,081. After the Yankees were eliminated, the average price jumped to $1,279.

But $1,300 would have been considered a bargain for really good seats to Game 3, which was played on a perfectly crisp Saturday night. One online site listed front-row seats near the Rangers dugout for $95,000. Per seat.

While bank accounts were drained to pay for tickets, at least the Rangers made a deposit in their fans' memory banks.

Naturally, Nolan Ryan threw out the ceremonial first pitch of the first World Series game ever to be played in North Texas, and instead of lobbing one in to former Rangers catcher Ivan "Pudge" Rodriguez, "Big Tex" was clocked with a 68 mph fastball.

That pitch set the tone for "C.L.," who was once again at his best, proving why he was—without question—the overall post-season pitching star for the 2010 Rangers. "C.L." is a reference to Colby Lewis, not Cliff Lee.

While Lee was spectacular leading up to the World Series, Lewis was Mr. Consistency throughout the postseason. Lewis kept the Giants off-balance, limiting San Francisco to two runs in 7⅔ innings. In the process, Lewis improved to 3–0 with a 1.71 ERA in four postseason starts in 2010.

"He's just been tremendous," American League MVP Josh Hamilton said of Lewis after Game 3. "He's been just as good as Cliff [Lee] and C.J. [Wilson]. It's pretty awesome to be out there in center and watch him pitch."

"Tonight was the Colby Lewis show," Young said afterward.

True, but rookie first baseman Mitch Moreland and Hamilton also had key roles.

In the bottom of the second inning of a scoreless game, Moreland, the nine-hole hitter, came to the plate with two runners on and two out against San Francisco starter Jonathan Sanchez. Moreland, displaying the patience and persistence of a veteran, fouled off four straight off-speed pitches after the count evened to 2–2. On the ninth pitch of the at-bat, catcher Buster Posey set up on the inside part of the plate and called for a fastball.

Sanchez hit his spot. But Moreland hit it out of the park, drilling a three-run homer into the right-field bleachers. It was his first major league homer against a left-hander.

Hamilton added to the lead with his first home run of the World Series in the fifth inning off Sanchez, who had held left-handed hitters to a .181 average and five home runs in 138 at-bats during the regular season.

San Francisco outfielder Cody Ross hit a solo home run in the seventh, and Andres Torres hit another solo shot off Lewis in the eighth. With two outs in the eighth, Lewis hit Aubrey Huff with a pitch, which brought the tying run to the plate in Posey.

But in the tensest moment of the game for the Rangers, reliever Darren O'Day induced a weak ground ball from Posey to shortstop Elvis Andrus to end the inning.

That left the ninth for Texas closer Neftali Feliz, who set down the side in order to preserve the first-ever victory in a World Series game for a major league team from the Lone Star State.

14
Game 5 of the 2015 ALDS: The Call, the Chaos, the Errors, and the Bat Flip

Following a 14-inning, four-hour and 57-minute marathon, the Texas Rangers boarded a south-bound plane on the night of October 9, 2015, and headed back to Arlington with a 2–0 lead in the ALDS. The Rangers, who pieced together four consecutive two-out hits in the top of the 14th inning to beat Toronto 6–4 in Game 2, returned to the Lone Star State needing just one victory to return to the ALCS for the first time since 2011.

Home-field advantage, however, was not so advantageous for Texas. Troy Tulowitzki launched a three-run homer to lead the Blue Jays to a 5–1 win in Game 3, and Toronto jumped all over Texas starter Derek Holland in Game 4, scoring six runs on five hits before the lefty was pulled in the third inning. The Rangers rallied, but still lost the game 8–4, as well as their chance to clinch the series at home.

Instead, both teams headed back to the Rogers Centre tied 2–2 for what turned out to be one of the most memorable and bizarre games in the 2015 postseason.

With the deciding game knotted at 2–2 in the top of the seventh inning and Rangers second baseman Rougned Odor at third base, Blue Jays reliever Aaron Sanchez delivered a high fastball to Shin-Soo Choo to run the count to 2–2. Toronto catcher Russell Martin's return throw caromed off Choo's hand and rolled down the third-base line.

An alert Odor immediately broke for home and crossed the plate. Initially, plate umpire Dale Scott called timeout as Odor was halfway home. But Odor kept going, and Texas manager Jeff Banister emerged from the dugout to make his case.

"I've been involved in that play before. I've done that play before," said Banister, a former minor league catcher. "I've done that exact play as a catcher where I've actually thrown it off of the hitter's hand/bat before, so I was aware of the rule."

Banister was obviously one of the few inside the packed stadium who did understand the rule.

After a lengthy discussion with Banister and a conference with the rest of the umpiring crew, Dale Scott awarded Odor the run, giving Texas the lead. Blue Jays manager John Gibbons stormed emphatically out of the dugout to argue the call as the Toronto fans littered the field with beer cans, paper cups and practically everything else. Gibbons decided to play the rest if the game under protest as the game moved on to the bottom of the seventh.

That's when things became even crazier. With Texas starter Cole Hamels pitching well, Russell Martin led off the bottom of the seventh with a routine, broken-bat ground ball to shortstop Elvis Andrus, who muffed it, allowing Martin to reach safely.

The next hitter, Kevin Pillar, fell behind 1–2 and then bounced a routine ball to first baseman Mitch Moreland, who threw to Andrus at second to begin what could have been a 3-6-3 double play. At the very least, it should have forced Martin at second for the first out of the inning. Instead. Moreland's throw short-hopped Andrus, who could not handle the bounce.

Both runners were safe, which brought the No. 9 hitter, Ryan Goins, to the plate. Goins bunted the ball sharply to third baseman Adrian Beltre, who fielded it cleanly and threw to Andrus who was covering third. The throw was in plenty of time and hit Andrus in the glove. Inexplicably, Andrus dropped it to load the bases.

"Unimaginable," Rangers' radio play-by-play announcer Eric Nadel said during the broadcast. "The Rangers, who have made just two errors the entire series, have now made three errors on three routine plays in a row."

Ben Revere followed with a grounder to first base, which resulted in a force at home. At that point, the Rangers easily could have recorded five outs in the inning. After throwing 111 pitches,

Elvis Bounces Back in a Big Way

After three straight disappointing seasons and one absolutely disastrous inning in the 2015 ALDS, many Rangers' fans were led to believe that Elvis Andrus' best years were behind him. A leadoff hitter on the 2010 World Series team and the two-hole hitter in 2011, Andrus signed an eight-year, $120 million contract extension with the Rangers in April 2013, as he was entering his age-24 season, and then proceeded to watch his overall game decline.

His offense steadily declined from 2013 to '15, stabilizing with OPS+ marks of 82, 81, and 80 in those three seasons. His defense also deteriorated. From to 2011 to 2013 he averaged plus-9 defensive runs saved per season; in 2014 and 2015, his totals were minus-13 and minus-1.

Then there was the seventh inning of Game 5 of the 2015 ALDS in Toronto. The Rangers entered the bottom of the seventh with a 3–2 lead, but two errors by Andrus (it could have been three) allowed the Blue Jays to score four times as Toronto recorded a 6–3 win and advanced to the ALCS.

Andrus carried a heavy burden into the offseason.

"It was the toughest moment of my career," Andrus told Jeff Wilson of the *Fort Worth Star-Telegram*. "If I make those two plays, especially the first one, I think the story would be a lot different. Where I was at the moment in my career, I needed a change. It was an eye-opening experience for me, and the way I was feeling was not a great feeling. I was going to do everything in my power to never feel that way again."

Andrus bounced back in terrific fashion in 2016, posting a team-best .302 batting average, the first .300 season of his career.

In early June, his batting average was a respectable .273, but from that point forward, he was the Rangers' most steady offensive player, hitting .322 and launching six of his career-high eight home runs from that point, plus one homer in the postseason. He was also especially clutch, as Andrus batted .351 (20 for 57) with runners in scoring position and two outs.

Third baseman Adrian Beltre, whom Andrus admires like an older brother, spoke to the shortstop after the Game 5 disaster and encouraged him to use it as motivation.

"For me, it's not a secret, it's not a surprise to me that he can put up a season like that," Beltre said. "I expect it every year because he's that good."

Hamels was pulled from the game with the bases loaded and one out.

Sam Dyson entered the game and then jammed Josh Donaldson, who blooped a ball in the direction of Odor. It should have been the second out of the inning—or the sixth—but Odor misread it and the ball fell just beyond his reach. Odor handled the bounce quickly enough to force out the runner at second, but Pillar scored from third to ties the game.

The ball had barely left the infield, but the Rangers' mistakes had allowed Toronto to tie the game. The next hitter was Jose Bautista, who definitely managed to drive the ball out of the infield…and out of the ballpark.

Bautista launched a soaring, searing three-run home run to break a 3–3 tie and lead the Blue Jays to a 6–3 win on a wild afternoon of tension and drama. He punctuated the home run with a demonstrative, declarative bat toss toward the Rangers' dugout. The homer and the bat toss electrified the crowd of 49,742 inside Rogers Centre and propelled Toronto into the ALCS.

In the other dugout, the entire scene left an extremely sour taste in the mouths of the Rangers.

15 Rougned Odor and the Shot Heard Around the Baseball Universe

Rougned Odor first burst onto the local scene when, as a 20-year-old rookie, he was called to Arlington on May 8, 2014, to take over second base when Donnie Murphy went on the disabled list and Josh Wilson (the 2014 Opening Day starter at second) was designated for assignment.

Odor, wearing the No. 73, debuted in the Rangers' lineup on May 8, 2014, at home against the Colorado Rockies, and he collected his first MLB hit the following night in an 8–0 home win over the Red Sox, a game where Yu Darvish narrowly missed a no-hitter. Throughout the rest of his debut season, Odor proved he belonged in the big leagues in many ways. He played in 114 games, hitting .259 with 14 doubles, seven triples, nine home runs, and 48 RBIs.

Most notably, he displayed a presence and swagger on the field that belied his age. He impressed his teammates, and former Rangers great Michael Young right away. In the midst of Odor's rookie season, Young told radio hosts Ben Rogers and Jeff "Skin" Wade of 105.3 The Fan:

"[Odor] might be one of my top five favorite players in the game. That kid is animal. I love watching him play. I think he comes to whoop your ass, man. That's what the big leagues is all about. It's one thing to show up and enjoy it and have fun, which is great. When I see that kid at [game time] he's ready to go out there and whoop some ass."

Young was speaking figuratively. And quite prophetically, as well.

Roughly two years after first making a name for himself in Arlington, Odor burst onto the national scene by displaying Michael Young's ass-whooping description of him.

On May 15, 2016, the Rangers rallied from a 6–4 deficit against the Toronto Blue Jays and took a 7–6 lead on a three-run homer by Ian Desmond in the bottom of the seventh. In the top of the eighth, reliever Matt Bush, making just his second appearance for the Rangers, hit Jose Bautista with a 96-mph fastball. Clearly, the pitch had a purpose, dating back to Bautista's flamboyant bat flip in Game 5 of the 2015 ALDS.

Bush was pulled from the game and received a standing ovation from the Arlington crowd. Later in the eighth inning, Bautista slid

Matt Bush: From the Golden Corral to Bullpen Gem

Throughout the franchise's history, the Rangers have witnessed some great stories of players coming back from addiction to make key contributions to the squad. Josh Hamilton may be the best story of all, but the remarkable tale of right-handed reliever Matt Bush may be worthy of a Hollywood movie, as well.

By the end of the 2016 season, Bush, a 30-year-old rookie, had emerged as one of the Rangers' most reliable bullpen pieces. A year earlier, he was serving what ended up being a 39-month stay in prison for a DUI causing great bodily injury at a work release center in Jacksonville, Florida.

"I'm just happy to be here, happy to be with this team," Bush said, as reported by MLB.com's Ryan Posner. "I'm happy to have a job in society and that it's with the Texas Rangers. It's a thrill to still have a job and still play baseball."

Bush, the No. 1 overall draft pick by the Padres in the 2004 Draft as a shortstop out of Mission Bay High in San Diego, was sentenced on December 18, 2012, to 52 months in prison after being charged on three felony counts for crashing into a 72-year-old motorcyclist while drunk, driving over his head, and then leaving the scene of the accident. Anthony Tufano, who was left unconscious with his brain hemorrhaging, a collapsed lung, and eight broken vertebrae, survived.

Bush was sent to prison, and after sitting out of organized baseball for four years and playing only for his prison softball team, he made his MLB debut with the Rangers on May 13, 2016. During the rest of the season, he played a huge role in helping the Rangers to the best record in the American League. As a rookie, Bush averaged 97.8 miles per hour on his fastball, the fifth highest among all Major League pitchers with at least 500 fastballs thrown.

Bush's triumphant return to baseball was due in part to the efforts of Rangers special advisor Roy Silver, who also helped to resurrect Hamilton's career. Silver watched Bush and played catch with him in a Golden Corral parking lot, where Bush was working near his release facility in Jacksonville.

"[Silver] followed Bush through his whole situation while being incarcerated," Rangers general manager Jon Daniels said. "Not because he thought [Bush] was going to work one day with a team as a Major League reliever, but because that's where his heart was—sincere and genuine. You look up now and see how that's manifested for the organization."

hard into Odor at second as he was attempting to turn a double play. Odor turned immediately toward Bautista, who bowed up.

Odor pushed Bautista hard once and then delivered a wicked right punch to Bautista's jaw. His sunglasses went flying and he probably would have wound up on the ground if not for being bear-hugged by Rangers third baseman Adrian Beltre. Both benches quickly emptied, and the punch and the ensuing brawl drew national media attention and made Odor a well-known name across the country.

Odor was ultimately suspended for eight games for inciting the brawl, but he proved he had plenty of punch with the bat the rest of the season. Odor led the Rangers with 33 homers during the 2016 regular season, and he proved throughout the year that he has an extremely bright future in the Major Leagues.

Odor also proved he could handle the role of Public Enemy No. 1 in the 2016 postseason when Texas visited Toronto for Game 3 of the ALDS. Despite a chorus of boos each time his name was announced at Rogers Centre, Odor scored two runs and hit a two-run homer in the Rangers' 7-6, extra-inning loss.

His throwing error in the 10th inning allowed the winning run to score, which was especially meaningful for Toronto fans, who hung a sign on one of the stadium's railings that stated: "Would rather get punched in May than get knocked out in October."

Chances are good that Odor will forever be booed north of the border. But his toughness and tenacity will likely keep him quite popular among Rangers fans for many years to come.

16 2011 Rangers Complete Best Regular Season in History

The haunting image of the Giants celebrating the 2010 World Series championship on November 1 at Rangers Ballpark in Arlington motivated the 2011 Rangers to go further than any other team in franchise history.

It galvanized them when one of the game's most prominent pitchers departed for Philadelphia and left the Rangers without a true ace. It fueled their focus during one of the hottest summers on record, when the first-pitch temperature in Arlington was above 100 degrees 27 times. It sustained them during a slew of injuries early in the season. And it stuck with them as they battled the Angels in the American League West, the Rays in the ALDS, the Tigers in the ALCS, and the Cardinals in the World Series.

Through the highs and lows, the sultry home stands and red-eye road trips, the regular season and the postseason, the Rangers had a singular mission in mind: win it all...and replace that lingering image of the Giants.

Unfortunately, the Rangers didn't completely accomplish the mission of the season, falling one win short of the World Series title. Nevertheless, the 2011 Rangers were historic in many ways, winning more regular-season (96) and postseason games (10) than any previous ballclub in franchise history.

"They are champions, although we didn't get the World Series trophy," former manager Ron Washington told his players, as reported by MLB.com's T.R. Sullivan following the Game 7 World Series loss. "Those guys committed themselves to getting here this year and winning this, and they did it. A lot of times it's nothing but talk, but it wasn't talk in that Texas Rangers clubhouse. We just didn't get it done. We got beat by a good club."

In hindsight, the Rangers acknowledged that beating the Yankees in the 2010 ALCS and reaching the World Series seemed like the ultimate destination. Then the Giants, armed with a dominant pitching rotation that hit its stride in the postseason, destroyed the euphoric feeling that had emanated the Rangers' clubhouse and engulfed North Texas with claw-and-antler fever.

Initial hopes for bigger things in 2011 hinged on the team's ability to re-sign Cliff Lee, who was spectacular in his first three postseason appearances with Texas. But Lee stunned the Rangers and Yankees by joining Philadelphia's phenomenal rotation, because, he said, he believed the Phillies gave him the best chance to win a World Series.

Meanwhile, Jon Daniels, Nolan Ryan, and company began developing plans to improve the team without Lee. The Rangers made their biggest off-season move by signing third baseman Adrian Beltre, who bolstered their defense and added a big bat to the lineup. They also acquired Mike Napoli and Yorvit Torrealba, who proved to be outstanding additions. Other off-season moves (Brandon Webb, Arthur Rhodes, Dave Bush, and Yoshinori Tateyama, to name a few) eventually had far less of an impact. But heading into the season, the Rangers liked their chances of repeating in the American League West…as long as their young pitchers stepped forward.

The 64-year-old Ryan, who'd years earlier demanded that the club stop babying young pitchers with pitch counts, issued the "it's time" challenge to the expected trio of young pitchers (Tommy Hunter, Derek Holland, and Matt Harrison) behind C.J. Wilson and Colby Lewis in the rotation. But Hunter, the most experienced starter of the trio, strained a groin muscle just prior to the beginning of the season. Washington then inserted another youngster, Alexi Ogando, into the rotation.

The Rangers opened the season by playing host to the overwhelming favorites to win the American League pennant, the Boston Red Sox. Texas swept the Red Sox and burst out of the starting blocks with a 9–1 record. Ogando and two relievers blanked Justin Verlander and the Tigers 2–0 on April 11, and the Rangers appeared to have all systems going toward a dream-come-true season.

2011 Rangers Fans Brave Brutal Heat to Set Attendance Record

Despite the record-breaking misery of constant triple-digit temperatures during the summer of 2011, Rangers fans certainly didn't bail on their boys or refrain from rooting for the home team in person during the team's run to a second consecutive World Series.

In fact, Rangers fans responded to the record-breaking heat by breaking the team's all-time attendance record. The 2011 Rangers drew 2,946,949 fans, breaking the previous single-season attendance record of 2,945,244 set in 1997. Those fans were treated to a team that went 52–29 during the regular season.

"If I had to script it, I probably couldn't have scripted it any better than what's happened," former Rangers CEO and president Nolan Ryan said, as reported by Louie Horvath of MLB.com. "As far as how the club's played and what we've accomplished, the fans have come out and supported us. You look at 2008, we drew [1.9 million] fans, and now we're sitting here drawing a million over that.

"Any time that you're knocking on the door of 3 million; obviously, we'd like to go break that number and surpass 3 million and be one of the elite clubs in all of baseball with attendance."

The Rangers' players were also extremely appreciative of the fan support. While many people associated with the organization anticipated increased attendance in the year following the team's first World Series appearance, the weather didn't help the Rangers' cause.

During the 2011 regular season, the first-pitch temperature was over 100 degrees 27 times, including 15 straight home games during August.

"It's been an incredible summer for the fans, and it's probably been the hottest summer of my life," former Rangers second baseman Ian Kinsler said. "It's been over 100 degrees I don't know how many times, but they show up and continue to support us. That's huge for us."

One day later, however, reigning American League MVP Josh Hamilton fractured a bone just below his right shoulder. Before the end of April, closer Neftali Feliz joined him on the disabled list with right shoulder inflammation, and reliever Darren O'Day followed with a torn labrum in his left hip. In early May, Nelson Cruz also joined the DL gang with a strained right quadriceps.

The Rangers weathered the injury storms fairly well, and when they did hit rough patches—like losing eight of 10 games in June—team leaders refused to allow things to slide completely out of control. Washington held a productive team meeting—the only one he called all season—in the midst of the June swoon in Minnesota.

The Rangers won 12 in a row in July. Their bullpen was bolstered by late-July trades to acquire Mike Adams and Koji Uehara. And with the Angels close in the standings at the end of August, the Rangers kicked it into sizzling postseason gear, going 19–6 in September to secure the No. 2 seed in the American League. That gave Texas the home-field advantage—as it played out—in both the ALDS and the ALCS.

En route to winning a second consecutive American League West title, those young pitchers whom Ryan had challenged—Holland, Harrison, and Ogando—combined to go 43–22, and while each one of them had lapses along the way, they all rebounded impressively. And it's not a stretch to say that the traditionally pitching-challenged Rangers won the West again largely on the strength of their starting pitching. Overall, Texas starters went 74–40 with a 3.65 ERA, third-best in the American League during the season.

"You don't understand what commitment is until you go through a full 162-game season," Washington said. "Those kids grew up. They stepped up to the challenge."

17 Acquisition of Lee Lifts Rangers to the World Series

Right up until Rangers general manager Jon Daniels received the phone call from Cliff Lee on the night of December 13, 2010, Texas fans and team officials had remained hopeful that the lefty would turn his back on big-money suitors from the Bronx and choose Arlington's convenient location over the Yankees' bottomless pockets.

Rangers fans had been reminded that Lee was quite the family man, and Arlington was the closest major league city to his hometown in Benton, Arkansas, which had allowed Lee, for the first time as a big leaguer, to fly home on off days after he was traded to Texas.

"This is great for my family to be this close to home," Lee said after the Rangers eliminated the Yankees in Game 6 of the 2010 ALCS. "I love this situation I'm in. I love this team. I love my teammates. It's been a fun ride. It's been an unbelievable experience."

Yeah, whatever. Lee pulled a fast one on both the Rangers and the Yankees, leaving both organizations at the altar. Instead, he exchanged vows with the Phillies…presumably because Philadelphia is practically a suburb of Benton.

Again, whatever. Rangers fans should never have bought into Lee's words, especially since his actions spoke so convincingly that he'd already made a decision not to return to Texas. Consider the conclusive video evidence from Game 1 of the 2010 World Series in San Francisco. With the Rangers holding a 1–0 lead in the top of the second and Bengie Molina at first with one out, Lee squared to bunt against Giants ace Tim Lincecum, pulled the bat back, and lifted a double into the left-center-field gap.

His teammates went nuts, leaping to the top row of the dugout and extending their arms skyward as they performed the trademark "claw" in Lee's direction. Instead of joining the fun with a reciprocating claw, Lee shrugged his shoulder and smiled, as if he didn't want to participate in the Rangers' reindeer games.

He then blew the 2–0 lead and surrendered seven runs (six earned) on eight hits and a walk in an 11–7 loss. He pitched much better in Game 5 in Arlington, but he was too stubborn to walk one of the Giants' hottest hitters with first base open and the game on the line. Instead, Edgar Renteria's two-out, three-run homer off Lee in the top of the seventh inning silenced Rangers Ballpark and propelled the Giants to the World Series title.

Mr. October, as Lee had been dubbed, was human. Many Rangers fans were also initially quite upset at him when he chose to sign with the Phillies after indicating at one time that he was leaning toward returning to Texas.

But even though he ultimately turned his back on Texas, Rangers fans should always be grateful to Lee. While he blew a tire in the World Series, he was the ultimate rental in Rangers history, leading Texas into the Fall Classic for the first time ever.

Make no mistake: the Rangers would not have made it to the World Series without Lee. No way.

He pitched two absolute gems against Tampa Bay in the ALDS, including the road clincher in Game 5, and then he stifled the Yankees 8–0 in Game 3 of the ALCS to give the Rangers a lead in the series. In those three postseason appearances for the Rangers, he was 3–0 with an 0.75 ERA and struck out 10 or more hitters in each game, becoming the first pitcher to do that in one postseason.

Texas already had the largest divisional lead in baseball when Lee was acquired on July 9 in a trade that sent starting first baseman Justin Smoak and minor leaguers Blake Beavan, Josh Lueke, and

Matthew Lawson to the Mariners for Lee and injured reliever Mark Lowe.

Fortunately for Texas, the Rangers didn't need Lee to make it to the postseason because, quite frankly, he was pretty mediocre once he joined the team. In closing out the regular season, Lee was 4–6 with a 3.98 ERA with the Rangers.

Once the regular season turned into the postseason, however, Lee lit a fire under the Rangers. The trade for Lee put the Rangers in the World Series. He was the rental that made the first World Series ride in franchise history possible.

18 Ron Washington: The Winningest Manager in Rangers History

Perhaps it was because Ron Washington, while running in place or waving his arms wildly in the dugout as Rangers players circle the base paths, sometimes resembled a team mascot as much as the manager.

Maybe it was because he was so often grammatically incorrect in his postgame comments. English teachers cringed and journalists snickered at Wash-isms like, "That's the way baseball go."

Or possibly it was because he was not as calculating as Tony La Russa, as intimidating as Mike Scioscia, as dignified as Joe Girardi, as experienced as Jim Leyland, or as witty as Joe Maddon.

For whatever reason, Washington was regularly overlooked by national—and even regional—media when identifying the top managers in the game during his Rangers tenure. Washington routinely received more criticism for personnel moves and in-game decisions than he has received credit for improving the Rangers' record in each of his first five years in Texas (2007–11).

Nevertheless, at the time of this writing, Washington is still the only manager to lead the Rangers to a World Series. In fact, he remains the only manager to lead Texas past the ALDS.

With back-to-back American League pennants to his credit, Wash certainly earned a place in the hearts of Rangers fans for his ability to mentor champions. His dugout dances and silly, giddy grins were quite memorable, as well. The bottom line is that his players enjoyed his high-energy style and absolutely loved to play for Washington.

"When the leader of the team, the skip, is having a good time and messing around, it allows us to be free and do that," Josh Hamilton once said. "When we're playing, he feels like he's out there with us. He treats his players very well and doesn't do anything to embarrass them."

Washington cared deeply about the players, and he stood up for them routinely with his words and actions. When Nelson Cruz was struggling miserably at the end of the 2011 regular season and went 1-for-15 in the ALDS, Washington defended Cruz and kept him in the lineup.

Cruz then dominated the ALCS, making history with six homers.

Same thing with Michael Young and his 2011 postseason struggles in the first nine games. Young then delivered two RBI doubles and a homer in the ALCS-clinching game. When Ian Kinsler struggled early in the year at the leadoff spot, Wash remained his biggest supporter.

"We trust Wash," Kinsler told ESPNDallas.com's Jeff Caplan. "He believes in us, and it goes the other way in that we believe in him. He knows we have his back, and it just makes it easier for him to believe in us."

The trust factor was never more obvious than on the day Washington first publicly admitted he'd made a "huge mistake" when he used cocaine and failed a Major League Baseball drug test.

Ron Washington reacts during Game 2 of the 2011 World Series. The animated manager led the Rangers to consecutive American League pennants in 2010 and 2011. (AP Images)

Immediately, Young spoke some prophetic words regarding what would become the first pennant-winning season in Rangers history.

"Based on the kind of person that Wash is, the kind of person that we know him to be, we support him 100 percent," Young said on March 17, 2010, as reported by Bob Baum of the Associated Press. "This isn't going to be any kind of distraction in terms of us getting ready for the season. If anything, it's going to make us rally around him even more."

Against some remarkable odds, that's exactly what the Rangers did, rallying around Washington all the way to the franchise's first World Series appearance.

Still, the American League Manager of the Year Award went to the Twins' Ron Gardenhire..

Washington often managed by his "gut feel" more than by the traditional baseball book, and his moves often left observers scratching their heads. But up and down the roster, it was obvious that the Rangers thoroughly enjoy playing for their manager, and there's little doubt that Washington played a huge role in leading Texas to the 2010 and 2011 World Series as the team embraced his style of play.

While the Rangers had long been known for hitting homers, Washington began preaching the importance of winning in a variety of ways when he replaced Buck Showalter following the 2006 season. The culture didn't change overnight, but the Rangers continually improved their pitching, defense, and base running during Washington's first couple of seasons. In 2010–11, Texas appeared to be a reflection of what Washington had been stressing for years.

The 2010 Rangers, for example, led the majors with a .276 batting average, but the team total of 162 homers was the Rangers' lowest since 1992. Texas base runners advanced from first to third on singles 122 times in 2010, 22 more than the major leagues' next-best team. The Rangers also had fewer than 1,000 strikeouts for the first time since 2000, while leading the American League with 53 sacrifice bunts.

Washington led the 2012 Rangers to 93 wins and a Wild Card berth, and the Rangers won 91 games and played a tie-breaking 163rd game in 2013, as Texas recorded its fourth consecutive season with at least 90 victories.

Thanks in large part to a barrage of injuries, however, the winning ways came to an abrupt halt in 2014, as Texas went 67–95. Toward the end of that season—September 5, 2014—Washington resigned for personal reasons. Two weeks later, he acknowledged that personal reason was a result of his infidelity.

"I was not true to my wife, after 42 years," Washington said as his wife, Gerry, sat nearby during a news conference. "I broke her trust. I'm here today to own that mistake and apologize to her, and to those I disappointed, and those who have trusted in me, and I let them down. Today, I'm at a very low time in my life. I'm sorry for breaking the trust that I had with my wife and for disappointing my players, for disappointing my coaches, disappointing Major League Baseball, and for disappointing the Texas Rangers."

After making his statement, Washington stepped off a small stage and put his arm around his wife's shoulder, and she put her arm around his waist as they walked off together.

Washington retired with a 664–611 record in his eight seasons with the Rangers. He is the franchise's leader in regular-season wins and games managed, and he guided Texas to an 18–16 record in three postseason appearances.

In June 2015, after Washington had been hired as a hitting instructor with the Oakland A's, Washington conducted a radio interview with The Shan and RJ Show on Dallas-based 105.3 The Fan. During the interview, he was asked about what he missed being in Texas.

"I miss everything about Texas," he said. "I miss the hospitality. I miss the fans. I miss the players. I miss the front office. I miss everyone. But I'm onto a new chapter in my life and I'm moving on....I love all.[the Rangers fans]. I love 'em all, and that will not change."

19 Johnny Oates: No Ranger Will Ever Wear No. 26 Again

Throughout much of his tenure as the manager of the Rangers from 1995 to 2001, Johnny Oates' genuine passions for his faith, family, players, and the fans of the Dallas–Fort Worth area were often best revealed during engaging and introspective interviews with radio personalities like Norm Hitzges, then of KLIF.

So when Oates struggled continuously to find the words he wanted in a radio interview in October 2001, he suspected something might be seriously wrong.

Unfortunately, he was right. Medical tests revealed he had an aggressive tumor called glioblastoma multiforme. Patients diagnosed with that condition typically have a life expectancy of one year.

Just as he had often done as manager of the Rangers, however, Oates exceeded expectations. He died in Virginia on Christmas Eve in 2004, a month shy of his 59th birthday. Following the terminal diagnosis, he lived long enough to attend the wedding of his daughter, see the birth of a grandchild, attend the 2003 ceremony in Arlington when he was one of the first four inductees into the Rangers Hall of Fame, and spend three more quality years with his wife, Gloria.

"Gloria said one of their prayers was that he would be in heaven before Christmas," former Rangers manager Buck Showalter, who played for Oates in the minor leagues, said in '04. "I bet there will be a heck of a baseball game up there tomorrow...no, the day after tomorrow. It will take John time to get organized."

Oates was known as one of the most organized and meticulous men in baseball long before he was hired by the Rangers. Those traits allowed him to catch in the major leagues for 11 seasons, although he was primarily a backup.

"I still don't know how I got to the big leagues, because I wasn't that good," Oates said in 2003. "I was a slap hitter. I couldn't throw a lick."

Nevertheless, he was valued for his ability to handle pitchers. He made his debut with the Orioles in 1970 and also caught for the Braves, Phillies, and Dodgers before concluding his playing career with the Yankees in 1980–81.

Yankees pitcher Tommy John provided *The New York Times'* Dave Anderson with an indication of Oates' commitment to preparation in 1981 prior to a game against Toronto: "We'll go over the Blue Jay hitters. Johnny will want to know what they've done to me in the past, what I think their strengths and weaknesses are. Then he'll tell me how he wants me to pitch to them. I've never had a catcher who spends that much time with me before a game."

When his playing career ended, Oates managed in the Yankees' and Orioles' farm systems and served as a coach with the Cubs and the Orioles before succeeding Frank Robinson as the Baltimore manager in May 1991. The Orioles produced winning records in 1992 and 1993 and were in second place in the American League East in August 1994 when the players' strike ended the season. Despite his success, he was fired by Peter Angelos in September and hired as the Rangers' manager the following month.

Oates made an immediate impact in Texas, although he did not start the '95 season with the team. He took a 16-day leave of absence to attend to Gloria, who was suffering from emotional and physical exhaustion. That was a perspective-altering time for Oates, and he talked about it often in the ensuing years.

"Last year I wasn't wrapped as tight as people thought, but I was very defensive, and I took things personally," Oates told *Sports Illustrated* in 1995 after being involved in a number of confrontations with media members in Baltimore. "And I wasn't being a good husband. I had a mistress…a mistress called baseball. I was more concerned about what a writer wrote or what [Angelos] said in the 'Style' section. My family was crying out for help, but I wasn't listening."

Texas' players obviously listened to Oates. The Rangers made significant improvements in '95 and won their first division title in franchise history in '96, when Oates shared the American League Manager of the Year Award with Joe Torre. The Rangers also won the West in '98 and '99, losing to the Yankees in the ALDS in each of those seasons.

"A good manager is always one of the keys to a successful ball-club," said former *Fort Worth Star-Telegram* columnist Jim Reeves, who grew especially close to Oates. "You've got to have good players, and those were good teams. They barely had enough pitching. They didn't have great pitching, but they had good pitching and they had great chemistry in the clubhouse.

"Johnny—like Ron Washington—left the clubhouse to the players. That was their domain. He left that to his team leaders to take care of, for the most part. Much like Wash did. Johnny knew the game, and he had a strong presence about him. He knew when to remain calm. Johnny was also the most organized person in baseball that I have ever seen. He had a place for everything. Routines were very important to him. Everything on his desk was in just the right spot."

Oates, who compiled a career regular-season record of 797–746, resigned early in the 2001 season after the team lost 17 of its first 28 games following the off-season addition of free-agent shortstop Alex Rodriguez. He was considering a return to baseball when he was diagnosed with cancer. When he was inducted into the Rangers Hall of Fame in '03, Showalter had the manager's office at the Ballpark in Arlington named for Oates.

"I've been real careful through the years to say that I've been exposed to a lot of good baseball people, but he is the best," Showalter said of Oates in '03. "I can tell you right now that no one impacted my life and my professional career more than John Oates.

He was and is the most ethical, moral man I ever was around. He was the best manager I ever played for."

Following his death, the Rangers permanently retired Oates' No. 26 in an emotional ceremony in August 2005. Right up until he took his last breath, Oates spoke openly about his faith and his appreciation of the players and fans he met throughout his career. He shared this message with the fans in Arlington at his induction into the Rangers Hall of Fame in '03:

"Just know that we have an awesome God, and He's in control. To be part of an honor like this is part of the joy that He allows us to have here on Earth. All these trophies and all these awards, for which I am very thankful for, won't help you one bit getting into heaven. There is no guarantee, and please don't be fooled into thinking otherwise. I thought I was going to play major league baseball forever. I thought I was going to live forever, and we know now that nobody is. So we just pray that we're ready when that day comes."

20 Bannister Leads Worst-to-First Bounce-Back in His Rookie Managerial Season

From 2010 to 2013, the Rangers won 370 regular-season games (an average of 92.5 per year), represented the American League twice in the World Series, earned three consecutive playoff appearances, and hosted the tie-breaking game for the final wildcard spot in 2013. It represented the best four-year stretch in franchise history.

And after trading for Prince Fielder and signing Shin-Soo Choo to a seven-year, $130 million deal in the offseason, the expectation was that Texas would once again be a playoff contender with World Series potential in 2014.

It didn't take long into the 2014 calendar year to realize that Rangers were being governed by Murphy's Law (and not the law of David Murphy, who along with Nelson Cruz, Ian Kinsler, Joe Nathan, and A.J. Pierzynski departed Texas following the 2013 season). One week into January 2014, Derek Holland, who was projected to be the No. 2 starting pitcher in the rotation, tore cartilage in his knee while stumbling over his dog on the stairs at his home, the first of many stumbles by Holland over the course of the next three years.

The injury required surgery and cost Holland five months of the season. It was a sign of things to come in what may have been the most disappointing season in franchise history.

The Rangers set Major League records by using 64 players in 2014, including 40 pitchers. Twenty-three rookies were among those 64 players, as the Rangers used the disabled list a Major League-high 26 times. The rash of injuries resulted in the Rangers producing a 67–95 record, the most losses for the team in a single season since the 1985 Rangers lost 99 games.

The most telling number, however, may have been 637. That's how many runs the Rangers scored the entire season. In comparison, the 2011 Rangers scored 855 runs—218 more runs than the '14 squad.

Before the miserable season came to an end, the Rangers also lost manager Ron Washington, who resigned on September 6 for personal reasons. Bench coach Tim Bogar served as interim manager for the remainder of the season, and Bogar's final month of the season was one of the brightest spots of the entire year. Bogar pieced together a roster that went 14–8 in the final 22 games, and many fans assumed that he had done such a good job in an interim role that he would be given the opportunity to guide the 2015 ballclub.

In a bold move, however, that would dramatically shape the Rangers' future in a positive manner, general manager Jon Daniels announced that, after a 12-person team of Rangers baseball-operations personnel vetted about 40 candidates over a three-week interview period, former Pittsburgh Pirates bench coach Jeff Bannister had been hired as the Rangers' manager.

Bannister didn't immediately generate any miracles, as the Rangers were nine games out of first place as late as July 22, 2015, and eight games behind the Houston Astros on August 2. At the July 31 non-waiver trade deadline, however, Texas received a huge boost that energized the squad by trading for starting pitcher Cole Hamels and relievers Sam Dyson and Jake Diekman.

Displaying the toughness and tenacity of its manager, Texas climbed into the Wild Card race in early September and swept the Astros in a four-game series in mid-September to move into first place. The Rangers ultimately won 37 of their last 58 games and ended up being only the sixth team since division play began in 1969 to win a division title after trailing by as many as eight games in August. The 2015 Rangers were the fifth team to reach the postseason after having a league-worst record the previous season. The others were the 1991 Braves, 1998 Cubs, 2007 Cubs, and 2008 Rays.

Texas was eliminated in the postseason one game short of reaching the American League Championship Series, but Bannister, after leading the Rangers to a 21-game turnaround from 2014 to '15, was named the American League manager of the Year. He beat out A.J. Hinch of the Astros and Paul Molitor of the Twins to become the Rangers' first Manager of the Year since Buck Showalter in 2004. He also became the first AL manager to win the award in his first season.

In his second season as manager in 2016, Bannister again led the Rangers to an AL West title, leaving the Mariners (nine games back) and the Astros (11 back) in the dust. Texas was especially poised in close games under Bannister. The 2016 Rangers went 36–11 in one-run contests during the regular season, the best record in such games in Major League history.

21 Adrian Beltre: Worth Every Penny of Big-Money Contract

Following the run to the 2010 World Series, the Rangers did everything they could to re-sign free agent starting pitcher Cliff Lee. When that didn't work out, GM Jon Daniels and company began their Plan B attack.

Without Lee, priority No. 1 was to sign third baseman Adrian Beltre, who was also seriously considering a contract offer from the Rangers' top AL West rival, the Los Angeles Angels of Anaheim.

Texas paid a hefty price to land Beltre ($80 million guaranteed for five years and a $16 million option). Many critics, including former MLB commissioner Bud Selig, said the Rangers overpaid, especially since the rap against Beltre, who was entering his age-32 season, was that he was only at his best in a contract year.

The critics were wrong. Dead wrong.

Beltre made an instant impact with the Rangers, leading the team to the 2011 World Series. With his colorful and playful personality—he does practically everything with flair—he quickly emerged as a fan favorite. In fact, Rangers fans voted him in 2015 as among the "Franchise Four," representing the most impactful players in franchise history. The other three franchise players were Nolan Ryan, Pudge Rodriguez, and Michael Young.

In the clubhouse and dugout, Beltre became just as popular and clearly developed into the leader of the team, especially after the departure of Young.

He's played through immense pain a variety of times in his career with the Rangers and has led by example ever since arriving in Arlington, helping to develop younger players of all ethnic backgrounds. Beltre plays the game with tremendous intensity, but he does it with joy and style, tap dancing at the plate, making highlight reels with his antics on the basepaths, and scowling as teammates attempt to touch his head—a Beltre pet peeve—after he hits home runs.

He has also appeared to be virtually ageless at the plate, launching home runs as he drops to one knee and continually delivering clutch hits. Through the end of the 2016 season, Beltre had hit for the cycle three times in Arlington—once in 2008, against the Rangers while with the Mariners, and twice with the Rangers in 2012 and '15.

His offensive numbers alone, dating back to when he broke in with Dodgers as a 19-year-old in 1998, have made him a likely Hall of Famer. Add in his range and knack for making magnificent plays at third base, and he appears destined for Cooperstown. According to baseball-reference.com, Beltre ranks 13th all-time in defensive wins above replacement for all position players through the 2016 season.

"I think at the end of the day he's going to be a first-ballot Hall of Famer," said longtime slugger Albert Pujols in 2016. "The numbers speak for themselves."

Beltre's continued greatness and overall value to the team is why the Rangers signed him to a two-year extension worth $36 million that locked him up through 2018.

After all he has done since joining the Rangers in 2011, the signing of the extension was celebrated by Rangers fans, and no one was criticizing Texas for investing in the most valuable third baseman to ever play for the Rangers.

The Sad Saga of the Rapid Rise and Fall of David Clyde

If it had been up to then–Rangers manager Whitey Herzog, Texas wouldn't have done anything different on draft day in 1973. Even knowing now what he couldn't have known then, Herzog says the team did the right thing by choosing Kansas City–born, Houston-raised David Eugene Clyde, a left-handed power pitcher with virtually unlimited potential.

It's what happened after draft day that Herzog wishes he could change, according to what he wrote in his autobiography, *White Rat*. What happened after draft day wasn't about baseball. It was purely business.

It went a long way toward saving the Rangers' bottom line in 1973, but it also ruined Clyde's psyche...and probably his golden arm. It was a Short-sighted move, to say the least.

Bob Short–sighted, to be exact.

Short was the owner when the franchise moved from Washington, D.C., to Arlington and played before mostly empty seats during the inaugural season in Texas in 1972. Despite Short's numerous marketing and promotional ploys, the Rangers averaged about 6,000 fans per night for home games throughout the '72 season and much of '73. Texas lost a combined 205 games those two seasons, making a comedy of errors along the way.

The reward for so much bad baseball was that the Rangers owned the No. 1 overall pick in the 1973 draft. Choosing Clyde was a no-brainer. Scouts unanimously anointed him as the best pitching prospect since Bob Feller, and his high school coach, Bob French, figured he was destined to become the next Sandy Koufax.

Koufax was Clyde's idol, and he had done a nice imitation of the former Dodgers star in high school, when he'd compiled a 35–2 record over his last two seasons, including an 18–0 mark as a senior. During his sensational senior season, Clyde recorded 14 shutouts, five no-hitters, and two perfect games while striking out 328 batters and allowing only three earned runs all year.

According to Mike Shropshire's book, *Seasons in Hell*, Phillies scout Lou Fitzgerald once appeared at a Westchester High School game in Houston and left after watching Clyde pitch only three innings: "Why waste time?" Fitzgerald said. "We're picking second."

By selecting Clyde, the Rangers passed on future Hall of Famers Dave Winfield and Robin Yount. No matter, though. Clyde also had that kind of potential. He first made a major impression on Herzog while pitching for Westchester in the Texas high school state championship tournament in Austin. When Herzog returned to Arlington, he told reporters his vision for Clyde's future.

"Start him off in an all-rookie league, where he'll get used to being away from home with some guys his own age, then pull him all the way to Double A or Triple A next year," said the typically quick-witted Herzog. "I think the kid will be primed for the majors by the time he's 20. And after that we can bottle his sperm."

Unfortunately for Clyde and the franchise's long-term perspective, Short intervened. Against Herzog's strong opposition, Clyde, his parents, and Short concocted a plan where, after receiving a hefty signing bonus, Clyde would make his major league debut in Arlington. He'd pitch two home games for the Rangers, hopefully attract big crowds, and then move to the minors where he could develop secondary pitches and become less of a thrower and more of a pitcher.

While Herzog didn't like that plan, he could at least stomach it because it involved pitching the kid in only two major league games. But in the days following the draft, Short's plan generated plenty of publicity. When Clyde made his debut as a starting pitcher on June 27, 1973, against Minnesota, the traffic was so thick around Arlington Stadium that the game's start was delayed to accommodate the crowd. Clyde received a pregame telegram from Koufax, which read, "Go get 'em Number 32."

Once he stepped on the hill before a sold-out crowd of 35,698, Clyde walked the Twins' first two batters, Jerry Terrell and Rod Carew, on nine pitches. But he proceeded to strike out the side to end the inning. It was that kind of night, as Clyde pitched five innings and left with a 4–2 lead. He ended up winning the game, allowing just one hit (a two-run homer), while striking out eight and walking seven.

Before that game even ended, fans were lining up to buy tickets for his next start. The next evening, when it was business as usual at Arlington Stadium, a crowd of 3,200 showed up to watch the Twins beat the Rangers.

The excitement was all about Clyde, who pitched well in his second outing before an Arlington crowd of 33,000. Clyde pitched six innings and left with a 4–3 lead, which the bullpen later relinquished. That should have been it for "King David." After two games, he had not been exposed by big-league hitters, and he had accomplished what Short had desperately needed, drawing nearly 70,000 fans for two home dates.

Instead of sticking to the original plan, however, Short demanded that the 18-year-old Clyde stay in the Rangers' rotation…and continue putting butts in seats. It was a terrible mistake. Clyde and the Rangers lost his next start 17–2 at Milwaukee. He made 18 starts in '73, finishing the year with a 4–8 record and a 5.01 ERA.

By the end of that season, Short fired Herzog and hired Billy Martin to replace him. Martin turned the Rangers' fortunes around in '74, but not Clyde's. In his second season, Clyde went 3–9 with a 4.38 ERA in 28 appearances.

"David Clyde was one of the best young left-handed pitchers I've ever seen," Herzog told Dave Anderson of *The New York Times* in 2003. "He was really mishandled. He was wild and the other hitters started sitting on his fastball. He never had the advantage of going to the minors and pitching against kids his own age. And he was really a good kid himself. It was a tragedy."

In 1975, just before Martin was fired in July, Clyde was 0–1 before finally being sent to the minors. In 1976 his arm troubles began. He was traded to the Indians in 1978, where he went 11–15 in two seasons before he damaged a rotator cuff.

Although he signed a contract with the Astros in '81, Clyde ultimately decided at 26 years old to walk away from baseball with an 18–33 career record and an overall ERA of 4.63 in 84 games.

Globe Life Park: Home of the Heat Index

Newsflash from Captain Obvious: summertime temperatures in Arlington can turn the open-air, brick ballyard in the middle of the Metroplex into a stifling, sultry, suffocating sauna where thermometer readings often exceed the radar-gun calculations for fastballs. Fans don't merely do the wave at Globe Life Park; they perform the heat wave.

Those attending games in the summer (even night games… and even late spring and early fall contests) should expect to sweat. Players should anticipate water-weight loss. And everybody who complains about the excessive, oppressive heat should be grateful that the Rangers have plans in place for a retractable roof stadium and that the team no longer plays at Arlington Stadium.

The old muddle of metal, once located a quarter of a mile across the parking lot from Globe Life Park, was more of a furnace than a sauna. Because of the positioning of Arlington Stadium's playing surface, the lack of shadows, and the metal construction, players were in the sun longer, and the facility held the heat deep into the night.

Bobby Jones, who played for the Rangers in the 1970s and '80s and later became the team's Triple A manager, told former beat writer Phil Rogers that he remembered looking up at the thermometer on the Texas-shaped scoreboard of the old stadium one particular day and seeing that the temperature read 107 in batting practice. Nearly two hours later, it was 112 when the game started at 7:00 PM.

That was one of the reasons the Rangers needed a new stadium. Revenue potential—from suites, club seats, seat licenses, and many other bells and whistles—was the primary reason, however.

Tom Schieffer, a member of the George Bush–Rusty Rose ownership team that bought the Rangers in 1989, spearheaded the political maneuvering to find funding for the new stadium, and the Rangers and the city of Arlington announced an agreement on October 24, 1990, to build a new ballpark. Arlington voters in 1991 approved a sales tax increase to finance municipal bonds for constructing the stadium, and construction began in April 1992. The new Ballpark in Arlington was opened on April 1, 1994, to rave reviews.

In fact, the new stadium earned the nickname "the Temple" because of its classic beauty. The red brick façade, arches, and columns were a throwback to turn-of-the-century ballparks. The double-decked, covered home run porch in right field resembled old Tiger Stadium in Detroit.

The 49,000-seat stadium, designed by HKS Inc., David M. Schwarz Architectural Services, also incorporates plenty of unique features, such as the four-story office complex in center field, a 17,000-square-foot baseball museum, and an interactive area in Vandergriff Plaza that includes a wiffle ball park, tee-ball cages, speed pitch locations, and picnic tables. The stadium is also a revenue generator with 5,704 club seats and 126 luxury suites.

Its opening in 1994 instantly gave the Rangers credibility they never had in the old stadium and provided the team with added revenue to improve the roster. On July 11, 1995, the Rangers

For Whom the Ameriquest Bell Tolls

In May 2004—10 years after the opening of The Ballpark in Arlington—Ameriquest Mortgage Company bought the naming rights to the stadium for $75 million over 30 years. The new name: Ameriquest Field in Arlington.

"We think it will give us the ability to be more competitive," said then–Rangers owner Tom Hicks. "In today's economics it probably means one more good pitcher a year, and that gives us a chance to be more competitive."

That wasn't the case over the long haul, as the Rangers endured four consecutive losing seasons from 2005 to 2008. But the corporate deal did deliver one big, goofy bell.

As part of the agreement with the California-based mortgage company, a 15'-high bell was placed in the left-field terrace. It rang each time a Rangers player hit a home run or when the Rangers scored. The bell was Ameriquest's trademark, and the addition of it in the outfield was hokey, to say the least.

In mid-March 2007, however, it was announced that Ameriquest Field in Arlington was no more.

"I feel great," Hicks said. "We're getting our brand back. Based on our research with our fans, the prevailing feeling is that our ballpark is our biggest asset and we needed to have our brand on it."

That wasn't the only reason. During the three years of the partnership, Ameriquest had been involved in numerous difficulties, including layoffs, outlet closings, and lawsuits. In May 2006 Ameriquest announced it was closing all of its retail offices. The handwriting of trouble on the horizon for the company was on the wall...and the bell.

The Rangers lost $2.5 million per year from the naming rights, but they regained a number of advertising outlets at the ballpark and they no longer had to listen to the *ding-dong*.

The Promise of a New Stadium

In July 1993, Rangers president Tom Schieffer told the *Associated Press* that the team's new stadium—The Ballpark in Arlington, which was then nearing completion—would have such a distinctive Texas flavor and become so iconic that fans would immediately recognize where the game was being played simply by flipping on the television.

"You will know instantly when you turn on your TV that you're seeing Texas, just like you know right away that a game is at Wrigley Field or Fenway Park," Schieffer said. "We're building this for 100 years."

Unfortunately, it was not built for 100 degrees, which is why the Rangers, in the spring of 2016, unveiled plans for a new $1 billion, air-conditioned retractable roof ballpark through a public-private partnership where the baseball club and the City of Arlington is each paying for half of the sports complex.

The stadium is being built in parking lots A and B south of Globe Life Park and connected to a separate $200 million development of shops and restaurants known as Texas Live!, where patrons will have a view of ballgames from an outfield courtyard area.

The ballpark, which was approved by Arlington voters in a November 8, 2016, referendum, is tentatively scheduled to be completed by Opening Day of 2021. The Rangers' 30-year lease at Globe Life Park was slated to end in 2024. The partnership for the new stadium, however, extends that lease to January 1, 2054.

"We want to be proactive and continue this 45-year relationship, which has been so successful for us, for the team and the North Texas region," Arlington Mayor W. Jeff Williams said in a statement in 2016. "This is where [the Rangers] belong and this deal keeps them here for generations to come."

Plans for the mixed-use portion of the project include an upscale hotel, retail shops and a music venue, as well as dining and entertainment options.

The Rangers' economic impact is estimated to be $77.5 million for Arlington and $137.6 million for Tarrant County, according to a 2016 study commissioned by the Arlington Convention and Visitors Bureau. The club's continued presence from 2016-2054 will have an estimated economic impact of $2.53 billion for Arlington and $4.49 billion for Tarrant County.

played host to their first All-Star Game, as 50,920 fans packed into the new park. One year later, the Rangers played their first-ever playoff games in Arlington, playing the Yankees in Games 3 and 4 of the 1996 ALDS.

The new ballpark alleviated or eliminated many of the issues that restricted the team while operating out of an overgrown minor league facility. But it did not dramatically address the heat element that continually hounds and hampers the club.

The Ballpark in Arlington (a naming right deal changed the name to Globe Life Park in February 2014) was built in the early 1990s at a cost of $191 million. At that time, retractable-roof technology did exist. The SkyDome in Toronto (now the Rogers Centre) opened years earlier in 1989 at a cost of $570 million. It was funded largely by the Canadian federal and provincial governments. The Rangers didn't have that option.

Years later, the cost of retractable-roof technology dropped significantly. The Astros built Enron Field (now Minute Maid Park) with a 242'-high retractable roof in downtown Houston, opening the facility in 2000 at a cost of $250 million.

Quite frankly, the Rangers were victims of timing and a lack of technology when the Ballpark in Arlington opened. The team investigated possible solutions for heat issues, but attempting to build a roof on the existing facility is so expensive that it is not plausible.

In 2008 team officials met with a German company that designed the sun-screen apparatus that has been utilized by some European soccer stadiums. The company conducted studies and determined that with the addition of permanent shades, which would be hung on cables from support beams, the temperature inside the stadium could be lowered by up to 15 degrees.

Unfortunately, the price was exorbitant. The estimated cost for a shade that provided cover for 40 percent of the stadium was $70 million; $100 million for 60 percent shade. Again, it was not a realistic option.

Even before the unveiling of plans for a new, air-conditioned ballpark, the ownership group led by Ray Davis and Bob Simpson hired Populous in 2014 to look into the idea of installing a shade structure. The team, which has spent $60 million on improvements to the stadium since 2010, was looking for a similar, retrofitting solution to the summer heat.

A metal canopy would have cost at least $80 million and extended up to 100 feet over sections of the current seating area. While shading at least 75 percent of the stadium's spectators, it still would have left those closest to the field exposed to the sun during a day game.

The proposed structure would have only lowered the temperature by a few degrees, taken at least three baseball seasons to build, and would have made it difficult to keep the natural playing surface.

As such, Rangers fans, players, and even team executives will continue to battle temperatures in the "home of the heat index" until the completion of the new retractable roof stadium.

24 Josh Hamilton: The Good, the Bad, and the "Baseball Town" Thing

During his first tenure in Texas (2008–12), Josh Hamilton enjoyed stretches—sometimes prolonged and sometimes momentarily—when he was clearly the most dominant, mesmerizing and magnificent offensive player in the game and in the history of the Rangers' franchise.

There was the 4-for-5 performance against the Red Sox on August 13, 2010 when Texas overcame an 8–2 deficit to win in extra innings; the upper-deck walk-off home run against the A's on July 9, 2011—two days after a fan fell to his death attempting to catch a ball Hamilton tossed into the crowd; the two-homer performance at Yankee Stadium in Game 4 of the 2010 ALCS; the four-homer game in Baltimore in May 2012 when he accounted for 18 total bases, an American League record; and the go-ahead two-run homer in the 10th inning of Game 6 of the 2011 World Series, to name a few shining moments.

With the insanely talented Josh Hamilton, though, head-scratching moments often followed jaw-dropping stretches. When Hamilton slumped, flailing at breaking balls in the dirt, he sometimes looked like the least-disciplined hitter in the game. And at times, he didn't seem to care.

Hamilton also battled the demons of drug and alcohol addiction, suffering two alcohol relapses (2009 and again in 2012) during his first tenure with the Rangers.

Quite frankly, he was often as perplexing to watch as he was spellbinding. And years of drug abuse obviously affected his health, as Hamilton landed on the disabled list numerous times. When he played, he was worthy of triumphant cheers and boisterous boos—sometimes in the same homestand.

"You guys have seen what he can do," Rangers third baseman Adrian Beltre said of Hamilton in January 2016. "He's one of the best hitters in the game when he's of the right mind and he's healthy."

Whether he was locked-in or zoned-out, Hamilton was certainly one of the most memorable players in Rangers history and represents one of Jon Daniels' best trades. Four days before Christmas in 2007, Texas sent talented pitcher Edinson Volquez and reliever Danny Herrera to Cincinnati in exchange for Hamilton, who had once been the No. 1 overall pick in the MLB Draft before his life spiraled out of control because of addiction. He resurrected his career in Cincinnati and came to Texas in December 2007.

"It's a very Merry Christmas that Jon Daniels and [former owner] Mr. [Tom] Hicks have brought to the Texas Rangers in Josh Hamilton," Ron Washington said at the time of the trade.

Added Daniels: "Obviously, we've done as much homework on this guy as we've ever had on anybody [because of his prior alcohol and drug addiction problems]. We feel very comfortable about where Josh has been and that he'll be a big part of our team. He has been through a lot over the past few years, and we feel he's over the hump."

Right from the start, Hamilton was an impact player with the Rangers. In April 2008, he hit .333 with six home runs and 32 RBI. He followed that up by hitting .322 with eight home runs and 29 RBI in May. In both months, he was named American League Player of the Month. Hamilton was the star of the 2008 All-Star festivities in New York, hitting 28 homers in the first round of the Home Run Derby.

The debut season in Arlington was great. In 2009, however, Hamilton's season ended after just 89 games and 336 at-bats. He finished '09 at .268 with 10 home runs and 54 RBIs after hitting .304 with 32 home runs and 130 RBI in 156 games the previous year.

He was on the disabled list from April 27 to May 11, 2009 with a strained intercostal (rib area) muscle and again from June 1 to July 5 with a torn abdominal muscle that required surgery. His back began bothering him at the end of August, and he missed most of September.

The following year, he helped put the Rangers over the hump, leading the team to the American League West title for the first time in 11 years with an MVP season in 2010. And even though he missed most of the final month of the 2010 regular season with two fractured ribs, he carried the franchise all the way to its first-ever World Series appearance, winning the ALCS MVP with a heroic series against the Yankees.

Josh Hamilton hits a home run at Yankee Stadium during the ninth inning of Game 4 of the 2010 ALCS. Hamilton was named the MVP of the series after batting .350 with four home runs. (AP Images)

During the six games against New York, Hamilton hit .350 with four homers and reached base in 15 of 28 plate appearances.

In 2011, he missed more than a month early when he sustained a fracture in his upper right arm after diving into home plate at Detroit. But Hamilton played a huge role in leading the Rangers to consecutive American League pennants.

In 121 regular-season games in 2011, he hit .298 with 25 homers, 94 RBIs, and a .346 on-base percentage. Hamilton's power numbers dipped late in the season because of a groin injury that hampered him throughout September and the entire postseason. Nevertheless, he hit .308 with five RBIs in the ALCS and stood to be the hero in

Read Josh Hamilton's Book *Beyond Belief*

Virtually every Rangers fan—and possibly every fervent baseball fan—has likely heard and/or read some variation of Josh Hamilton's unlikely rout from golden-boy prospect to tattoo-covered drug addict, and from rock bottom to Home Run Derby hero and American League MVP.

But unless you've read *Beyond Belief: Finding the Strength to Come Back*, Hamilton's 2008 autobiography, you probably have no idea just how low he managed to sink into a self-destructive, drug-induced hell without losing his life. And the spiritual warfare that transpired in Hamilton's life is practically beyond belief. It is haunting, horrifying, and ultimately heartwarming and inspiring.

Beyond Belief is 272 pages of gripping, head-shaking, perspective-altering, and eyebrow-raising high, lows, twists, and turns. It is exasperating, enlightening, and, in the end, uplifting. It is also exceptionally well written, as Hamilton's co-author, Tim Keown, does an outstanding job of vividly describing Hamilton's roller-coaster ride from the strapping, 240-pound top pick of the 1999 Major League Baseball Draft to the 180-pound junkie on death's door.

The book is written from a Christian perspective and is published by FaithWords. Because it is ultimately a tale of Hamilton's Christian salvation and God's saving grace in his life, the book is particularly powerful in detailing the spiritual warfare that surrounds Hamilton as he finally attempts to overcome his addictions by following the words of James 4:7: "Submit yourselves, then, to God. Resist the devil, and he will flee from you."

Before Hamilton ever started drinking or using drugs, there was a foreshadowing of something evil on the horizon. During his first summer as a pro player, while playing in the outfield at Hunnicutt Field in Princeton, West Virginia, a thunderstorm moved in from the west as Hamilton looked into the skies.

"I have difficulty describing what happened next," Hamilton wrote. "The clouds kept moving, and suddenly a demon's face appeared, superimposed on the clouds. It was jumping out at me, and it made me rock back on my heels. I got chills. The face was grinning, almost taunting."

Shortly after detailing Hamilton's initial use of cocaine and receiving one of his last tattoos, Keown pinpoints the official beginning of the battle with drugs and for Hamilton's soul in a powerful one-page, 93-word chapter that can be read again and again.

The last three lines of the chapter, describing two tattoos on Hamilton's right leg, are riveting:

"The soulless demon.

"The face of Jesus.

"The battle had begun."

Throughout the ensuing four-year battle with drugs, alcohol, hopelessness, and depression, Hamilton makes one horrendous decision after another. Four days after his daughter was born, for example, Hamilton went on an errand to pick up a prescription for his wife. Instead he went to a bar and disappeared for three days of drinking and cocaine abuse.

Toward the end of the road to rock bottom, Hamilton describes himself, "as a shell of a human, a soulless being. I had stripped myself of self respect and lost my ability to feel love or hope or joy or even pain."

Only God could have saved him from his relentless quest for cocaine. And with the help of Hamilton's granny, that's exactly what happened. But read the book for complete details. It's a page-turner that you will likely complete in a couple of days, and it's one that will stay with you for a lifetime.

the World Series—if Texas had held onto the lead—when he blasted a two-run homer in the 10th inning of Game 6.

The 2012 season was the biggest roller coaster of all for Hamilton. He was amazing at time (like the four-homer night in Baltimore), but he was the poster player of the Rangers' late-season collapse. Texas lost seven of its final nine regular-season games, including the final three in Oakland. In the final game, the A's overcame a four-run deficit to win 12–5 in a comeback that was punctuated by Hamilton's dropped fly ball on a routine plat in centerfield.

Oakland moved into first place for the first time all year on the final day of the season. As a result, the Rangers were forced to play in the AL Wild Card Game against Baltimore. The Rangers lost the game 5–1, as the offense went silent.

Hamilton went 0-for-4 and struck out twice. He was also booed during that loss. The Wild Card game only continued a trend, as Hamilton struck out in 18 of his last 39 at-bats.

In the offseason, Hamilton signed a five-year, $125 million deal with the Angels…without giving the Rangers an opportunity to match the deal.

Then, in February, Hamilton enraged Rangers' fans. "There are true baseball fans in Texas, but it's not a true baseball town," said Hamilton in a television interview.

The fans didn't forget. In his first game in Arlington as a member of the Angels (also the Rangers' 2013 home-opener), "Hambo" was greeted by a chorus of boos from the crowd of 48,845. When the fans began chanting "Baseball town, baseball town," Hamilton began playfully imitating a quarterback's throwing motion, even pretending to take a few snaps from center. "Yeah, I messed with them a little bit," he said. "You gotta encourage them a little bit."

Unfortunately for Hamilton, his numbers nosedived from a .285 batting average, 43 homers and 128 RBI in his final season in Texas to .250, 21 homers and 79 RBI after switching uniforms. Then he missed nearly half of 2014 with injuries, produced a career-low of 10 homers and 44 RBI and went hitless, while being lustily booed, in 13 playoff at-bats as the Angels were swept by Kansas City in the division series.

In February 2015, Hamilton underwent right-shoulder surgery and then did not report to spring training in Arizona after informing MLB of a drug relapse in the offseason. Hamilton also filed for a divorce from his wife, Katie, during that offseason.

On April 3, 2015, an arbitrator ruled that Hamilton had not violated his drug treatment program, so Hamilton did not have to go into a rehabilitation program and could not be suspended.

Angels management was livid. The team had already pulled Hamilton-related merchandise from team stores and refused to issue him a locker in the Angel Stadium clubhouse.

At wit's end, the Angels traded him back to Texas in late April 2015, paying him about $60 million to play for an American League West rival, a reflection of just how much owner Arte Moreno wanted to rid himself of Hamilton.

Hamilton was embraced by his teammates and the fans when he returned, and he played a role in helping the Rangers win their first AL West title since 2011 by playing in 50 games in 2015 and hitting .253 with eight homers and eight doubles. He wasn't the old MVP Josh, but he again had his moments.

For example, on May 31, 2015, Hamilton delivered a pinch-hit, two-run double with two outs in the bottom of the ninth to lift the Rangers to a 4–3 victory over Red Sox, moving the Rangers over .500 for the first time in 360 days.

Unfortunately, moments like that were few and far between, and they came to an end in 2016 when Hamilton missed the beginning of the season while recovering from knee surgery. Upon his return in late April, he appeared in just one rehab game before having to take additional time off. He underwent another operation in June to repair a torn ACL and cartilage damage, ending his season. In August 2016, the Rangers released him.

"We plan to monitor Josh's progress as he continues his rehab process and is medically cleared this winter," said General Manager Jon Daniels. "Given the rules in place, releasing him before the end of this month allows us to keep the door open to extending the relationship in the future."

Perhaps there will be yet another chapter in the Hamilton-Rangers book. Regardless, it's been one helluva entertaining—and at times perplexing—read.

Surviving the Near-Disastrous Slide of 1996

The 1996 Rangers scaled some unprecedented heights, winning the organization's initial division title and the franchise's first-ever playoff game. Before reaching an unparalleled summit, however, the Rangers tortured their fans by nearly sliding out of the playoff picture with a collapse that would have ranked among the biggest choke jobs in baseball history.

On September 11, 1996, the Rangers' lead over second-place Seattle ballooned to nine games. But after being swept by the Mariners in a four-game series at the Kingdome on September 16–19 and losing an extra-inning game in Anaheim on September 20, the lead was cut to one game, and the red-hot Mariners were tied with Texas in the loss column.

The Rangers needed more than a shot in the arm; they appeared in desperate need of the Heimlich Maneuver.

"I wouldn't say anybody associated with the team slipped into panic mode," Rangers play-by-play radio announcer Eric Nadel recalled. "But the mood was definitely tense in the dugout before the games in Seattle and during [batting practice]. Clearly, they were not loose the way they had been all year. I think [manager] Johnny [Oates] kept the team from going into complete panic, and I think [second baseman Mark] McLemore was responsible, too.

"But there's no doubt that things got tight. Very early in the first game in Seattle, Dean Palmer made an error that led to six Seattle runs. They went to Anaheim, and they lost the first game even though they were leading in the 10th. That loss knocked the lead down to one. The next game is when [John] Burkett pitched a gem, and they definitely needed it."

Burkett, who'd been acquired from Florida in August, pitched eight innings on Saturday night (September 21) to lead the Rangers to a 7–1 win over the Angels in what was—at that point—the most important victory in franchise history. One day later, Ken Hill

Dave Valle: An Unsung Hero of the 1996 Playoff Team

Prior to surviving the slide of September, the Rangers had already endured a mini-avalanche in August. Two losses in Detroit cut the Rangers' lead over Seattle to just two games in early August, and on the plane to Toronto from the Motor City, backup catcher Dave Valle told relief pitcher Dennis Cook that he felt like he needed to say something to the team.

"But Dave wasn't sure if it was his place," recalled Jamey Newberg, creator and author of the *Newberg Report*. "'Cookie' told Valle, at the time a 13-year big league veteran with only 62 at-bats in four months as Pudge [Rodriguez's] backup, that he'd earned the right to speak up."

Valle asked manager Johnny Oates for permission to hold a team meeting on August 9 in Toronto. Oates approved and asked when he and the coaches should leave the room.

"Valle responded by saying that nobody was excused from the room," Newberg wrote. "Valle then got in the face of every man in that clubhouse—the players, trainers, equipment guys, the bullpen catcher, and even the manager—and challenged each of them, saying: 'Are you willing to do what it takes to win?' Picture a second lieutenant lining up the troops, side by side, barking the same question, the same command, at each of them."

Oates responded by saying, "Yes, sir."

The Rangers went on a seven-game winning streak to increase the lead over the Mariners to seven. Texas would need every game of that lead during the September nosedive.

And when the Rangers needed a win in the worst way—with the lead in the American League West down to one game on September 21—Oates put Valle in the lineup to catch John Burkett, sitting Rodriguez on the bench. Valle was up to the challenge, homering to left off Jim Abbott in the seventh to highlight a 2-for-4 night in a 7–1 Rangers win.

delivered an equally important clutch pitching performance, going the distance in a 4–1 victory. On that same Sunday afternoon, Seattle had its 10-game winning streak snapped in a 13–11 loss to Oakland.

"Those two games in Anaheim stopped the bleeding," Nadel said. "They were big in so many ways."

Texas left Anaheim and split a pair of games with Oakland to finish the road trip at 3–6 overall. It wasn't pretty, but it was so much better than it could have been after going 0–5 to begin the trip.

"I think the atmosphere is different than when we left Seattle," Oates said after winning the final game of the trip 7–3 in Oakland. "Now we can go home and get a chance to do what needs to be done."

That's exactly what happened, as the Rangers finished the season with six wins in their final eight games. Texas clinched the division on September 27, despite losing a 15-inning marathon to the Angels in Arlington. Oakland beat Seattle to eliminate the Mariners before the end of the California-Texas game, which allowed everyone inside the Ballpark at Arlington to finally breathe easy.

Until those two big wins in Anaheim on September 21 and 22, most Rangers fans had been holding their collective breath as media across the country compared the Texas nosedive to the historic collapses of the '64 Phillies, the '69 Cubs, and the '78 Red Sox.

But before a crowd of 24,104 on Saturday night at Anaheim Stadium, Burkett pitched eight strong innings, allowing seven hits but just one earned run. The Rangers backed Burkett with all the run support he needed in the top of the third, as No. 9 hitter Kevin Elster led off with a double against Angels starter Jim Abbott and was bunted to third by Darryl Hamilton. Elster scored on Pudge Rodriguez's sacrifice fly, then Rusty Greer homered to right, and Juan Gonzalez followed with a homer to right-center.

The next day, Gonzalez hit his club-record 47th homer, singled twice, and drove in two runs to raise his season total to 141.

Meanwhile, Hill allowed eight hits but just one run in a complete-game effort.

"Kenny Hill was on top of his game today, just like Burkett was last night, and those are the kind of outings their staff is going to have to have if they're going to win the division," said Rex Hudler, who scored the Angels' only run on September 22.

26 Jim Sundberg: Reluctant Ranger to Lone Star Legend

It doesn't take a rocket scientist to figure out why Jim Sundberg was originally tagged with the nickname "Sunny." But in the grand scheme of his role in Rangers history, that moniker has so much more meaning than merely serving as a catchy shortening of his surname.

When Texas produced some really good teams in the 1970s, Sunny shone brightly behind the plate and in the batter's box. And on so many forgettable teams in the '70s and early '80s, Sunny was the bright spot for the franchise. The six-time Gold Glove–winner has also built a glowing résumé in the team's front office, as it was Sundberg, now the team's senior executive vice president, who laid the groundwork for Nolan Ryan's return as team president in 2008.

Sundberg, born in Galesburg, Illinois, attended college at the University of Iowa and won his only World Series ring with Kansas City in 1985. But he has spent so much of his professional life in the Lone Star State that he now claims Texas as his home state. Appropriately, he was one of the four original inductees into the Rangers Hall of Fame in 2003, joining Ryan, Charlie Hough, and Johnny Oates. And if there had been a popularity vote among

Rangers fans in the late 1970s, Sundberg would have been the runaway winner.

In his first stint with the Rangers (1974–83), Sundberg played on teams that finished a combined 132½ games out of first place. While he played on a 94-win team in '77, Sundberg played on five losing teams, including the 98-loss Rangers of 1982.

In good times or bad, Rangers fans could count on Sundberg to be the catcher of class. He was much more than just a brilliant defensive backstop, though. He became the face of the franchise, the most radiant of all early Rangers, outlasting fellow 1974 rookie Mike Hargrove on the team's roster, outhustling and outworking so many players who came and went, surviving an era of often terrible trades, and providing legitimacy for a franchise that craved it.

Ironically, the man who now cherishes his revered stature in Rangers lore once loathed the idea of wearing a Texas uniform. Sundberg had first been drafted by the Athletics in 1969 coming out of high school. Then in 1972, the Rangers picked him in the eighth round. Prior to the '72 draft, one of the Rangers' scouts gave Sundberg good reasons not to sign with the team and to harbor adverse feelings about playing in Arlington.

"Being drafted by the Rangers was not something I initially enjoyed," said Sundberg, who finally signed with Texas after he was the team's first-round-pick in the January 1973 secondary phase of the first-year-player draft. "The scout ripped me up one side and down the other. He said, 'You can't hit, can't catch, you throw everything into center field, and you're never going to make it to the big leagues. But I'll give you a chance anyway.'

"That didn't sit too well with me, so I wasn't very happy when they drafted me in the ['73] draft. I called a friend who said the Rangers didn't have any catching, and I had a good chance at working up in the system quickly, so I should consider signing with them."

Sundberg took the fast track to the show, making his first Rangers start on April 6, 1974, when he caught Fergie Jenkins' one-hitter against the world-champion Athletics.

"I had a couple of hits in that first start and threw out [future Rangers teammate] Bert Campaneris," Sundberg said. "That was a memorable way to start my career. In my last game with the Rangers, I caught Nolan Ryan [on September 24, 1989], and had [a key] RBI. So, I came in and went out as a player on memorable notes."

In between, he played in an additional 1,960 major league games, building a legacy in the Lone Star State and adding to his glowing reputation with a couple of other teams. Sundberg finished fourth in the 1974 Rookie of the Year balloting (won by Hargrove) and made the first of three All-Star appearances that season.

He won the first of six straight Gold Gloves in 1976 and was sensational in '77 when the Rangers went 94–68 and finished eight games back of the Royals, who won 102 games. Sunny hit .291 and threw out 56 percent of attempted base stealers in '77, when he was voted as the team's MVP.

Sundberg continued to be a steadying force in ensuing years, but the dreadful '82 Rangers attempted to trade Sunny to the Dodgers for Orel Hershiser and Dave Stewart. Sundberg, who was being short-changed in his contract, rejected the trade. On December 8, 1983, however, the Rangers made an abysmal trade that Sunny approved, sending him to Milwaukee for Ned Yost and Dan Scarpetta.

"The first trade is the hardest," said Sundberg, who in 2000 wrote a very good book with his wife, Janet, called *How to Win at Sports Parenting: Maximizing the Sports Experience for You and Your Child.* "Your feelings are hurt. They tried to trade me to the Dodgers, so I had a little bit of a taste at what being traded felt like. By the time I was traded to Milwaukee, I was ready to go."

Sundberg was an All-Star in '84 with the Brewers and was then dealt to Kansas City, where he spent the '85 and '86 seasons. He helped solidify a young pitching staff for the '85 Royals and came up big in the postseason.

In Game 7 of the '85 ALCS, Sundberg's three-run triple in the sixth broke open the game, leading the Royals to a 6–2 win over the Blue Jays. In the World Series, Sunny hit safely in six of seven games.

"There's nothing better than playing on a championship club," Sundberg said of his time in Kansas City. "It's the pinnacle of anyone's career. That was a thrill, but my heart was always in Texas."

Sundberg spent the '87 season and part of '88 with the Chicago Cubs before returning to the Rangers on July 21, 1988. He retired as a player following the conclusion of the 1989 season and spent six years as the team's television analyst. He left the organization from 1996 to 2001 before returning in 2002 as minor league catching coordinator. He first moved into the front office in 2004, where he once again served as a beacon of hope during the dark days of four consecutive losing seasons (2005–08).

In helping to bring Ryan back to the franchise as team president in '08, Sunny also played a huge role in leading the Rangers to consecutive World Series appearances in 2010–11.

"I had a major hand in [Ryan's return], which felt good because he brought a pitching philosophy and an element to our organization that we didn't have," Sundberg said. "That's a big reason why we went to the World Series. He and Jon Daniels have teamed up pretty well. They're at two different ends of the spectrum in age, experience, education, and backgrounds, but they've turned out to be a good team. And to see the Rangers in the World Series was a dream come true for me."

Fittingly, Sunny also had a dream role in the Rangers' first World Series. Prior to Game 5 in Arlington in 2010, he caught the ceremonial first pitch from Fergie Jenkins, who had pitched so splendidly in Sunny's first major league start more than a quarter of a century earlier.

"It's been a great ride," Sundberg said. "Hopefully, there are plenty more adventures."

27 No Ranger Crushed a Baseball Quite Like Juan Gonzalez

During the course of his career with Texas, Michael Young has watched plenty of powerful hitters deliver majestic home runs for the Rangers. Young was a member of the team when Alex Rodriguez set the club record with 57 homers in '02.

He watched Rafael Palmeiro tie his own team record for homers by a left-handed hitter with 47 in 2001 and witnessed Mark Teixeira deliver 43 homers in 2005, still a club record by a switch hitter. And, of course, he's seen Josh Hamilton and Nelson Cruz crush some of the longest homers in team history.

So, who is the hardest masher of them all? None of the aforementioned folks.

"Juan was the most gifted hitter I ever played with," Young told ESPNDallas.com's Richard Durrett of the two seasons he played with Gonzalez in Texas (2002 and 2003). "To this day, I've never seen a guy hit balls as hard as Juan.... His homers were 2 irons. They stayed low and hard. He didn't hit many high, majestic homers. They were bullets that didn't stop.... Two things stick out: how hard he hit the ball and his nose for the RBI."

Gonzalez still holds the single-season club records for most RBIs (157 during the 1998 season), the highest slugging percentage (.643 in 1996), and the most extra-base hits (97 in 1998).

Juan Gonzalez is the Rangers' all-time home run leader, hitting 372 of his 434 career long balls in a Rangers uniform. (AP Images)

But what made "Igor" one of the most feared hitters in baseball during his first stint with the Rangers (1989–99) was his ability to hit the ball out of the ballpark in the blink of an eye. Gonzalez didn't benefit tremendously from the "jet stream" that often produces cheap home runs to right field at Rangers Ballpark in Arlington.

Gonzalez was a pull hitter—a line-drive-hitting, laser-producing machine who hit more home runs (372) in a Rangers uniform than any other player in team history. He twice led the American League in home runs (43 in 1992 and 46 in '93), which may not seem too surprising. But consider that he did so while playing half his games in pitcher-friendly Arlington Stadium, where winds often caused long fly balls to die on the warning track.

"Arlington Stadium was not a friendly park for home run hitters," said former Rangers player and general manager Tom Grieve. "But Juan would crush the baseball on a line. He would hit a laser beam that would leave the stadium in no time, and everybody would kind of look around and say, 'Wow.' He was an aggressive hitter who'd also strike out quite a bit and could look really ugly doing so. But when a pitcher made a mistake or when Juan zeroed in on his pitch, he was something else."

Gonzalez, who hit at least 20 homers in eight seasons, was in a class of his own in the 1996 and '98 regular seasons, his two American League MVP seasons. But he was never more sensational than in the 1996 ALDS. In the four-game series, Gonzalez hit five home runs, collected nine RBIs, and hit for a .438 average. The rest of the Rangers combined to hit .190 with one homer and seven RBIs.

"He was amazing in the '96 ALDS," Grieve recalled. "That may be the definition of being in 'the zone.'"

Following the 1999 seasons, Texas traded Gonzalez, Danny Patterson, and Gregg Zaun to Detroit for Frank Catalanotto, Francisco Cordero, Gabe Kapler, Bill Haselman, Justin Thompson, and minor league pitcher Alan Webb. The trade really didn't work out as hoped for either side. After a short stint with the Tigers and then with the Indians, Gonzalez re-signed with Texas in January 2002.

In hindsight, then-owner Tom Hicks said that was one of the biggest mistakes he made. In 2007 Hicks said he suspected Gonzalez had been slowed and injury-prone later in his career because of steroid use.

"I have no knowledge that Juan used steroids. His number of injuries and early retirement just makes me suspicious," Hicks wrote in an email to the Associated Press in 2007. "In any event, we paid him $24 million for very few games. Juan Gonzalez for $24 million [over two years] after he came off steroids, probably, we just gave that money away."

Frank Catalanotto Reaches Base 13 Consecutive Times

Before the 2000 season, infielder Frank Catalanotto joined the Rangers as part of the nine-player Juan Gonzalez trade with Detroit. He didn't waste time making an impact in Texas.

From April 21 to May 18, Catalanotto reached base safely 13 consecutive trips to the plate (10 hits, three walks). The streak still stands (through 2011) as the Rangers' franchise record for consecutive appearances reaching base.

Because of a pulled groin, Catalanotto went 29 straight days without making an out. He started his streak in late April and then went on the disabled list.

In his return to the starting lineup on May 17, Catalanotto went 5-for-5 against the Devil Rays. One night later against Baltimore, Catalanotto extended his streak of consecutive at-bats without making an out with first- and third-inning singles. The streak ended when he grounded out in the fourth.

Catalanotto's breakout year came in 2001 when he finished fifth in the American League in batting average with a .330 mark, slugged a career-best .490, and stole 15 bases.

Sidelined by a torn ligament in his right thumb and a right calf injury, he played in only 152 of 324 games in 2002–03, hitting .288 with 32 homers and 105 RBIs. He finished his career by playing 33 games with Kansas City in 2004 and one game with Cleveland in '05, tearing his hamstring in his only at-bat with the Indians.

28 Rangers Trade Teixeira to Atlanta for Prime Prospects

Mark Teixeira could have been a lifelong Ranger. Fortunately for Texas, he had absolutely no desire to make that kind of commitment to the team.

Just before the Rangers pulled the trigger on a blockbuster seven-player trade with the Atlanta Braves in July 2007, Texas offered an eight-year, $140 million contract extension to "Tex" and his agent, Scott Boras. Teixeira, who'd been chosen by the Rangers with the fifth overall selection of the 2001 draft out of Georgia Tech, declined. Politely but emphatically.

In hindsight, it worked out exceptionally well for both Teixeira and the Rangers.

Texas sent its switch-hitting All-Star first baseman to the Braves, along with left-handed reliever Ron Mahay, in exchange for rookie catcher Jarrod Saltalamacchia and four minor leaguers. Two of those young prospects (shortstop Elvis Andrus and pitcher Neftali Feliz) proved to be instrumental in leading the Rangers to their first World Series appearance in 2010.

Andrus, a runner-up for 2009 American League Rookie of the Year, served as Texas' leadoff hitter and best defensive infielder throughout much of the 2010 season. Feliz was the 2010 American

League Rookie of the Year after setting a record for saves by a rookie with 40, and closed out the ALCS Game 6 clincher against the Yankees. Teixeira wasn't on the field for the Yankees in Games 5 and 6 because he'd suffered a hamstring injury in Game 4.

Prior to that, however, Teixeira had not been a factor. Against his old team, Teixeira was 0-for-14 in the ALCS. It was the worst oh-fer in Yankees postseason history, surpassing Joe Collins' 0-for-12 in the 1952 World Series, according to ESPN Stats & Information.

In fairness to Teixeira, he did help the Yankees to the 2009 World Series title, and he also helped the Angels into the 2008 postseason.

He also performed valiantly with the Rangers throughout the early years of his career without coming seriously close to reaching the postseason. Teixeira won two Gold Gloves and also claimed two Silver Slugger Awards with the Rangers.

When he declined the team's contract extension in July '07, Texas was woefully out of the playoff race. Meanwhile, on the day he was acquired by the Braves, Atlanta was 4½ games behind the Mets in the National League East and in the middle of the wild-card chase.

"We've got the team to win the World Series," Atlanta catcher Brian McCann said after it was announced that the Braves had acquired Teixeira.

That didn't happen. Tex played well with Atlanta, homering in each of his first three games. And in 54 games with Atlanta to close out 2007, Teixeira batted .317 with 17 homers and 56 RBIs. But it wasn't enough to put the Braves into the postseason, and in July 2008, Teixeira was traded to the Angels for Casey Kotchman and minor league pitcher Stephen Marek. Then in December 2008, Tex signed an eight-year, $180 million free-agent deal with the Yankees, his fourth team in 17 months.

Injuries prevented Saltalamacchia from becoming a star in Texas, and the Rangers sent him to the Red Sox on July 31, 2010, for minor league prospects Chris McGuinness, Roman Mendez, a player to be named later (Michael Thomas), and cash.

During the 2011 season, left-handed pitcher Matt Harrison, another prospect acquired in the trade, became a key component of the starting rotation that helped the Rangers return to the World Series, adding even further value to the Teixeira trade. Even before Harrison's breakout season in '11, the trade had been widely considered as one of the best—if not the best—in the Rangers' history because it delivered two cornerstones for the franchise's back-to-back World Series runs in Andrus and Feliz. Once Harrison also emerged as an outstanding starting pitcher (he was an All-Star in 2012 before back issues derailed his career in Texas), there was not much doubt that this trade was one for the ages in Arlington.

"[Teixeira] was a great player and a valuable one, but it was obvious that at that point in his career [2007] and where we were in our winning cycle, they weren't synced up," Rangers GM Jon Daniels said to Richard Durrett of ESPNDallas.com. "There's no harm in that. He recognized it. We recognized it. Ultimately, it worked out for him and us."

29 2016 Rangers Starting Pitching Disappears at Worst Possible Time

Entering the 2016 postseason, the Rangers owned the best record in the American League and, by virtue of the AL's win in the All-Star game, Texas could envision having home-field advantage in the playoffs throughout the World Series for the first time in franchise history.

More significantly, though, the 95-win Rangers entered the 2016 postseason with their best 1–2 punch in team history at the top of the rotation. By running away with the AL West, Texas was able to position its starting pitching perfectly for the ALDS rematch with the Toronto Blue Jays: aces Cole Hamels and Yu Darvish for the first two games, postseason warrior Colby Lewis for Game 3, and possibly Hamels and Darvish again in the fourth and fifth games, if necessary.

Unfortunately, the fourth and fifth games weren't necessary in large part because those aforementioned starters often looked like they were throwing batting practice to the Blue Jays. In the course of being swept out of the playoffs, Hamels, Darvish and Lewis combined to allow 16 hits and 17 runs (16 earned) in 10.1 innings in the three straight losses (a 13.94 ERA).

In Game 1 (a 10–1 loss before a sold-out crowd at Globe Life Park), Hamels allowed seven runs (six earned) in 3.1 innings. It was an uncharacteristic October performance for the 32-year-old Hamels, and the shortest postseason outing of his career. It was also only the second time in six career playoff-opening starts that he took a loss.

Next up for the Rangers was Darvish, who had actually been much better in the final month of the regular season than Hamels. But after displaying electric "stuff" in the first inning, Darvish delivered a 2–0 fastball in the second inning to Troy Tulowitzki, who sent it over the wall in left-center field for a two-run shot in second inning.

Toronto broke the game wide open in the fifth inning with three solo homers off Darvish, who became the first pitcher to allow four homers in a postseason game since the Twins' Rick Reed in 2002.

Overall, the Blue Jays managed only six hits during the entire game in winning 5–3, but four of them left the ballpark. With their two best starters on the hill, the Rangers became only the second team in postseason history to allow six home runs to six batters over the first two games of a series.

By losing the first two games of the series in Arlington, the Rangers also fell to 1–11 all-time in ALDS games at home. Hitting the road didn't produce any different results, though.

Facing elimination in Game 3 in Toronto, the Rangers turned to Colby Lewis, who had won more postseason games than any pitcher in Rangers history. Like his teammates, though, the 37-year-old right-hander was rocked early in the series-deciding 7–6 loss.

Lewis left in the third inning and was charged with five earned runs on five hits. He allowed two homers in the first inning as the Jays erased a brief 1–0 deficit. A two-run homer by Edwin Encarnacion and a solo homer by Russell Martin came on sliders left out over the plate by Lewis.

Lewis was taken out with no batter retired in the third inning after a single and ground-rule double by Josh Donaldson put Toronto up 4–2.

As a result, the Rangers' 2016 season—the first in franchise history in which the team compiled the best record in the American League—ended once again at the expense of the Blue Jays, who won the final three games of the 2015 ALDS to put together a six-game postseason winning streak against Texas.

As they had done all year, the Rangers showed plenty of grit in rallying back to take the lead in Game 3, but ultimately the Rangers were eliminated because they lost a one-run game for just the 12th time in 2016. Texas went 36–11 in one-run contests during the regular season, the best record in such games in Major League history.

In the regular season, the 2016 Rangers were 60–31 against teams that had a winning record, which seemed to be a good omen entering the playoffs. The .659 winning percentage against teams with winning records was the third highest ever in American League history behind the 2001 Mariners (.676) and the 1910 Athletics (.662). But it didn't work out in the 2016 postseason.

30 The 1974 Season: The First Signs of a Pulse

After only two seasons in Arlington, the one thing that could be said about the early Rangers was that they were remarkably consistent. Unfortunately for local fans (and the word *fans* should be used loosely in this instance), the Rangers were dependably dismal.

The first team in Arlington went 54–100 in the strike-shortened 1972 season for manager Ted Williams, finishing 38½ games out of first place (a .351 winning percentage). The second edition, managed by Whitey Herzog for most of the year, produced an almost identical winning percentage (.352) and finished 37 games out of first place with a 57–105 record.

Just prior to the end of the '73 season, however, the Rangers' front office made a move that breathed life—actually hot air—into the team for the 1974 season. On September 8, 1973, the Rangers, at 47–91, announced that Herzog had been fired as manager, and he was being replaced by the fiery and controversial Billy Martin, who'd been fired by Detroit in August. Martin arrived in Arlington on a mission and with a message for the lowly Rangers.

"When Billy Martin joined the team for the last month of the season, he came into the clubhouse and said, 'I don't want anyone in here to think I'm here to try to make us better or to try to be respectable,'" recalled Tom Grieve, a 25-year-old outfielder for the '73 Rangers. "He clearly made the point that the only reason he was here was to win. He said, 'I expect that we will win next year, and if anyone in this room doesn't feel that way, come into my office. No questions will be asked, no grudges will be held, but I'll get rid of you because I came here to win.'

"It was inspiring, but when he got done speaking, the players looked at each other and thought that he must not have seen us play this year."

While the team continued to struggle throughout the rest of September, the front office made another major move in the off-season that would have a monumentally positive effect on the '74 season. On October 25, 1973, the Rangers sent third baseman Bill Madlock and second baseman Vic Harris to the Cubs for right-handed pitcher Fergie Jenkins.

That move, along with the decisions to provide plenty of playing time to rookies at first base (Mike Hargrove) and catcher

Rangers' 1972 Opening Day Cancelled

The 1972 major league season was the first to ever have games canceled by a players' strike, delaying the opening of the year by a week and a half because of disputes regarding pension and salary arbitration. Perhaps it was fitting that 1972 was also the Rangers' first season in Arlington.

Before the '72 Rangers ever officially stepped on the field, they already had a strike against them.

It was a sign of things to come.

The Rangers' first-ever Opening Day was originally scheduled for April 6. That game and seven others were canceled, as Texas played only 154 games in 1972.

But fewer games didn't mean the Rangers could avoid triple-digits in the loss column. Texas went 54–100 in its first season, finishing 38½ games behind Oakland in the American League West.

Despite the overall atrocious record, Texas actually started the season decently. On April 29, the Rangers beat Boston 7–6 to improve to 7–5 for the season. And on May 21, the Rangers swept a doubleheader against Minnesota to run its winning streak to five and return to .500 at 15–15.

That was the last sniff the team had of .500, however, as Texas lost eight of its next nine to end May. But the worst month of the year—by far—was September. Texas went 3–23 in the final full month of the season, including a 15-game losing streak to end September.

(Jim Sundberg) for the 1974 season, made a world of difference. With Martin punching many of the right buttons and the 31-year-old Jenkins serving as the ace of the staff, the Rangers completed April at 13–8 and hovered at .500 until July 4.

The team slipped a little in early July, losing 10 of 13 during one stretch to fall five games under .500. But the Rangers righted the ship in August. Second baseman Dave Nelson punctuated the end of the summer months by tying a major league record on August 30, stealing second, third, and home in the first inning against Cleveland.

By mid-September, the Rangers had won nine of 11 to move to a season-high 11 games over .500 (79–68). Texas was in second place in the American League West, 4½ games back of Oakland and 5 ahead of third-place Minnesota.

The Rangers could never move any closer, and they finished the year at 84–76, 5 games behind the eventual world champion Athletics. Nevertheless, it was a tremendously successful season on so many levels.

After hitting .301 and driving in 118 runs, outfielder Jeff Burroughs was selected as the American League MVP. Hargrove, who produced a .323 batting average in 131 games, was American League Rookie of the Year. Martin was the league's Manager of the Year. And Jenkins, who went 25–12 with a spectacular 2.82 ERA, was chosen as Comeback Player of the Year.

Perhaps most important, the '74 Rangers etched a place in the consciousness of the local sports fans. After drawing 662,974 fans in '72 and 686,085 in '73, the 1974 Rangers attracted 1,193,902 fans to Arlington Stadium.

"We had a good team," Grieve said. "We didn't win the division, but we made it competitive, and we drew a million fans for the first time. That was a significant accomplishment."

Indeed, it may have signified that Rangers could make it in Arlington.

31 The Short Union of Nolan Ryan and Chuck Greenberg

In retrospect, the ownership union of Hall of Fame pitcher Nolan Ryan and Pittsburgh sports attorney Chuck Greenberg—once perceived as a blissful baseball match—was as flawed as many of the mega–movie star marriages that often dissolve within months of matrimony.

Ryan and Greenberg, the high-profile front men of an ownership group called Rangers Baseball Express LLC, won a controversial auction in a Fort Worth federal bankruptcy court to buy the team from Tom Hicks and were approved as owners in August 2010. By early March 2011, Greenberg was out, announcing he had resigned—against his own desires—as CEO and managing partner in a breakup as bizarre as the bankruptcy hearings.

While the Greenberg-Ryan team didn't stand the test of time, Greenberg's role in the formation of Rangers Baseball Express should be recognized and respected by the team's fans. Greenberg was the behind-the-scenes organizer and most outspoken proponent of the ownership group that included Ryan and principal investors Bob Simpson and Ray Davis.

That group had the public backing of Major League Baseball and the financial stability to beat a nearly $600 million offer from Dallas Mavericks owner Mark Cuban and Houston businessman Jim Crane. If Cuban and Crane had won the bid, it could have been ruinous for the Rangers.

Ryan, the team president at the time of the auction, probably would have immediately resigned from his working relationship with the Rangers. Losing Ryan from the front office would have been a public-relations nightmare, and it would have abruptly halted the positive energy and progress the team had made in many areas since Ryan became president in 2008.

As unofficial team captain Michael Young said: "Nolan Ryan gives anything he is associated with instant credibility. And when you talk about the Texas Rangers, this is the team he's most associated with. We definitely appreciate what it means to be associated with him."

Greenberg's legwork assured that Ryan would be associated with the team for years to come. Immediately after it was announced that the Greenberg-Ryan team had made the winning bid for $593 million, which included $385 million in cash, the packed courtroom erupted in cheers shortly before 1:00 AM on August 5, some 10 hours after the auction had begun. It had been a back-and-forth process all day, with opposing lawyers cursing in the hallways, haggling behind closed doors, and jockeying for position in the courtroom.

The winning bid came through as the Rangers were in the midst of defeating the Mariners 11–6 in Seattle. In fact, Young hit a grand slam at just about the same time the winning bid from the Greenberg-Ryan team was announced in Tarrant County. Even Major League Baseball seemed delighted with the results.

"I'm very pleased, and I look forward to Chuck Greenberg and Nolan Ryan leading the team for many years to come," league president Bob DuPuy told ESPNDallas.com.

From the outside looking in, the Greenberg-Ryan team immediately began punching all the right buttons. They lowered prices at the concession stands; they made plenty of public appearances; and the Rangers, under their guidance, went to the World Series, with Greenberg and Ryan celebrating every trophy and triumph in the spotlight.

But according to *Fort Worth Star-Telegram* beat writer Jeff Wilson, the partnership began to disintegrate almost immediately. About five weeks after the World Series, members of the Rangers' baseball operations staff were flustered by how involved Greenberg became in daily internal discussions during the 2010 winter meetings. Ryan was especially angered when Greenberg made a third trip to Arkansas to see Cliff Lee in the team's failed bid to re-sign the ace left-hander.

Later in the year, the Greenberg-Ryan relationship was further strained during negotiations for an extension for Jon Daniels. Greenberg sold the suite at Rangers Ballpark that Daniels had used to host families of front-office personnel and to conduct meetings. The suite, supposed to be part of Daniels' extension offer, was sold despite Ryan's objections.

Those were just two of many differences between Ryan and Greenberg, and Ryan apparently extended a "me or him" ultimatum to Simpson and Davis. They quickly sided with the iconic Ryan, and on March 11, 2011, the Rangers sent out a release in the morning and held a press conference that afternoon announcing Greenberg's resignation. It was also announced that Ryan would add the title of CEO and oversee all baseball and business operations for the organization.

Just like that, Greenberg, who was not a majority owner, was gone. Compared to Simpson and Davis, he had an extremely small financial ownership stake. His major investments had been time and energy in organizing the ownership group. For that, Rangers fans should forever be thankful to Greenberg, who learned a little too late what Robin Ventura had discovered on August 4, 1993, at Arlington Stadium: you don't confront Big Tex without taking a beating.

32 Ryan Fans Rickey, Records Strikeout No. 5,000 at Home

Playoff baseball didn't come to Arlington until October 1996, three years after the Rangers had played their final game in Arlington Stadium. The World Series didn't make its North Texas debut until October 2010, 16 years after the old ballpark was demolished.

But that doesn't mean that the old minor league ballpark was never supercharged with an electric, combustible, playoff-like atmosphere. Arlington Stadium's finest night—perhaps the Rangers' finest moment to that point—occurred on August 22, 1989, as a fervent, capacity crowd of 42,869 shoehorned into the ballpark to witness history in the making.

It had nothing to do with the home team. Or the visitors, the first-place Athletics, who would go on to win the '89 World Series. Camera-clutching fans treated their ticket stubs like keepsakes, jostled for position to buy programs in the crowded concourses, and braved 101-degree pregame temperatures to see Superman go where no mortal man had been—to witness baseball's strikeout king, Nolan Ryan, add a phenomenal jewel to his crown.

Ryan, then 42 years old and in his first season with the Rangers, took the mound that night needing six strikeouts to reach 5,000. Only one other pitcher in major league history, Steve Carlton, had concluded his career with more than 4,000 strikeouts (4,136) at that time. The previous King of the Ks, Walter "Big Train" Johnson, held the record of 3,508 strikeouts for six decades.

Ryan had blown past Johnson's record six years earlier, and he seemed to be improving with age. Entering his historic August 22 start, Ryan had struck out at least 10 batters for the Rangers in 12 of his 25 starts. He'd also completed four of those starts and was limiting opponents to a league-low .183 batting average.

So, there was not much of a question regarding "if" he would record six strikeouts on this particular night, only questions regarding when and against whom.

"It really was a magical atmosphere," longtime Rangers radio announcer Eric Nadel said. "Nolan pitched two no-hitters as a member of the Rangers, but you couldn't plan for that. The way the '89 season progressed, it was obvious on that particular night that he was going to have a great chance of getting the 5,000[th] strikeout before the home crowd. The fans were very energized, to say the least."

They were feverish once the Rangers and Ryan took the field in the first inning. Rickey Henderson dampened the mood with a leadoff double, but the energy level ratcheted back up when Ryan struck out Jose Canseco to escape the first inning. Dave Henderson and Tony Phillips struck out in the second, and although Walt Weiss scored on Canseco's single in the third, Ryan struck out Rickey Henderson and Ron Hassey in that same inning to bring his total career strikeout total to 4,999.

Cameras throughout the stadium flashed as Ryan released every pitch in the fourth inning, but no strikeouts were recorded.

Rickey Henderson led off the fifth, taking Ryan's first two pitches, both called strikes. He worked the count to 2–2 and fouled off the fifth pitch. The sixth pitch was inside, running the count full. With the crowd growing louder with each pitch, Ryan threw his best heater, low and away at 96 mph.

Henderson swung. Henderson missed. History was made.

"If you had asked me before the game how I wanted to get it, I would have said swinging on a fastball," Ryan said afterward.

Even Henderson did not seem to mind being the victim. "It was an honor to be the 5,000[th]," he said. "As Davey Lopes says, 'If [Ryan] ain't struck you out, you ain't nobody.'"

Ryan finished the game with 13 strikeouts, the season with a league-high 301, and his career with 5,714. During his amazing career, Ryan struck out 44 Hall of Famers and five father-son duos.

But even Ryan has acknowledged that No. 5,000 may have been the most meaningful of all of them. At Ryan's request, the game was not stopped, and the Rangers stayed in the dugout, although his teammates on the field did come to the mound to congratulate him. Ryan had left 57 tickets for family and friends, making this particular accomplishment extra special.

Oh, by the way, the Rangers lost the game, 2–0. None of the fans seemed to mind. That wasn't why they packed the stadium with all the energy of a deciding playoff game.

33 Home Sweet Home: Winning a Playoff Game in Arlington

The 2010 Rangers had already removed one humiliating stigma from the franchise's horrific history of playoff ineptitude, dispatching Tampa Bay in five games to win the ALDS and claim Texas' first-ever postseason series victory.

With that monkey removed from their backs, the Rangers, on October 16, also struck the first of four lethal blows to the team's King Kong–sized tormenter.

In three previous trips to the postseason (1996, '97, and '99), the Rangers had been manhandled by the mighty Yankees. Texas was eliminated at home by the New Yorkers in all three of those postseason appearances, failing to win a game in Arlington.

Despite winning the series against the Rays, the Rangers' home struggles had continued, as Tampa won both games played at

Rangers Ballpark in Arlington before Texas claimed the deciding fifth game at Tropicana Field.

To make matters worse—much, much worse—the Rangers had opened the 2010 ALCS before a standing-room-only home crowd on October 15 by building a 5–0 lead over the Yankees in Game 1...and blowing it in a 6–5 Yankees win.

That loss stretched the Rangers' all-time playoff losing streak at home to seven games, and it increased the Yankees' playoff winning streak against Texas to 10 games over 14 years. It also made virtually every long-suffering, Yankees-cursing Rangers fan wonder if Texas would forever be burdened by the Bronx Bomber curse.

The resounding, "hell no" answer came less than 24 hours later, as Colby Lewis pitched exceptionally well and Texas did just about everything right in a 7–2 victory on a perfect Saturday afternoon. The Rangers players did not refer to the win as particularly poignant, but most of the 50,362 fans inside the stadium—and all those Texas fans watching the national telecast—breathed a huge sigh of relief.

The Pinstripe persecution was finally over. Anything, including a trip to the World Series, suddenly seemed possible.

"We knew [the heartbreaking nature of the previous night's loss] wasn't going to be an issue," said Michael Young, as reported by T.R. Sullivan of MLB.com. "By the time we got here, had breakfast, and got into our routine, Game 1 was forgotten about."

Game 2 should probably never be forgotten, as it set the tone for Texas' ALCS series victory in six games.

Lewis held the Yankees to two runs over 5⅔ innings. He also had plenty of support from his teammates, who showed early that they were going to be extremely aggressive in putting the previous night's memories out of their minds.

Elvis Andrus reached safely on an infield hit leading off the bottom of the first, moved to second on a wild pitch, and stole third with one out. With Josh Hamilton at first, Yankees starter Phil Hughes struck out Vladimir Guerrero for the second out and had a chance to escape the inning without the Rangers scoring.

But with Nelson Cruz at the plate, Ron Washington signaled for the double steal. The Rangers executed it perfectly. On a 1–1 pitch, Hamilton broke for second. Catcher Jorge Posada threw down, while Andrus broke for home as Hamilton stopped short of the base and second baseman Robinson Cano fired home. Andrus beat the throw for the game's first run.

"It was an aggressive play," Andrus said. "That's what we have to do against these guys: try and take it to them."

They did throughout the rest of the day...and the series. During the momentum-altering Game 2 win, David Murphy drove in two runs with a homer and a double, Cruz had two doubles, and Andrus and first baseman Mitch Moreland had two hits each. Lewis and the Rangers bullpen did the rest, cruising to a 7–2 win and fatally wounding King Kong in the process.

34 Charlie Hough: Best Bargain in Franchise History

At the first-ever induction ceremony of the Rangers Hall of Fame in August 2003, former pitcher Charlie Hough joked frequently with fans and former players that he was the one member of the inaugural class, which also featured Nolan Ryan, Jim Sundberg, and Johnny Oates, who was probably "outclassed."

During his later years with Texas, for example, Hough had been a teammate with Ryan, and he pointed out all that the two pitchers accomplished together.

"We had seven no-hitters between us," Hough said during the weekend induction ceremonies. "Of course, Ryan was responsible for all seven of them."

All joking aside, though, Hough certainly produced numbers worthy of the club's Hall of Fame, as he is still the all-time leader in wins (139), strikeouts recorded (1,452), and innings pitched (2,308). In his 11 seasons in Texas, Hough won the Rangers Pitcher of the Year six times, baffling opposing hitters—and his own catchers—with his dancing, darting knuckleball.

"Playing with Charlie was a lot of fun," Sundberg said. "Catching him was not."

Hough, who was originally selected by the Los Angeles Dodgers in the eighth round of the 1966 amateur draft, first learned to throw the knuckleball in 1970 in an attempt to salvage his career.

Following a strong season in the minors in 1967, Hough suffered a serious injury to his right shoulder but did not notify team officials because he was afraid he would be released. He pitched through the pain but was not particularly effective, leading the Texas League in home runs allowed at one point. With his career at a crossroads, Hough met with the Dodgers' Tommy Lasorda, then a manager in the minor league system, and scout Goldie Holt, who both encouraged him to learn a new pitch: the knuckleball.

Hough proved to be a quick learner, taking advice from knuckleballers like Phil Niekro. At Triple A Spokane in 1970, Hough won 12 games and posted a sparkling 1.95 ERA, and by '73 he was promoted to the major leagues, where he was an effective member of the Dodgers' bullpen.

He played exceptionally well with the Dodgers until '78, when he reinjured his right shoulder, reducing the effectiveness of his knuckleball. The following year, his ERA skyrocketed to 5.57 in 32 innings of work. Midway through the 1980 season, the Dodgers sold Hough's contract to the Rangers via the waiver wire. Former

Tiny Crowd Treated to Pitching Perfection to Close 1984 Season

By the end of the 92-loss 1984 season, North Texas sports fans had grown terribly tired of "Dreadful" Doug Rader and the rest of the rag-tag Rangers. So it wasn't too surprising that an announced crowd—that means it was actually much less—of 8,375 gluttons for punishment showed up at Arlington Stadium on "fan appreciation day" to watch the season finale against the mediocre California Angels (80–81 overall at game time).

Those who showed up, however, were treated to one of the most spectacular pitching performances in Rangers history.

It ended in a loss for Texas, like most other games in '84. But it was a work of art by two pitchers on top of their games.

Before plenty of empty seats on September 30, 1984, the Angels' Mike Witt tossed the 11th perfect game in major league history (the sixth in American League history), beating Texas knuckleballer Charlie Hough, who nearly matched him pitch for pitch, allowing just one run.

Witt needed only 94 pitches in one hour and 49 minutes to etch his name into baseball history in a 1–0 win for the Angels.

The game was scoreless into the seventh when the Angels' Doug DeCinces led off with a single. Texas catcher Donnie Scott missed a knuckleball from Hough, sending DeCinces to second, and he advanced to third on a ground-out by Brian Downing. Reggie Jackson then grounded to first, but DeCinces beat the throw home to score the game's only run.

Witt had struck out nine batters through eight innings and, after he fanned Tom Dunbar leading off the ninth, the small crowd began to cheer for the visiting pitcher. Bobby Jones hit a dribbler to second for out No. 2, and Marv Foley took three straight curveballs before grounding out to Rob Wilfong to end the game.

"His stuff was awesome," Hough said of Witt. "I saw Jerry Reuss and John Candelaria pitch no-hitters, but this was by far the most overpowering. I mean, this was no contest."

Interestingly, less than two years later, Hough hooked up in another classic pitching duel against the Angels and took a no-hitter and a 1–0 lead into the ninth inning in Anaheim on June 16, 1986. But left fielder George Wright, who'd entered the game in the ninth as a defensive replacement for Gary Ward, badly misplayed a fly ball, dropping it for a two-base error. A single by Wally Joyner—the Angels' only hit of the game—scored the tying run.

After a passed ball moved Joyner to second, Hough struck out DeCinces and then issued an intentional walk to Jackson. With two out and two on, Hough struck out George Hendrick, but a passed ball allowed Joyner to score the winning run when Hough forgot to cover the plate.

The Angels scored two runs on just one hit as Kirk McCaskill picked up the win for the second-place Angels over the first-place Rangers.

Rangers general manager Eddie Robinson paid the bargain price of $20,000 to acquire Hough.

Even in 1980 dollars, that was quite a steal, especially considering the way Hough pitched in Texas.

For the most part, Hough stayed in the bullpen for the Rangers throughout the 1980 and 1981 seasons before moving into the starting rotation in 1982, when he went 16–13 to lead the team in wins.

In his 11 years as a Ranger, Hough went 139–123 with a 3.68 ERA. Remarkably, he also pitched a complete game 98 times among his 313 games started as a Ranger. And in perhaps the ultimate example of rubber arm–resolve, Hough pitched 13 innings in a game in 1986 at Minnesota, still a club record.

Hough also holds the dubious club records for most homers allowed (238), most wild pitches (99), and most batters hit (89)—all examples of knucklers that didn't dance or ones that broke too much. But Hough posted double-digit win totals in every season he started with the Rangers, including 17 wins in '86 and 18 in '87.

"I think I was kind of an underdog type," Hough told Scott Burchett of MLB.com in '03. "I was never really good or anything. I got an opportunity to pitch a lot of innings [in Texas] and [it was] probably the best I did in my career. It was special, special times."

Fergie Jenkins: Triumph and Overcoming Tragedy

The Rangers' media guide is filled with bizarre tidbits and peculiar nuggets of nostalgia. But perhaps one of the oddest facts involves the greatest single-season pitching performance in club history.

The first Rangers pitcher to ever prove he could thrive in the summertime heat in Texas—the man who won 25 games in 1974 to establish a club record that still stands today—was a Canadian. A former hockey player, as a matter of fact.

Ferguson Jenkins, who grew up in Chatham, Ontario, and originally signed with the Phillies, helped make the '74 season the first truly memorable one—at least from a positive standpoint—for the team in Arlington by compiling a 25–12 record with a spectacular 2.82 ERA. Jenkins also established team records for most wins in a month (six in the sweltering heat of August) and most complete games in a season (29).

"Before Fergie, it used to get boring in the field," 23-year-old outfielder Jeff Burroughs told Ron Fimrite of *Sports Illustrated* in 1974. "Our pitchers would walk so many hitters and get behind so many others [that] you'd lose your concentration. Fergie is always around the plate, so you have to be alert."

Added then-25-year-old shortstop Toby Harrah: "Ferguson Jenkins is the greatest pitcher I've ever played behind."

The 6'5" Jenkins was undoubtedly the first great pitcher in Texas. Strangely, three teams, including the Rangers, gave up on him in a span of six years. The first puzzling move came from the Cubs, where Jenkins had won at least 20 games six consecutive seasons (1967–72). When he stumbled to a 14–16 record in '73, Chicago dealt him to Texas for infielders Bill Madlock and Vic Harris.

That could have been considered a win-win move, as Madlock enjoyed three exceptional years with the Cubs and won four batting titles in his career. But the Rangers made a baffling transaction after Jenkins went 17–18 with a 3.93 ERA in '75, shipping him to Boston for Juan Beniquez, Steve Barr, and Craig Skok. Beniquez was a solid outfielder for three seasons in Texas, but he was hardly worthy of being exchanged for a frontline pitcher like Jenkins.

Fergie Addresses His 1980 Arrest

In his book, *Fergie: My Life From the Cubs to Cooperstown,* co-written with Chicago-area sports journalist Lew Freedman, Fergie Jenkins acknowledges he used drugs recreationally—"not heavily, not a lot, but as a fun thing at parties"—during his time in the major leagues. But he also addresses the lowlight of his time as a Ranger when, on August 25, 1980, he was arrested in Toronto for possession of "small amounts" of cocaine, hashish, and marijuana at Exhibition Stadium.

The ensuing publicity and brief trial caused quite a stir in Canada, where Jenkins was viewed as a hero.

"I was stunned by the situation," Jenkins wrote. "I did not put drugs in my suitcase, and I did not know what was going on. Things got very strange. I have contended that I was set up for this arrest and that I committed no crimes. I am pretty sure I know who did it, but that is not something I will reveal publicly."

At a trial in Brampton, Jenkins was convicted of possession of four ounces of cocaine, while the other charges were dropped.

"Just an hour into his deliberations, Judge Jerry Young put aside the conviction and erased it from my record," Jenkins wrote. "The legal term was an 'absolute discharge.' The effect of that action was as if I had not been convicted."

But the negative press may have postponed Jenkins' induction into the Hall of Fame. He made it on his third attempt in 1991.

While Jenkins won 284 games in his career, it easily could have been more. He lost 13 games by the score of 1–0, despite going the distance. He also suffered 45 shutout losses playing for mostly mediocre teams.

Fortunately for the Rangers, the Red Sox reciprocated with a boneheaded move of their own, trading Jenkins back to Texas following the '77 season for John Poloni and cash. Poloni never played for the Red Sox, while Jenkins returned to elite form with the Rangers, going 18–8 in 1978 and compiling an overall record of 51–42 in his final four seasons in Texas. He then returned to the Cubs to pitch two more seasons and complete a 19-year major league career.

Throughout his Hall of Fame career, Jenkins exhibited exceptional control. He often toyed with hitters, painting the black with the precision of a surgeon. He was the first pitcher in history ever to strike out more than 3,000 hitters with fewer than 1,000 walks.

Unfortunately for Jenkins, the control and triumph he consistently enjoyed on the mound did not translate into his personal life, which often seemed to career completely out of control.

Jenkins never played on a championship team, but he has never dwelled on that fact. In his autobiography, *Fergie: My Life from the Cubs to Cooperstown*, he explained why he never allowed baseball to consume him…and why he always kept it in perspective.

His mother, Delores, went blind after giving birth to Fergie and died of cancer in 1970 at the age of 52. Close friend Jerry McCaffrey, an English teacher in Chatham who recommended Fergie to the area scout for the Phillies, died of a heart attack in the late 1960s at age 32. Tony Lucadello, the Phillies scout who signed Fergie, committed suicide in 1989 by shooting himself in the head.

His first marriage ended in divorce after 23 years. In 1988, when he was working as pitching coach with the Rangers' Triple A affiliate in Oklahoma City, he married Mary-Anne Miller, but she died after being injured in a major automobile accident and coming down with pneumonia in 1991, a couple days after Jenkins learned he'd been elected to the Baseball Hall of Fame.

In the fall of '92, he was preparing to accept a coaching position with the Reds, but his new fiancé killed herself and Jenkins' three-year-old daughter, Samantha, by carbon monoxide poisoning in the Oklahoma countryside.

Through it all, however, Jenkins, who is now married to the former Lydia Farrington and oversees the Fergie Jenkins Foundation, remains steadfast in one conviction regarding his life: he's been blessed.

"For me it's always good to be remembered," Jenkins said when he was inducted into the Rangers Hall of Fame in 2004. "To be voted into the Hall of Fame is a great honor. Nolan Ryan did it, Charlie [Hough] and Jim Sundberg, Johnny Oates, and now Buddy [Bell] and myself. To be remembered in the city where you played is a great honor."

Ian Kinsler: Love or Loathe Him, You Had To Respect Him

In 2011 *Moneyball* hit the silver screen, with Brad Pitt playing the role of Oakland general manager Billy Beane. The film version of Michael Lewis' book focuses on Beane's ability to build a winner without being a slave to standard baseball statistics. Among other things, the movie emphasizes that the number of runs scored by a player is ultimately a more important statistic in evaluating his worth than his batting average.

Rangers manager Ron Washington was part of the Athletics' coaching staff when Beane was making his then-revolutionary personnel decisions. Washington was even portrayed in the movie by Brent Jennings. That background information should explain why Washington was steadfast in his decision to insert Ian Kinsler into the leadoff role in 2011 and to stick with Kinsler through thick and thin.

A fantastic run producer, in 2011 Ian Kinsler became the 12th player in major league history with multiple seasons of at least 30 home runs and 30 stolen bases. (AP Images)

Kinsler was not the typical leadoff hitter. He liked to swing for the fences, and he sometimes appeared to be in love with an uppercut swing that produced an array of pop-ups. His batting average fell from a career-best .319 in 2008 to .286 in 2010. And he hit .255 in 2011.

But 2011 may have been his best year ever. Kinsler finished second in baseball behind only Curtis Granderson with 121 runs scored. He walked 89 times (ninth best in both leagues) and became just the 12th player in major league history with multiple seasons of at least 30 home runs and 30 stolen bases.

In the Rangers' best season ever, Kinsler was a win-producing, run-scoring, table-setting machine.

"Look at all the runs he's scored," Washington toldESPNDallas.com's Richard Durrett. "Look at the production. That's why I never moved him out of the No. 1 spot. He's been tremendous for us in that leadoff role."

He was at his best in the 2011 World Series, helping the Rangers steal Game 2 in St. Louis with his daring base running and finishing the Fall Classic with a .360 batting average and a .500 on-base percentage. But even when he was not compiling impressive numbers in Texas, Kinsler could be effective.

Take the first game of the 2011 ALCS, for example. Facing Tigers ace Justin Verlander, Kinsler went 1-for-3 with an RBI and a walk. Not bad, right? But look beyond the typical numbers. In the first at-bat of the game, Kinsler worked an eight-pitch walk. Later, after Kinsler drove in the Rangers' second run in a 3–2 victory, he worked Verlander for nine pitches before striking out. One of the primary reasons Verlander could not come back after a rain delay was that he'd thrown 19 pitches to Kinsler in three at-bats.

"The most important thing about leadoff is setting the table for the guys behind me," Kinsler said. "That's it. You have to be able to give them a situation. When you're hitting with runners on

Kinsler Goes 6-for-6 in Recording Rare Cycle

Thanks to the comprehensive documentation of the Elias Sports Bureau, journalists covering the Rangers' 19–6 win over the Orioles on April 15, 2009, in Arlington were able to accurately depict the historical significance of Ian Kinsler's 6-for-6 cycle with a mind-boggling statistical nugget to accompany the uncanny detail that a second baseman produced such a feat on Jackie Robinson Day, honoring perhaps the greatest of all second basemen.

According to Elias, Kinsler became the first player to produce six hits without an out in a game in which he hit for the cycle since 1890, when William Farmer Weaver of the Louisville Colonels—apparently a major league team at that time—did the same.

Let's put that into perspective. In 1890 future U.S. president Dwight Eisenhower was born, and Kinsler was still 90 years from being born. At the beginning of 1890, Idaho and Wyoming were not yet states, and a ballet called "Sleeping Beauty" was making its debut with music provided by a Russian composer named Tchaikovsky.

In other words, Kinsler's feat was beyond rare; it was literally once-in-a-century.

"It was a career-type of ballgame," then-Rangers third baseman Michael Young said, as reported by MLB.com beat writer T.R. Sullivan. "To hit for the cycle and have a couple of extra hits thrown in, that's an incredible game."

At the time of this writing, only two other players had recorded six hits en route to the cycle. Rondell White went 6-for-7 in 1995 for the Expos in a 13-inning game, and Detroit's Bobby Veach hit for the cycle in a 12-inning game in 1920. But Kinsler was only the second player to pull off the feat in a regulation game, dating back to Weaver in 1890.

And to do it on the day that Major League Baseball annually honors Robinson added extra significance to the accomplishment, especially because Robinson was the type of player who could have pulled off such a feat.

"It is more special to do it on Jackie Robinson Day," Kinsler said, 62 years after Robinson broke the color barrier. "He's the guy who could do everything in the game—hit triples, hit home runs, steal bases, score runs, do everything. It is weird that it's Jackie Robinson Day and I'm playing second base, but it's great it happened that way."

After the Orioles took a 2–0 lead in the first, Kinsler started his historic day with a leadoff double and followed that with a solo homer in the third. With the Rangers leading 4–3, Kinsler singled in the bottom of the fourth and eventually stole third base. He added another single later that inning when the Rangers broke it open with an eight-run outburst.

That left him a triple shy of the cycle—almost always the toughest hit to complete the feat. He came to the plate in the sixth against reliever Brian Bass with the Rangers leading 13–4. Kinsler worked the count full and ripped a monster shot toward the 407' sign in right-center, which fell just beyond the reach of center fielder Adam Jones and bounced against the wall.

He made it to third easily and added a double in the eighth for his sixth hit of the exceptionally rare night.

base, most guys are better. The ultimate goal of a hitter is to touch home plate."

In addition to his proficiency in reaching base and scoring runs, Kinsler was a lightning rod for drawing the ire of the opposition. Following a Rangers win over the Angels in 2009 in Arlington, Kinsler "encouraged" the visiting team to "get the f—— off our field." No wonder former Angels pitcher John Lackey was tossed from a later 2009 game after throwing only two pitches in the first inning. The first was behind Kinsler's head. The second one plunked him.

In Arlington, Kinsler was a gutsy, gritty grinder who played the game with a chip on his shoulder, his pants legs pulled up high, and his emotions on his sleeve. He was a little cocky; he was unafraid to speak his mind; he was quirky in the batter's box; and he played second base with an extreme swagger.

He was also a top-flight middle infielder, with tremendous range and sensationally quick hands. In 2011 Kinsler was second among American League second basemen with 16 defensive runs saved.

Whether he was popping up or popping off to opponents, or whether he was hitting bombs into the bleachers or dropping f-bombs toward opposing dugouts, Kinsler made a powerfully positive impact for the Rangers, which made trading him difficult.

Kinsler spent eight years with the Rangers before being traded to Detroit for Prince Fielder prior to the 2014 season. The trade definitely proved to be more beneficial for the Tigers, as Kinsler became a fixture for the Tigers at second base. Surgeries kept Fielder off the field in 2014 and eventually ended his career in 2016. He appeared in only 289 games during three seasons with the Rangers.

In a 2016 return to Arlington, Kinsler expressed sympathy for Fielder, who broke into tears at the retirement press conference.

"Prince and me are always connected, even though I don't know the guy that well," Kinsler said. "I think it affects everybody in the league when you see a guy like Prince Fielder have to end his career early. It's sad to see. I watched his press conference, and it just kind of brings you into respecting what we do day in and day out, and how it can go away quickly."

Kinsler also commented on the trade, saying, "It's been nothing but positive for me. Toward the end of my time in Texas, things got kind of stale. To be traded to an organization like Detroit really allowed me to be who I was as a player and what I needed to do to improve. It's been nothing but great things."

The trade was made with an eye toward creating an opening at second for Jurickson Profar. His shoulder injury in the spring of 2014 started a two-year ordeal, but it also cleared the way for Rougned Odor to become a star at second.

37 1977: One of the Best and Most Bizarre Seasons

The 1977 Rangers began one of the most peculiar seasons in team history by making outrageous headlines before the regular season began. Second baseman Lenny Randle's assault on manager Frank Lucchesi in March represented a turbulent beginning to a tumultuous and terrific season in which the Rangers were memorable for both their mayhem and magnificence.

On one hand, there was owner Brad Corbett, lamenting a 1–0 loss to Kansas City on July 4 and telling the media, "I'm selling this team because it's killing me. They are dogs on the field, and they are dogs off the field."

On the other hand, there was Willie Horton, who'd been acquired from Detroit in April, becoming the first Ranger to hit three homers in a game in a 7–3 win on May 15, also against the Royals.

"That was on the footsteps of a fight that broke out with the Royals," former Rangers catcher Jim Sundberg recalled. "Willie Horton was in the middle of that. We went to Kansas City the next week, and they booed him unmercifully. It was amazing seeing how the fans were all over him and then to see how he cranked three home runs. It was a great highlight of watching a teammate perform."

There were many other great highlights. On August 8 the Rangers turned their first triple play. With runners on first and second, Oakland's Manny Sanguillen hit a hard grounder to third baseman Toby Harrah, who stepped on third and threw to Bump Wills at second for the force. Wills relayed to Mike Hargrove at first to complete the triple play.

Less than a month later, on August 27, Harrah and Wills hit inside-the-park homers on consecutive pitches at Yankee Stadium. And on September 22, Bert Blyleven tossed the Rangers' second no-hitter, blanking the Angels in Anaheim, 6–0.

All those magical moments contributed to a 94-win season. That's still, as of 2011, the third-most wins in team history, behind the 95-win club in 1999 and the 96-win team in 2011. In the midst of landmark breakthroughs and accomplishments, however, the '77 Rangers went through four managers in a one-week midseason span.

"Sheer madness," former Rangers beat writer Jim Reeves wrote in describing the '77 season for the *Fort Worth Star-Telegram*. "There's really no other way to describe it. In 1977, the Texas Rangers suffered through one of the most traumatic and chaotic seasons in the history of Major League Baseball. By comparison, the Bronx Zoo Yankees were mere choirboys.... Yet, from the midst of the chaos and incredible turmoil, like a phoenix from the ashes, arose what some like to call 'The Best Texas Team to Never Win a Championship.'"

Corbett and team president Eddie Robinson had assembled an impressive pitching rotation that included future Hall of Famers Gaylord Perry and Bert Blyleven, along with free-agent acquisition Doyle Alexander. The Rangers later purchased the contract of Dock Ellis, who claimed he pitched a no-hitter in 1970 for the Pirates while under the influence of LSD.

Despite the stellar pitching and solid offense from the likes of Sundberg, Hargrove, Harrah, Horton, Claudell Washington, and others, the Rangers were a .500 team in June when Corbett and Robinson decided to make a managerial change. Robinson initially pushed for Baltimore third-base coach Billy Hunter. But Corbett preferred Eddie Stanky, a former major league second baseman and manager who was coaching at South Alabama University.

Following a Rangers loss in Minnesota on June 21, reporters informed Lucchesi that Stanky was on his way from Mobile, Alabama.

"In the tiny visiting clubhouse at old Metropolitan Stadium, not even afforded the luxury of a manager's office, Lucchesi began to weep," Reeves wrote. "The change came with the Rangers sitting at 31–31, in third place in the division and just four games out of the lead."

Stanky managed the Rangers to a 10–8 victory over the Twins the following day. Harrah had three hits, and Washington delivered a big home run as Darold Knowles picked up the win in relief of Blyleven and Adrian Devine. Meanwhile, Stanky took notes in the dugout.

"[Stanky] was very professional and kind of stern," Sundberg told FOX Sports reporter Emily Jones. "We knew from the past he would probably be a disciplinarian-type of guy. He took notes during the game, and he didn't say anything after the game. But the next morning we got a call saying that Eddie decided he was leaving. He had made a mistake, he wanted to be with his family, and he was going back home. He did call myself, Harrah, and Hargrove and said we needed to lead the team. So, he made those observations of the club. But the rumor was that the last time he had been in the game there were no hairdryers, and now guys were using hairdryers [laughing]. That might have been too much to handle."

Or, as Reeves wrote: "Maybe it was the sight of Dock Ellis, his hair in pink rollers, after the game."

Whatever the case, Stanky was gone after one game, and Robinson named third-base coach Connie Ryan the team's interim manager, the third skipper in three days. The Rangers offered the permanent job to another Hall of Famer, Harmon Killebrew, who declined. Finally, the Rangers went back to the first name on Robinson's list: Billy Hunter, who had been nicknamed "Little

Hitler" for his domineering style. Hunter took control of the team in Oakland on June 28.

"We had a great winning percentage [under Hunter]," Sundberg said. "We were a team that was waiting to have some kind of direction or guidance. It was kind of like a rebellious child who needed some leadership. He gave it to us, and by the time we were through, Billy Hunter had really kind of turned that club around."

The Rangers were 34–35 when Hunter became the manager. They finished the season by going 60–33. Unfortunately for Texas, it wasn't enough to catch Kansas City, which won 70 of its last 98 games en route to a 102-win season. Even with 94 wins, the Rangers finished eight games out of first place in what was easily the wackiest season in Texas history.

"It was an interesting, strange period, to say the least," Sundberg said.

38 Rogers Throws First Perfect Game in Rangers History

With two outs in the top of the eighth inning on July 28, 1994, California Angels second baseman Rex Hudler stood in the visiting on-deck circle, glanced toward Rangers left-hander Kenny Rogers on the mound, and began feeding Texas fans along the front rows a steady diet of trash talk.

Rogers had baffled Angels hitters, firing his 90 mph fastball by them, teasing them with a tantalizing curve, and keeping them off-balance by varying the speed of his pitches as the Rangers built a 4–0 lead. Twenty-three batters up, 23 Angels down.

Rogers, who entered the game with a 10–6 record, needed only 59 pitches to finish six innings, and Chili Davis—the leadoff hitter

Kenny Rogers acknowledges the crowd after recording the second out in the ninth inning of his perfect game against the California Angels on July 28, 1994.
(AP Images)

Kenny Loses His Cool

During his three stints with the Rangers (1989–95, 2000–02, and 2004–05), Kenny Rogers proved to be one of the greatest pitchers in team history, for which he was inducted into the Rangers Hall of Fame in 2011.

In addition to pitching the only perfect game in Rangers history in 1994, Rogers, who was drafted by the Rangers in the 39th round of the 1982 draft, still ranks second all-time with 133 wins as a Ranger (six behind Charlie Hough); first with 528 appearances; second with 1,909 innings pitched; and third with 1,201 strikeouts.

But for all Rogers did as a Ranger, his mostly outstanding career in Texas was tainted by a couple 2005 incidents in which Rogers apparently—at least momentarily—lost his mind.

Rogers fractured the fifth metacarpal bone in his right (non-pitching) hand on June 17, 2005, when he hit a dugout water cooler after being pulled from a game against the Washington Nationals. Rogers had allowed just one run in 6⅓ innings and earned the win. The 40-year-old made his next scheduled start against the Angels but lasted only 3⅓ innings and allowed six earned runs to take the loss. He then missed a scheduled start.

Media attention increased in the aftermath of the water-cooler incident, and before a game on June 29, 2005, Rogers shoved FOX Sports Net Southwest cameraman David Mammeli, who was shooting video of the pitcher on his way to a pregame stretch, and told him, "I told you to get those cameras out of my face." The pitcher then approached KDFW cameraman Larry Rodriguez and took the camera from him before throwing it to the ground and kicking it.

Rogers apologized a week later, but on July 18, while en route to turn himself in to the Tarrant County Jail after a Class A misdemeanor warrant was issued in connection with the assault on Rodriguez, Rogers had another confrontation with a cameraman. WFAA cameraman Mike Zukerman was videotaping the booking procedure when Rogers said, "You're getting really close, you know that? Do you hear me?"

A few seconds later, Rogers added, "You must be pretty proud of yourself, too."

Zukerman responded, "It's just my job, Kenny."

Rogers replied: "Yeah. Your job. That's just your excuse."

The Rangers declined to comment on the incident. But at the end of the year, the Rangers and Rogers parted ways, as Texas chose not to re-sign him. After going 32–17 for the Rangers in 2004–05, Rogers, who had also played with the Twins, Mets, A's, and Yankees earlier, finished his career in Detroit (2006–08).

The incidents cost Rogers more than his reputation. Commissioner Bud Selig issued Rogers a 20-game suspension (later reduced) and a $50,000 fine. Rogers was required to post a $1,500 bond after the Class A misdemeanor warrant was issued. Arlington police also mailed a Class C misdemeanor citation to Rogers, accusing him of assaulting Mammeli.

in the eighth—had been the only Angel to even hit a ball remotely hard against him.

But for some reason, as Rogers worked to retire J.T. Snow for the final out of the eighth, Hudler felt compelled to taunt the increasingly ecstatic Rangers fans.

"I was telling the fans in the first five rows that I was going to get him," Hudler said, as reported by Bob Nightengale of the *Los Angeles Times*. "I wanted him bad. I was going to hit an ugly bleeder that would piss off everyone."

Hudler led off the ninth and promptly fell behind 0–2 in the count. He then guessed fastball, and that's exactly what Rogers delivered.

As soon as the slicing line drive left Hudler's bat, the crowd of 46,581 inside The Ballpark in Arlington gasped, as everyone—including Rogers—instantly sensed that perfection had come to an end...just as Hudler had predicted the previous inning.

"When I hit it, I said to myself, 'Way to go. You did it,'" Hudler recalled afterward. "Then I started looking up, and the ball kept hanging up there. Then the guy dives. I couldn't believe what I saw."

"The guy," center fielder Rusty Greer, read the ball perfectly and began sprinting toward the gap in right-center. As the liner sunk toward the grass, Greer left his feet and was nearly horizontal when he made the backhanded grab to keep perfection intact.

"I never thought he was going to get it," Rogers said of Greer's heroic catch. "I thought that ball was going to drop, no matter what. Then, I thought the ball was going to pop out.

"I never thought about a perfect game. I wasn't thinking about the no-hitter until the last out. I just threw strikes. I got ahead of a lot of hitters, and that helped a lot. Rusty Greer, gosh, what can you say after a guy makes a catch like that? I didn't even know he caught it until he got up and threw the ball back in. It was spectacular. There are no other words to describe it."

Following Greer's catch, Chris Turner grounded out and Gary DiSarcina hit a fly ball to straightaway center. Greer—after momentarily misjudging it—caught it, jumping up and down along with everyone else at the stadium.

"I thought I hit it pretty good," said DiSarcina. "I took two, three steps out of the box, saw the guy wasn't moving, and said, 'Wow! He did it.'"

Rogers pitched the first perfect game since Dennis Martinez did it for the Expos, exactly three years earlier, in a 2–0 victory over the Dodgers. Ironically, the last perfect game in the American League had also come in Arlington with the Angels in town. On September 30, 1984, Mike Witt pitched a perfect game for the Angels against the Rangers.

In his gem, Rogers fanned eight, threw 98 total pitches, and went to a three-ball count only six times. After the game, Rogers wandered through the dugout in bewilderment until his wife, Becky, found him. They hugged, kissed, and slow-danced.

Rogers says he didn't sleep a wink that evening. The next morning he appeared on *Good Morning America*, and later in the afternoon, he rushed into the Rangers' clubhouse, asking teammates whether he should appear on Letterman or Leno. The Rangers voted on Letterman, and Rogers flew to New York to tape the show on August 1.

39 Ruben Sierra: Carrying the Weight of a Country with Class

In August 2009 Ruben Sierra and Toby Harrah entered the Rangers Hall of Fame together. It seemed fitting to pair the two, as Harrah had been a bench coach with the Rangers early in Sierra's career. When asked what he remembered most about the youthful Sierra's numerous tools and passion for the game, Harrah marveled at the way Ruben rounded the bases.

"I remember when Ruben first came up," Harrah told Daniel Paulling of MLB.com. "I enjoyed watching him hit a double or a triple more than a home run because you could see him run."

Considering how much weight Sierra carried on his muscular shoulders—from a metaphorical standpoint—the way he ran was even more impressive because he carted a country's expectations with him.

Over a 20-season major league career that included stints with nine teams, Sierra was a solid player who hit 306 homers, 428 doubles, 59 triples, and drove in 1,322 runs. In his first stint with the Rangers (1986–92), Sierra was often sensational.

In 1989 he made his first All-Star appearance and probably should have won the American League MVP, losing in a narrow vote to Milwaukee's Robin Yount. Sierra belted 29 home runs and hit .306 in '89, while leading the league in RBIs (119), total bases (344), slugging percentage (.543), extra-base hits (78), and triples (14). In head-to-head categories, Yount beat Sierra only in total batting average and doubles.

While he never quite duplicated the '89 season again, Sierra was an All-Star with the Rangers in '91 and in '92 before he was dealt to Oakland. He also was the 2001 American League Comeback Player of the Year with the Rangers. In his 10-season career with the Rangers, Sierra hit .280 with a .473 slugging percentage. As of 2011, Sierra ranked second in club history in triples (44), sixth in doubles (257), fifth in RBIs (742), and fifth in total bases (2,166).

Those numbers and many other contributions earned Sierra a place in the Rangers Hall of Fame. But the expectations for him were always so much higher. Long before he reached the Rangers, Sierra was branded as "the next Clemente" by many of the citizens of his native Puerto Rico.

Roberto Clemente, known as "El Magnifico" in Puerto Rico, was the Hall of Fame right fielder for the Pittsburgh Pirates who died in a plane crash on December 31, 1972. Because of Sierra's physical resemblance to Clemente, his position, and his remarkable skill set, Puerto Ricans hoped Sierra would follow Clemente all the way to Cooperstown.

Early in Sierra's career, it didn't seem like too much of a stretch to envision such future fame.

Sierra, seven years old when Clemente died in 1972, played on the same youth team with Roberto Clemente Jr. and stole the spotlight from the Hall of Famer's son. The Rangers signed Sierra as an amateur free agent in November 1982. At that time, he hit only right-handed. The following spring, the Rangers asked him to start switch-hitting. He practiced for a week, and in his first left-handed at-bat in a game, Sierra tripled.

It was a sign of things to come. Sierra made his major league debut on June 1, 1986, and homered in his second at-bat.

"He was one of the most exciting and explosive players ever to wear a Rangers uniform," said former Rangers general manager Tom Grieve.

After leaving Texas the first time, Sierra made just one more All-Star appearance in 1994 with the A's. He then became more of a journeyman than a middle-of-the-lineup staple. By the late 1990s, the comparisons to Clemente had stopped, but that doesn't diminish what Sierra accomplished, especially with the Rangers.

"I came from Puerto Rico and a humble background," Sierra said at his induction ceremony into the Rangers Hall of Fame. "My father passed away when I was four.... My mother raised five kids. My father's last words to my mother were, 'Take care of my little boy,' which is exactly what she did. My mother told me [that] to find success in life, you first have to find your passion, and then you have to do everything you can to keep that passion alive. I did exactly that...and my dream turned into a reality when I became a Texas Ranger."

To add to the fulfillment of that dream, Sierra beamed with pride when the Rangers drafted Ruben Sierra Jr. in the sixth round of the 2009 First-Year Player Draft. Father and son shared an emotional hug on the field at the '09 Hall of Fame induction.

40 Mark Holtz: Gone but Certainly Not Forgotten

Whenever he's on a road trip with the Rangers, radio play-by-play announcer Eric Nadel makes certain he is the last person from the team's traveling party to leave the bus.

Nadel isn't a dawdler. He's just appreciative. Leaving the bus last is his subtle reminder to always be grateful for his opportunity to broadcast baseball games for a living. And whenever he's counting professional blessings, he always thinks about his former partner, the late Mark Holtz.

"I end up thinking about him just about every day, especially during the season," Nadel said. "When we're at home, I think about him driving into the ballpark when I pass [Mark Holtz Lake on the north side of the stadium]. On the road, I think about him on the bus. Even at other times he'll creep into my consciousness at some point during the day. There was no one like Mark. He was the best of the best, and I am certainly not the only one with the Rangers who remembers him with tremendous admiration."

Not hardly. The lake outside the stadium was named in his honor in 1997, the same year he died after a bone marrow transplant during leukemia treatment. He was inducted posthumously into the Rangers Hall of Fame in 2005, and his trademark calls are still a part of every home game at Rangers Ballpark in Arlington and every Texas victory.

Chuck Morgan, the Rangers' vice president, in-park entertainment, welcomes fans to home games with this Holtz-ism: "It's baseball time in Texas." Following every home victory, Morgan makes certain Holtz's most revered call—"Hello win column"—flashes on the scoreboard.

"For Rangers fans, when things were going bad, Mark was the voice of hope; when things were good, he was the voice of celebration," Nadel said at the 2005 Hall of Fame ceremony for Holtz. "He is the best announcer the Rangers have ever had or will ever have. I can assure you that there will never be another one quite like him. I had the privilege of being his partner for 13 seasons. He was incredibly talented, and he had the perfect radio voice. He combined those beautiful tones with an infectious enthusiasm. He captured and described dramatic moments of the game better than anyone I have ever heard."

The classy and personable Holtz had been the voice of the Omaha Royals and Denver Bears in the 1970s, and he had also done some college football, basketball, and hockey before becoming the Dallas Mavericks' first radio broadcaster in 1980. Holtz's

The Story of "That Ball Is History"

For Rangers fans, four of the most fantastic words that can ever be heard while listening to the radio or an Internet broadcast are: "That ball is history."

That has long been the trademark home run call of Rangers radio play-by-play broadcaster Eric Nadel, who was first hired by the team to serve as a television broadcaster and advertising salesman in 1979.

The previous year—when Nadel auditioned for the vacancy by broadcasting four games into a tape recorder—one of the hip and cool phrases to say when exiting a room or saying "good-bye" was "I'm history." Nadel listened to the phrase, contemplated it, and figured it might be appropriate when describing a home run.

"I had been thinking about it for a while. But the first chance I had to use it was a surprise to me," Nadel recalled. "Johnny Grubb was the batter. He sliced it down the left-field line at the Kingdome in Seattle. As I was calling the ball, I was expecting it to go off of the wall or to be caught. I was expecting to say either 'caught' or 'off of the wall,' and 'history' is what came out. It wasn't obvious, but that came out, and it sounded natural, so I decided to go with it."

The rest, of course, is "history."

first assignment with the Rangers came as the team's cable play-by-play announcer in 1981. He then switched to the radio booth in 1982, when he joined Nadel to form one of the smoothest and most enjoyable broadcast teams in Dallas–Fort Worth history. They worked together from 1982 to 1994, and they were particularly good at improvising during lopsided losses—a frequent event during some dismal seasons.

"We clicked instantly," Nadel said. "There was chemistry between us that you don't often have. The first time we went to lunch we knew we were going to have a good time. We had the same philosophy: do the best job you can describing the game, but it's not brain surgery. If it's a bad game, use diversionary tactics to entertain the fans, and if it was a good game we'd talk baseball. We made it a point to know what was going on around the league, which wasn't easy without the Internet. We'd talk about movies or restaurants and other goofy stuff.

"In '82 we did 29 spring training games, so we spent a lot of time together driving across Florida getting to know each other and had a good time. People had already heard us when the regular season came. They liked the style. We were told to keep doing what we had been doing, even though the games counted now."

When Holtz left the radio booth, he returned to broadcasting televised Rangers games in 1995, where he remained until May 22, 1997, when his battle with leukemia forced him to retire. He died on September 7, 1997.

Among the memorable events Holtz called were two no-hitters by Nolan Ryan and perfect games by the Angels' Mike Witt in 1984 and the Rangers' Kenny Rogers in 1994. He was in the radio booth for Ryan's 5,000th strikeout and 300th win, and he lived long enough to see the Rangers participate in the 1996 playoffs.

"He never took for granted how fortunate he was to be living his childhood dream, and he prepared diligently," Nadel said. "No matter what was going on in his private life, you would never know by listening to him on the air. When Mark was on air, all was right in the world."

41 The Radio Voice of the Rangers: Eric Nadel

After 30 years of broadcasting Rangers games, Brooklyn native Eric Nadel entered the 2010 season having come to grips with the reality that he would likely never announce a World Series game. Or even an American League Championship Series.

While the marketing motto for the 2010 season was, "It's Time," Nadel had already served three decades of time with the team...and had never even announced a playoff series victory.

Nadel knew that *anything* was possible in baseball. After his beloved Dodgers left Brooklyn for the West Coast, Nadel eventually adopted the Mets as his team. He carried a transistor radio with him while attending classes at Brown University in 1969, listening to Lindsey Nelson and Bob Murphy document every magnificently remarkable moment of the Miracle Mets' run to the World Series title.

"I was always hopeful," says Nadel, who originally teamed with Jon Miller when he was first hired by the Rangers in 1979 as a television broadcaster and advertising salesman. "But for years, followers of the Rangers thought there was a jinx. [Former *Fort Worth Star-Telegram* columnist] Jim Reeves used to call it the 'Big Guy Theory,' as in, the Big Guy [in heaven] doesn't want the Rangers to win. There was always a big injury, or something crazy would happen that would keep us from winning when we had good teams. I had gotten to the point where I thought I'd never work a World Series game."

Nevertheless, Nadel never allowed mediocrity on the field to interfere with articulate and artistic brilliance in the broadcast booth. While his original professional goal was to broadcast hockey, Nadel first learned the intricacies of baseball from Miller and then joined Rangers radio play-by-play announcer Mark Holtz in 1982, forming a terrifically fluent and entertaining tandem throughout the 1980s and into the mid-1990s.

When Holtz transitioned to television in 1995, Nadel moved into the play-by-play seat and proved to be every bit as eloquent, descriptive, and dynamic in the lead role as his mentors and former partners. Nadel doesn't just describe the game; he paints vivid word pictures, creating mental images in the minds of listeners.

His delivery is a mix of passion and professionalism. He can be critical without being condemning, he's entertaining as well as informative, he is upbeat toward the Rangers without being degrading to opponents, and he is consistently compelling, regardless of whether the Rangers are in the thick of a playoff race or mathematically eliminated by early September.

"My mother and I both hated the Yankees, but when the Dodgers left, the only games I could listen to were Yankees games," Nadel recalled. "I'd listen to Mel Allen and Red Barber, and then Phil Rizzuto and Jerry Coleman. They did a great job broadcasting very good teams. Then, when the Mets came in '62, I listened to Lindsey Nelson and Bob Murphy doing the games. Even though it was the worst team in baseball history, they always sounded like they were having a great time and were happy to be there. They made it sound like the Mets had really good players, even though they went 40–120. They were the voice of hope. I kept that in mind many times when we were doing games when the Rangers were hopelessly out of the race."

The Rangers were certainly never out of the race in 2010, but it wasn't until July 9—the day Texas acquired Cliff Lee in a trade from Seattle—that Nadel allowed himself to ponder the possibility of calling a playoff series victory…and possibly much more.

Nadel acknowledges that he was a nervous wreck prior to the deciding Game 5 of the ALDS in Tampa Bay, where Lee pitched a gem to help the Rangers win their first-ever playoff series.

"I don't think I've ever been more nervous than before that game against the Rays," Nadel said. "I was sick to my stomach before the game. If we lose that game, everybody says: 'Same ol' Rangers, can't win a playoff series.' But if you win, it changes everything. That game was so important in the history of the franchise."

So was Game 6 of the ALCS on October 22…against the team that Nadel grew up hating: the Yankees. With the Rangers holding a 3–2 lead in the series, Colby Lewis pitched a masterful game,

Eric Nadel holds up his score book from the Rangers' record-setting 30–3 win over the Baltimore Orioles on August 22, 2007. Nadel has been calling Rangers games since 1979. (AP Images)

Hard-Working Radio Man Goes the Extra Mile

One of the most endearing on-air qualities of Rangers radio play-by-play personality Eric Nadel is his behind-the-scenes, personal knowledge of the Texas players—their personalities, their likes, their dislikes, and their general perspectives on life and the game.

That viewpoint doesn't come effortlessly. Nadel has gone to great lengths to make certain he is capable of developing a relationship with every player, regardless of his nationality.

Early in Nadel's career with the Rangers, Texas signed 17-year-old Ruben Sierra out of Puerto Rico in November 1982. In June 1986 Sierra made his major league debut with the Rangers and hit a home run in his second at-bat. But because Sierra could not speak English, Nadel had no way of gaining any insight into his background.

"When Sierra came to the big leagues in the mid-1980s, I couldn't talk to him," Nadel said. "I had to use Jose Guzman as a translator. It was very frustrating because Ruben was a key figure in the game two or three times a week, and I couldn't talk to him."

Nadel vowed to do something about that, and when baseball had a lockout in 1990, the radio man of the Rangers went to work.

"During the lockout in 1990, I sat at home and learned Spanish from cassette tapes instead of going to spring training," Nadel said. "All through the season I used those tapes and then took lessons in the off-season. I also started going to Latin America. I went to language school in Venezuela for two weeks. It's still a struggle, I'm not fluent.

"But I could tell Ruben was thankful. I was never good enough to talk to him when he was in Texas. But he was impressed that I could at least make statements to him. When he came back (to Texas in 2000 after spending eight years with the A's, Yankees, Tigers, Reds, Blue Jays, and White Sox), he knew how to speak English, but he still liked the fact I had learned his language. Over the years, it's been valuable in other ways, too. Other guys trust me a little more because I've made the efforts to learn, so they speak more frankly with me."

Consequently, listeners to the Rangers radio network tend to receive a little more insight than anyone else.

Vladimir Guerrero provided a big hit, and Nelson Cruz launched a game-altering home run to help the Rangers build a big lead entering the ninth. Closer Neftali Feliz entered the game and recorded two quick outs, bringing Alex Rodriguez to the plate.

Now, let's turn it over to Nadel for the call of the final out:

"One ball, two strikes, two outs, 6–1 Rangers lead in the top of the ninth. Feliz the high set. Here comes the pitch. Breaking ball. Strike three called! The Rangers are going to the World Series!"

For the next 36 seconds, Nadel said nothing, allowing the euphoric crowd noise, fireworks, and music inside Rangers Ballpark in Arlington to speak for itself. After the extended silence from Nadel, he delivered a typically well-expressed description of the magnitude of the moment:

"In the 50th year of the franchise, in their 39th year in Texas, under a full moon in Arlington, the Texas Rangers have won the American League pennant."

Nadel saw it and called it. He even received the red American League championship T-shirt, complete with the claw and antler logos, to commemorate the event. But just to make sure he wasn't imagining it all, Nadel took the T-shirt home and placed it on the floor next to his bed.

"I wanted to make sure it was the first thing I saw the next morning when I woke up [on October 23]," Nadel said. "I didn't want to rub my eyes in the morning and wonder if I was really going to get to call a World Series game. It was a magical moment and a terrific season. Now, of course, what I'd love to do is call the clinching game of a World Series victory."

Only time will tell if that happens. Regardless, Nadel won't change his delivery: He's the consummate pro regardless of the Rangers' place in the standings.

42 Rusty Greer Played the Game with a Marine's Mentality

In a 1999 spring training interview with *Sports Illustrated's* Gerry Callahan, Rangers outfielder Rusty Greer pointed to nameplates showing the names Palmeiro, Gonzalez, and Rodriguez above empty lockers in the team's clubhouse for emphasis and then explained that he—as the three-hole hitter—had the most enviable lineup position in all of Major League Baseball.

"Our four-five-six guys are as good as any in baseball," Greer said. "Me? I'm just one of the guys who's supposed to get on base for the big guns."

Greer's humility—in that interview and practically every other one during his splendid career with the Rangers—was one of the primary reasons he was such a beloved figure in the clubhouse and in the community from the time he made his debut in a Texas uniform in 1994 until the time he officially retired in 2005.

The other primary reason he was adored by so many fans and fellow players was that, while Greer resembled Opie Taylor, he played left field with the reckless abandon of Lawrence Taylor. The hard-nosed Greer raced into outfield walls and leapt belly-first onto outfield turfs with no apparent concern for his own health, generating highlight-reel catches and standing ovations throughout his career.

One of his first great catches came in the ninth inning of Kenny Rogers' perfect game on July 28, 1994. The California Angels' Rex Hudler led off the ninth with a humpback line drive toward right-center field that Rogers, Hudler, and practically everyone inside the Ballpark in Arlington believed was destined to be a base hit. But Greer, then a rookie playing center field, made a great read on the ball.

He sprinted toward the right-center gap, dove, and caught the ball, preserving the perfect game. He also recorded the final out of that game on a more routine liner.

"When Rusty did that, I thought, *Somebody wants me to do this*," Rogers said after the game. "I never thought he could catch that ball. He went at it like there was a no-hitter on the line."

Fittingly, Greer maintained that bold and daring style of play until the very end. He last started for the Rangers on June 2, 2002, against Kansas City. Playing left field and hitting leadoff, Greer singled in the first, stole second, and scored to ignite a five-run inning. In the eighth inning, he made the second of two diving catches, sprawling after Michael Tucker's sinking line drive.

Greer strained his back on the play. He never played the outfield again and had just three more at-bats the rest of the year. He then required a series of surgeries that ultimately prevented him from making a comeback.

"I don't regret [my style of play]," Greer told T.R. Sullivan of MLB.com prior to being inducted into the Rangers Hall of Fame in 2007. "That's just one of those things like being in a clutch situation; your teammates want you out there. When we went to the field, my teammates—particularly the pitcher—they wanted me to play left field because they knew I'd go after anything. That's the way I was wired. Will Clark was wired that way. Mickey Tettleton was wired that way, and Mark McLemore. I don't regret any of it."

Unlike many other big-name players on the Rangers' roster in the mid- and late 1990s, Greer was not particularly imposing from a physical standpoint. He was a decent-sized guy—6'0", 190 pounds—but he didn't possess the stature of Juan Gonzalez, the arm of Pudge Rodriguez, or the sweet swing of Will Clark.

Greer was more of an average-looking kind of guy, who played college ball at tiny University of Montevallo, some 30 miles south of Birmingham, Alabama. Montevallo was the only school that had shown interest in Greer prior to a senior-year all-star game in which he performed exceptionally well. When larger universities began expressing interest after the all-star game, Greer showed his loyalty by keeping his commitment to Montevallo.

He displayed that loyalty with the Rangers as well, staying in the organization throughout his entire career. Texas chose Greer with its 10th-round pick (279th overall) in the 1990 amateur draft, and while he had opportunities during his career to cash in on free agency, the Alabama-born Greer stuck with the team that first picked him. That also made him extremely relatable with the fans.

But Greer was much more than a run-of-the-mill player. In addition to showing the heart and hustle fans loved, he batted a career-high .332 with 96 runs scored, 18 home runs, and 100 RBIs in 1996, helping the Rangers win their first division title. In that breakout season, Greer earned $258,333.

In a four-year period from 1996 to 1999, Greer hit .315 while averaging 20 home runs, 106 runs scored, and 99 RBIs as Texas claimed three American League West titles.

"Rusty also prepared himself for the game as well as anyone and played hurt at times when no one knew it," said former Rangers general manager Doug Melvin. "I remember when I introduced Rusty at John Wetteland's press conference signing. John gave this serious look right into Rusty's eyes, gave him a firm handshake, and said, 'Rusty, you are my kind of player.' He played the game the right way and for the right reasons: enjoyment and to win. We don't win those divisions without Rusty."

Injuries abruptly ended his career, but when he retired, Greer had plenty of impressive credentials. His career .305 batting average ranks fifth highest in club history, and his six career grand slams were just one shy of most in Rangers history. Furthermore, Greer was greatest in the clutch, driving in the game-winning run in the Rangers' last at-bat 17 times.

"Rusty had a great career," former Rangers manager Buck Showalter said. "He could really show his consistency over a 162-game season. He was a great competitor and did things the right way, on and off the field."

Tom Grieve: The Player, the Executive, the Commentator

On the afternoon before he officially became the 13th member of the Texas Rangers Hall of Fame, Tom Grieve smiled broadly and regularly as the luncheon at the Arlington Sheraton turned into somewhat of a roast regarding Grieve's pedestrian productivity as a player.

"[Grieve] would hit .400 for a week, and then he'd hit .100 for a week," recalled Jim Sundberg, who was inducted into the Rangers Hall of Fame in 2003. "He was one of the hottest and coldest hitters. When he was hitting, he was fun to watch."

The personable, quick-witted Grieve would likely be the first to acknowledge that, as a big-league hitter, his numbers were often more representative of menopause than the mercury of a thermometer during August in Arlington. In other words, he'd generally have more hot flashes than extended hot streaks.

Grieve was the Washington Senators' first selection and the sixth overall pick in the first round of the 1966 Major League Baseball Draft, which also produced Reggie Jackson (second overall), future Rangers manager Johnny Oates (38th), and future Rangers pitcher Charlie Hough (159th overall). (Twenty-eight years later, one of Grieve's sons, Ben, was the second overall selection by Oakland in 1994, making the Grieves the first father-son combo to both be selected in the first round of the Major League Baseball Draft).

Tom Grieve made his big-league debut with the Senators on July 5, 1970, and he came to Texas with the team in 1972. He was a solid platoon outfielder and designated hitter for the Rangers from 1972 to 1977, and his best season was in 1976, when he hit .255, belted 20 homers, drove in 81 runs, and was the team's Player of the Year.

He was traded to the Mets in '78 and had a brief stint with the Cardinals in 1979. For his entire playing career, Grieve hit .249 with 65 homers and 254 RBIs in 670 games. He rejoined the Rangers in '79, playing in Triple A, but he decided to take a front-office job with the team in group sales instead of continuing his playing career in Japan. The Pittsfield, Massachusetts, native retired in 1980 with absolutely no illusions of ever becoming a Rangers legend of any sort.

But what no one—not even Grieve—could have possibly envisioned at the time was that he would string together some longevity numbers with the ballclub that would eventually earn him the nickname "Mr. Ranger." That's how television broadcaster John Rhadigan referred to Grieve at the Hall of Fame luncheon on July 23, 2010, in recognition of his 43 years—at that time—of service to the franchise as a player, front-office member, general manager, and broadcaster.

"I can't speak for the other guys who've gone into the Rangers Hall of Fame," Grieve said in response to the meaningfulness of being inducted by the team. "But I'm pretty sure it meant as much or more to me than it did to the other guys because I wouldn't have gone in based on my playing ability. The other players who went in…it was a foregone conclusion based on the way they played during their careers.

"That wasn't the case for me. For me, it was a sum of the parts—the fact that I was a player, the fact I worked in the front office, and the fact that I have worked as a broadcaster for a long time. That the Rangers would deem the sum of the parts to be worthy of the Hall of Fame was very significant to me. It was one of the best days I've had in baseball, and to have my family there against the Angels [on July 24, 2010,] with a full house just added to the memory."

Grieve's rise within the Rangers' front office ranks is certainly the most remarkable leg of his journey to the team's Hall of Fame.

From group sales under Brad Corbett's regime, Grieve worked his way into baseball operations and then on to player development, where he helped establish the Rangers as a pioneer in Latin America, especially Puerto Rico. Before the island fell under the amateur draft rules, Grieve and his staff landed future stars such as Ruben Sierra, Pudge Rodriguez, and Juan Gonzalez from Puerto Rico. And Grieve's ultimate success in running the farm system prompted then–club president Mike Stone to name Grieve as general manager, replacing Joe Klein on September 1, 1984, and making Grieve, then 36, the youngest general manager in baseball.

It was a great honor for Grieve...and an even bigger challenge. He inherited a team in '84 that was on its way to a 69–92 finish. And the farm system was in shambles from years of questionable trades and free-agent acquisitions.

Grieve first addressed the farm system by hiring San Diego's Sandy Johnson, and he gave him more power and freedom than any scouting director in baseball. Grieve then pieced together a roster for the '85 season, adding 37-year-old designated hitter Cliff Johnson, 36-year-old infielder Toby Harrah, and 35-year-old pitcher Burt Hooton in the off-season. The team's most popular player, third baseman Buddy Bell, desperately wanted to be traded, and Grieve obliged later that summer.

Predictably, the '85 Rangers were lousy, and in May, Grieve fired manager Doug Rader and replaced him with Bobby Valentine, a Tommy Lasorda protégé who had once roomed with Grieve with the Mets. Steadily, Grieve began building up the farm system, and Valentine began making the big-league team more competitive.

In December 1988 Grieve made one of the best trades in team history, a nine-player deal in which the Rangers acquired Rafael Palmeiro and Jamie Moyer from the Cubs for Mitch Williams and Curtis Wilkerson, among others. He also acquired future batting champion Julio Franco from the Indians for Pete O'Brien, Oddibe McDowell, and Jerry Browne. And in the big free-agent acquisition of the '88 off-season, the Rangers changed the perception of the franchise by adding Nolan Ryan to the team.

Those moves and many others made the Rangers competitive throughout much of Grieve's 10-year tenure as general manager. But with no division titles to his credit and a new ballpark in Arlington, management made a change, releasing Grieve from his general manager duties following the '94 season.

Perhaps all you really need to know about Grieve's popularity and perceived value within the franchise, however, is that right after then–club president Tom Schieffer fired Grieve as general manager, he hired him as a television analyst, where he has been ever since. And he has been quite entertaining in the television booth.

It should also be noted that when the Rangers took the field for their first-ever playoff series—the 1996 American League Division Series—five members of the starting lineup had been acquired by Grieve in some fashion.

As far as television color commentators go, who could possibly present a better perspective of the team—past and present—than Mr. Ranger?

44 Rangers Blast Yanks in 1996 ALDS Opener in Bronx

The modern Yankees dynasty can easily be traced back to the fall of 1996 when the Bronx Bombers won their first playoff series in 15 years. Beginning with that historic season, New York won four of the next five World Series and appeared in the Fall Classic six times in an eight-year span.

Ironically, the most dominating postseason run in baseball's modern era began more inauspiciously than favorably for the pinstripers. In fact, the typically overstated daily tabloids on the morning of October 2, 1996, warned of the potential imminent doom of the Yanks because of what had happened the previous night.

"Thanks to the muscle of the Power Rangers and some moxie from Texas pitcher John Burkett, the Yankees find themselves needing a victory tonight to avoid pushing their dream season to the brink of extinction," wrote John Giannone in the *New York Daily News* following the Rangers' 6–2 win in the series opener.

Much to the dismay of what was then a record-setting crowd of 57,205 at Yankee Stadium, Burkett was more masterful than New York ace David Cone in the ALDS opener. Burkett, acquired by the Rangers from the Marlins in early August, scattered 10 hits, but he stayed away from the big inning.

Meanwhile, Cone breezed through the first three innings with a 1–0 lead, but he ran into major issues in the fourth. Ivan Rodriguez opened the inning with a soft single to right, and Rusty Greer followed with a walk. Three pitches later, Juan Gonzalez muscled a belt-high fastball into the left-field seats to give the Rangers a 3–1 lead and silence the Bronx crowd.

Mark McLemore: One of the Rangers' All-Around Good Guys

Prior to the Rangers' July 15, 2011, game against the Mariners at Safeco Field, Mark McLemore tossed the ceremonial first pitch, kicking off a weekend-long celebration that honored the 10-year anniversary of Seattle's 116-win team from 2001.

It was purely coincidental that the Mariners celebrated the 2001 team with the Rangers in town. But it was fitting that McLemore threw the first pitch in a game pitting the two teams for which he played the most games in his career.

In 19 major league seasons, McLemore played nine of his last 10 years (1995–2003) with either the Rangers or the Mariners. In four seasons with the Mariners (2000–03), McLemore earned the title "supersub," playing a major role at multiple positions. McLemore was particularly valuable in 2001, playing 125 games at six different positions.

During that season, McLemore also participated in what he calls the most memorable event of his career. He and teammate Mike Cameron hoisted a U.S. flag and carried it around Safeco Field the night the Mariners clinched a playoff berth in 2001, just days after the 9/11 terrorist attacks.

McLemore never hoisted a flag in Texas, but he played a significant role in raising some division championship banners. McLemore, nicknamed "the Doctor of Defense," played five years (1995–99) and a total of 635 games with the Rangers. Texas won its first three American League West titles with McLemore as a fixture in the lineup, splitting time between second base and the outfield.

After starting his career with the Angels and then playing brief stints with the Indians and Astros, McLemore blossomed as a big leaguer under Johnny Oates from 1992 to 1994 in Baltimore. When Oates became the Rangers' manager following the 1994 season, McLemore was one of Texas' key free-agent acquisitions.

His best statistical year with the Rangers was 1996, when he hit a career-high .290 in 147 games. But there was so much more to his game than numbers could ever detail. He was one of Texas' all-time best chemistry guys in the clubhouse, a trait that also made him extremely popular in Seattle.

Following the conclusion of his playing career in 2004, McLemore continued to reside with his family in Southlake. He became an analyst for ESPN and later joined FOX Sports Southwest's Rangers television coverage, joining the broadcast booth during games and also co-hosting pregame and postgame shows. Prior to the Rangers' first ALDS home game against Tampa Bay in 2010—the first home playoff game for the team since 1999—it was fitting that McLemore and former Texas teammate Rusty Greer assisted eight-year-old Johnny Oates II, the grandson of the late Rangers manager, in throwing the ceremonial first pitch.

The Rangers weren't done in the fourth. Will Clark followed Gonzalez's blast with a single, and two batters later, Dean Palmer lifted a Cone slider two rows deep in the left-field stands.

That was all the offense Burkett needed, as he bent several times but never broke. Burkett featured exceptional control, throwing first-pitch strikes to 28 of the 38 hitters. Overall, he threw 122 pitches, 85 for strikes.

"He pitched a tremendous game," Yankees manager Joe Torre said of Burkett. "He was around the plate all night and around a lot of handles on our bats with tremendous movement."

He also was the beneficiary of sparkling defense, especially in the first when the Yankees seemed to be on the verge of taking early control. After Cone put the Rangers down in order, Tim Raines led off the bottom of the first by singling and going to third when the next hitter, Wade Boggs, doubled.

The third New York hitter of the game, Paul O'Neill, slashed a hard grounder between Palmer and the third-base bag. Palmer dove to his right, speared it cleanly, looked Raines back to third, and threw out O'Neill for the first out. Raines scored one batter later on Bernie Williams' groundout, but Burkett escaped the first without enduring major damage.

"That play Dean Palmer made in the first inning set the tone," said Texas manager Johnny Oates. "If O'Neill's ball goes in the corner, we're down two [runs] with nobody out and O'Neill on second. That was our first big play."

It may have been the play of the game, especially since Palmer had led the American League in errors as recently as 1994. But after an injury-shortened '95 season, he improved his defense dramatically in '96, which played a major role in the Rangers earning their first-ever playoff appearance.

There was more painful irony for Yankees fans on the morning of October 2, 1996 when Palmer credited his improved defense to former New York legend Bucky Dent, the Rangers' dugout coach at the time.

Heartbreak in the Bronx: Game 2 of the 1996 ALDS

History can be extremely unkind to players who make late-inning gaffes in postseason games. Ask Bill Buckner. Many kids, teens, and adults who were not even born in 1986 have been taught that Buckner cost the Red Sox their first World Series title since 1918 by allowing Mookie Wilson's grounder to go through his legs.

Never mind that reliever Bob Stanley uncorked a wild pitch earlier in the inning that allowed the Mets to tie it. Never mind that Buckner's blunder came in Game 6—not the finale.

People tend only to remember the mishap and to contemplate what might have been if it had not occurred. Dean Palmer's fielding error in Game 2 of the 1996 ALCS is one of those moments.

Palmer played 14 years in the major leagues, including a largely successful career as the Rangers' third baseman from 1991 to 1997. Palmer struck out too often (154 times in '92 and '93), but he hit for power (38 homers and 107 RBIs in '96), and he continually improved his defense during his tenure in Texas.

For all he accomplished, however, many Rangers fans remember Palmer most for his throwing error in the 12th inning of Game 2 of the 1996 ALDS. That error allowed Yankees rookie Derek Jeter to score from second base on a bunt by Charlie Hayes, giving New York a come-from-behind 5–4 victory that completely changed the complexion of the series and sent the Rangers reeling into a postseason abyss.

Beginning with that night—October 2, 1996—the Yankees won 10 consecutive playoff games against Texas, covering a span of 14 years. Meanwhile, Jeter and the Yankees began a run of postseason dominance unmatched in the modern era of baseball. New York rolled through the rest of the postseason, whipping the Orioles 4–1 in the ALCS and beating the Braves 4–2 in the World Series.

That begs the question: what if the Rangers had won that game and taken a 2–0 series lead with the next three games scheduled in Arlington?

That seemed like a distinct possibility when, in the top of the third, Juan Gonzalez blasted his second home run of the night (he hit a solo shot in the second off Yankees starter Andy Pettitte) and his third of the series. "Señor Octubre" crushed a three-run blast in the third to put the Rangers up, 4–1.

The Yankees chipped away against Rangers starter Ken Hill, tying it with one out in the eighth, when Cecil Fielder lined a hard single to right against ineffective closer Jeff Russell.

After scoring four runs in the first three frames, Texas did not push another runner across the plate in the ensuing nine innings. The Rangers went 1-for-9 with runners in scoring position, left 11 men on base, and, other than Gonzalez, no one drove in another run. The Rangers wasted plenty of scoring opportunities, including in the top of the 12th when Texas loaded the bases with two out and Palmer at the plate.

One night earlier, Palmer had been one of the biggest heroes in Texas' Game 1 victory, but on October 2, Palmer couldn't come through in the clutch. Reliever Brian Boehringer—the seventh pitcher of the night for New York—induced Palmer to a fly to right center in a play that nearly resulted in a collision between Paul O'Neill and Bernie Williams.

In the bottom of the 12th against Rangers reliever Mike Stanton, Jeter singled and Tim Raines walked to open the inning. Mike Henneman entered the game to face Hayes, who placed a bunt down the third-base line. Palmer picked it cleanly, but his throw was wild, and second baseman Mark McLemore—covering on the play—could not keep it from skipping down the right-field line.

Texas led the major leagues in fielding in 1996, and Palmer had been a big reason why the Rangers were an improved defense. But on that fateful night that possibly changed the playoff destinies of the Yankees and Rangers for many years to come, he could not make the play.

46 First Home Playoffs Produce More Agony in Arlington

After wandering aimlessly for most of their first 24 seasons in Arlington, the Rangers finally found the playoff promised land in 1996, and 50,860 fans packed the Ballpark in Arlington on October 4—an absolutely electric Friday night—for the first-ever postseason game in North Texas.

Unfortunately for the hometown fans, the first playoffs in Arlington produced emotions and results that had become synonymous with the franchise's first quarter of a century in the Metroplex: torment, torture, and tough losses.

Even though the Rangers had blown an early 4–1 lead and ultimately lost Game 2 of the 1996 ALDS in New York, Texas had accomplished what it needed to by gaining a split in the Bronx. The Rangers returned home needing to win two of the next three games in Arlington to eliminate the Yankees and move on to the team's first ALCS.

Simple enough, right? After all, the Rangers had already beaten the Yanks in five of six regular-season games in Arlington, outscoring the Bombers 44–15 in those contests. Moreover, the Rangers liked the pitching matchup in Game 3, as 14-game winner Darren Oliver, just shy of his 26th birthday, squared off against Jimmy Key, who'd gone 17–4 in 1994 but was essentially a .500 pitcher (12–11 overall) with a 4.68 ERA in '96.

Fourteen years later, Oliver—then in his third stint with Texas—played a key left-handed relief role in helping the Rangers finally win a playoff series and reach the World Series in 2010. But he may have been at his absolute best on the night of October 4, 1996.

After giving up a first-inning solo homer to Bernie Williams, Oliver cruised through the next seven innings, allowing no runs and just three hits. Meanwhile, the Rangers tied it in the fourth on a homer by—who else?—Juan Gonzalez, his fourth in three games.

The Rangers took a 2–1 lead in the fifth when Kevin Elster attempted a delayed steal and Yankees rookie Derek Jeter failed to cover second. New York catcher (and future manager) Joe Girardi threw into center field for a two-base error. One batter later, Ivan Rodriguez doubled to give the Rangers the lead.

It stayed that way into the ninth, and Johnny Oates elected to stick with Oliver instead of turning the game over to his questionable bullpen. The Rangers had already lost 12 times in 1996 when they needed only three outs for a win, so Rangers fans were hardly breathing easily entering the ninth.

Their worst fears were realized when Jeter started the ninth with a single and moved to third when Tim Raines singled. With two on and nobody out, Oates turned to closer Mike Henneman, who induced a game-tying sacrifice fly from Williams and then forced Cecil Fielder to ground out on a play where Raines advanced to second. The Rangers issued an intentional walk to Tino Martinez, bringing up free-swinging Mariano Duncan, who dropped a single into center to score Raines.

In 1997 the Rangers addressed their back-of-the-bullpen issues by adding John Wetteland. Unfortunately for Texas, he was still with New York in '96, and Wetteland closed out the 3–2 win by striking out Darryl Hamilton with the tying run at third.

"It was probably the maddest I've been after a baseball game," Oliver told *The New York Times* in 2010. "We were so close to winning. If it would have been a game like that nowadays, I probably wouldn't have been out there for the ninth. They put so much emphasis on the closer and the bullpen. That was a good team [we had in '96]. That was a team that probably could have gone all the way. If we had won that game and went on, I think we probably could have done some big things."

Instead, the Rangers followed a familiar script the next day: Jump out to a lead, watch Gonzalez homer, and lament about what could have been after the Yankees rally. Texas knocked out Yankees starter Kenny Rogers—a former and future Ranger—and built a 4–0 lead after three innings thanks, in part, to Gonzalez's fifth homer of the series. But then the Yankees knocked out Texas starter Bobby Witt, rallied to tie it in the fifth, and built a 6–4 lead in the ninth.

In the bottom half of the ninth, the Rangers put the tying runs on against Wetteland, but Will Clark flew out and Dean Palmer struck out to end the game and the series. The Yankees went on to win the World Series and build a dynasty. The Rangers wandered and wondered about winning a playoff game for the next 14 years.

47 George W. Bush: Leading the Rangers, Texas, and the USA

This could have been placed higher. Or lower. But it's only fitting that Mr. 43 makes the list at 43.

Long before he spent eight years in the White House, George "Dub-ya" Bush made a name for himself and created a brighter future for the Rangers by helping the team build and move into Arlington's most famous brick house.

Rangers Ballpark in Arlington, which opened in 1994, moved the team out of the "Bush leagues." It may have also propelled Bush into a political league of his own.

"The Ballpark is the legacy of Bush's five-year stint as managing general partner of the Rangers, a time in which he built up both the franchise's bottom line and his own, along the way honing many of the skills he draws upon in politics," wrote Joe Nick Patoski in a 1999 article in *Texas Monthly.* "Fundraiser Bush shook out $46 million from various investors during the depths of Texas' last economic bust in the run-up to buying the team. Consensus-builder Bush got the Ballpark referendum passed in Arlington when similar measures were being nixed by voters elsewhere. Manager Bush ran a business efficiently in the glare of the public eye. People-person Bush nourished the egos of the famous and the anonymous, from Juan Gonzalez to the groundskeepers, always addressing them by name."

With the Rangers, Bush proved to be more than a familiar name. He had spent much of 1988 campaigning for his father's successful bid to become the 41st president of the United States and then returned to Texas, where he'd previously been involved in starting several oil exploration companies. And it was one of his former oil-business partners in Midland, William DeWitt Jr., who informed Bush that Eddie Chiles was interested in selling the Rangers.

Chiles, a friend of the Bush family, had once flown George W's sister, Robin, to hospitals in his private plane after she was diagnosed with leukemia. He'd bought the Rangers in 1980 and was interested in selling the team to someone who would keep it in Arlington. Bush gathered an investor group that included Roland W. Betts, a movie financier who'd been one of Bush's fraternity

Greene's Hill Not Just Another Green Hill

One of the features of Rangers Ballpark in Arlington is the grass-covered hill in center field, where flag-waving girls in bejeweled Texas jerseys sometimes run following Rangers scores and fans scramble—and often dog pile—for souvenirs when a player blasts a homer to straightaway center.

The green grass serves as a natural batter's eye. But a devoted Rangers fan should know that it's not an ordinary green hill; it's "Greene's Hill," named in 1997 after former Arlington mayor Richard Greene.

Greene was first elected mayor in April 1987 after more than a decade of service as chairman of the city's Planning and Zoning Commission and as mayor pro-tem. He served five mayoral terms, and when competing cities in the Dallas–Fort Worth area attempted to convince the Rangers to leave Arlington in the late 1980s and early '90s, Greene developed a plan, with the blessings of the George W. Bush ownership group, to build a new ballpark for the team as part of a proposed public-private partnership. Arlington voters overwhelmingly approved the plan in the largest-ever voter turnout in a local election.

Greene's plan dedicated $135 million toward the new stadium by raising the sales tax by a half-cent.

brothers; Connecticut real-estate investor Craig Stapleton, who was Bush's cousin through marriage; former Marriott Corporation executive Fred Malek; and three Cincinnati investors.

Chiles immediately signed a letter of agreement with the Bush group, but baseball commissioner Peter Ueberroth wanted a group with more local investors. At Ueberroth's urging, Bush met Fort Worth financier Richard Rainwater, who later met with Bush, Betts, and Stapleton at the Highland Park home of Edward "Rusty" Rose, a financier who specialized in leveraged buyouts. After various meetings, the investment team came together with the agreement that Bush and Rose would run the team, with Bush serving as the public-relations front man and Rose operating as chairman of the board.

Bush contributed only $606,000 of his own money—the smallest amount of any major investor, for which he would later be criticized. Overall, 70 investors representing 39 limited partnerships bought a piece of the team for $86 million, and the sale was approved in April 1989. At the first meeting of the new Bush-Rose ownership group, it was decided that in order to turn the team's fortunes around, a new stadium was essential.

Tom Schieffer, a member of the ownership team who'd served three terms as a Democrat in the Texas House of Representatives and is the younger brother of *Face the Nation* host Bob Schieffer, was appointed as the stadium czar in July 1990. Schieffer did much of the legwork in selecting a site, developing a strategy to implement a half-cent local sales tax in Arlington to pay for the stadium. Schieffer also recruited Tarrant County judge Tom Vandergriff and Arlington mayor Richard Greene to help win voter support for the $135 million in bonds it would take to build the stadium.

The bond issue passed in January 1991 by a 2:1 margin.

"This eventually will give us the ability to compete on a payroll level that will put us with a whole new echelon of ballclubs," Bush said after the referendum passed. "We'll be able to pay the market price to keep our talent and, at the same time, keep ticket prices down."

Deservedly, much of the credit for building the Ballpark in Arlington, which opened in 1994, went to Schieffer. But Bush's behind-the-scenes involvement had been critical as well.

"The bond election, the ballpark, the financing technique, that was all George's deal," Arlington realtor Mike Reilly, one of the Bush-Rose ownership partners, told Joe Nick Patoski. "He quarterbacked the whole thing, but he never took the credit."

Bush took a leave of absence to run for governor in 1994, the same season the Ballpark in Arlington opened to rave reviews. He won the race for governor, defeating Ann Richards, and resigned as managing general partner. By the time Tom Hicks bought the team in 1998, Bush's 1.8 percent share of the ownership had ballooned to 11.3 percent, and he pocketed almost $15 million—$2.7 million as a return on his investment and a $12.2 million "general partner interest." But he actually gained much more than the millions he made.

"Before the Rangers, I told him he needed to do something to step out of his father's shadow," Betts said in the *Texas Monthly* article. "Baseball was it. He became our local celebrity. He knew every usher. He signed autographs. He talked to fans. His presence meant everything. His eyes were on politics the whole time, but even when he was speaking at Republican functions, he was always talking about the Rangers."

In 2009 the Rangers honored Bush by naming the owner's suite the President George W. Bush Owner's Suite.

"I've looked this up, and in the 133-year history of Major League Baseball, never has a president been an owner except President Bush," former Rangers owner Tom Hicks said. "I'm glad he's home and can reconnect with this place. We thought it would be fitting to have the suite named after him."

48 Mike Hargrove: Worth the Wait

One of the most well-known and commonly repeated baseball adages, originally attributed to Hall of Fame pitcher Warren Spahn, is that, "Hitting is timing. Pitching is disrupting that timing."

While virtually every player—from Little League to the major leagues—has accepted that theory since Spahn uttered those words, former Rangers first baseman Mike Hargrove always seemed intent on proving otherwise. Hargrove's painstaking pre-pitch routine at the plate disrupted a pitcher's pace, typically slowed the flow of the game, and threatened to alter the earth's rotation.

He wasn't merely a patient hitter; he was a patience-tester.

Hargrove's rituals often made his at-bats seem as long as the wait at a doctor's office or the DMV. He'd step out of the batter's box, bang the barrel of the bat against his spikes, lean the bat against his legs, adjust his helmet, and adjust one batting glove and then the other, paying special attention to how the gloves fit snuggly onto his thumbs. Then he'd pull on each sleeve of his uniform and wipe each hand against his pants before picking up the bat, stepping back into the box, and digging into the dirt.

Unless he reached base or was retired, he'd begin the whole routine again after the next pitch. And the next one. And every one afterward.

"He wasn't really a meticulous person in any other setting," said former Rangers teammate and fellow 1974 rookie Jim Sundberg. "But he was deliberate and meticulous in the batter's box. He lived up to his nickname."

The fitting moniker: "the Human Rain Delay."

Perhaps just as aptly, Mr. Precipitation burst onto the major league scene with the suddenness of a lightning bolt.

169

Dudley Michael Hargrove was raised in Perryton, a farming and oil-drilling community in the Texas panhandle. He didn't play high school baseball but was a football and basketball star. When Texas A&M backed away from its football scholarship offer, Hargrove attended Northwestern Oklahoma State on a basketball scholarship. At his father's urging, Hargrove also reluctantly tried out for the baseball team.

"I didn't want to embarrass myself," Hargrove told Larry Keith of *Sports Illustrated* in a 1975 story. "I didn't know how good I would be."

He proved to be exceptional, leading the conference in hitting his freshman year. In 1972 he was chosen in the 25th round by Texas, which assigned him to its rookie team in Geneva, New York. He hit .267 the first year, but after making a few tweaks to his stance, he turned heads by hitting .351 at Class A Gastonia in 1973. He played so well in '73 that he was invited to the Rangers' spring training in 1974, where he shocked everyone by hitting .486 in the Grapefruit League games, earning a spot on the Opening Day roster.

The gritty, 24-year-old Hargrove was a huge part of the Rangers turnaround in '74, winning Rookie of the Year honors by hitting .323 in 131 games. The next year, he made the All-Star team. When the '75 All-Star balloting began, local supporters in Perryton offered a trip to Kansas City to watch Hargrove play to the person who gave him the most votes. The winner turned in 18,000.

Hargrove played the first five years of his 12-season major league career with the Rangers, hitting .293 with an on-base percentage of .399. Hargrove had such a good eye and drew so many walks (435 in five seasons) that he often batted leadoff for Texas.

In October 1978 Texas sent Hargrove, Kurt Bevacqua, and Bill Fahey to San Diego for Oscar Gamble, Dave Roberts, and $300,000. Hargrove was dealt to the Indians the following summer, establishing quite a legacy in Cleveland—first as a player and then as a manager. He played seven seasons with Cleveland (1979–85) and began his managerial career with the Tribe in 1991. In nine years with the Indians, he compiled an overall record of 721–591, leading Cleveland to five consecutive American League Central Division titles from 1995 to 1999 and World Series appearances in 1995 and 1997.

Hargrove also managed in Baltimore and Seattle.

49 Will Clark: "The Sheriff" Brings Law and Order to Rangers

Ultimately, former Rangers general manager Doug Melvin probably made the right decision when Rafael Palmeiro called him on December 1, 1998. Palmeiro, a free-agent first baseman who'd spent the previous five seasons with Baltimore, wanted to return to Texas, where he played from 1989 to 1993. But he also wanted an offer from the Rangers right away...or else he felt compelled to take the Orioles' offer.

Melvin weighed the options: sign Palmeiro or re-sign incumbent first baseman Will Clark, who was coming off one of his best seasons.

Under the gun, Melvin chose Palmeiro. The Orioles, in turn, signed Clark.

That worked out well for the Rangers, as Palmeiro had a monster '99 season, hitting .324 with 47 home runs and 148 RBIs. Over the course of the next five seasons (1999–2003), Palmeiro hit 214 homers and drove in 608 runs for the Rangers. Meanwhile, Clark played only two more seasons in the majors.

But, while the second personnel decision involving Palmeiro and Clark was a good one for the Rangers, the first one—in the winter of 1993—was an even better one. At that time, Rangers general manager Tom Grieve had hoped to re-sign Palmeiro, but when negotiations broke down, Texas turned its attention to the sweet-swinging Clark.

"Our priority was to re-sign Rafael, but we couldn't go to six years or more than $30 million, and we couldn't risk losing Clark as well," Grieve said in November 1993. "It's imperative that we have a left-handed power hitter in our new stadium next year."

Clark brought so much more than a big bat to Texas. And he delivered more than Palmeiro ever could. Clark brought attitude, toughness, grit, heart, and a championship dimension to the Rangers' clubhouse.

In the strike-shortened 1994 season, Clark ranked fifth in the American League with a .431 on-base percentage and placed eighth in the league with a .329 batting average when the season was abruptly halted. Most significantly—even though the American League West was embarrassingly bad—the Rangers were in first place when the season ended.

"He's got the will to win and knows what is involved in getting it done," former Rangers manager Kevin Kennedy said in '94. "Not just some days, every day. It's the kind of intensity this organization needed."

Two years later, Clark helped to deliver what the organization really needed: its first division title. And in '98, his final season with the Rangers, Clark again helped to will the Rangers to the West crown.

In a key mid-September win against Baltimore in 1998, for example, Clark beat out two infield singles in the same game… despite playing with a broken toe. The second came in the ninth inning, one hitter before Pudge Rodriguez drilled a dramatic two-run homer to win the game.

"I thought Clark brought a very necessary sense of toughness and discipline to the Rangers," former *Fort Worth Star-Telegram* columnist Jim Reeves said. "His nickname was 'the Sheriff,' and he earned that title. He lived up to it. Will could be very caustic. He could give writers hell. But what he brought to the team was immensely valuable and needed.

"Those teams needed that, and then they brought other guys in who supported Will like Mickey Tettleton, Rusty Greer, and Mark McLemore. Those teams had a lot of guys who understood what it took to win as a team."

Clark hit at least .300 in four of his five seasons with the Rangers, but he provided so much more than numbers. He wasn't afraid to verbally challenge a teammate, confront a team official, or stare down an opponent. He didn't cut anyone slack.

In fairness, the far more laid-back Palmeiro did help the Rangers continue their postseason run, as Texas won its third American League West crown in four years in '99. But there may have never been a first division crown in 1996 without bringing the Sheriff to Arlington.

50 Buddy Bell: Pure Class at the Hot Corner

Earlier in the 1985 season, popular Rangers third baseman Buddy Bell had requested a trade and presented then–general manager Tom Grieve with a list of the 10 teams where he would most like to play. So no one was surprised on July 19, when it was announced that Bell was being dealt to Cincinnati for Duane Walker and a player to be named later (Jeff Russell).

Long before the deal went down, it was a foregone conclusion that Bell would be moved. But that didn't make it any easier for Bell to say goodbye to his Texas teammates.

As he left Detroit—where the Rangers were playing the Tigers—to catch a flight to Cincinnati, Bell had to continually fight back the tears.

"I'm really very happy," Bell told *Sports Illustrated's* Craig Neff, "even if it doesn't look that way."

Most Rangers fans understood completely. They hated to see the classy, hardworking, and personable Bell leaving their hometown team. The charismatic smile, the spectacular diving plays and backhand stabs he made at third, and the overall gutsy way he performed from 1979 to 1985 made him one of the most popular players in franchise history.

But after toiling for the first eight years of his career with the lowly Cleveland Indians and then laboring the next six and a half years with the typically run-of-the-mill Rangers, most Texas fans were at least happy that the then-33-year-old was finally going to be able to play for a contender. Additionally, he was returning to Cincinnati, where he'd lived as a kid when his father, Gus, starred as an outfielder with the Reds in the 1950s.

Bell played for several second-place teams in Cincinnati before being traded to the Astros in 1988. He then finished up his career in Texas, playing 34 games for the Rangers in 1989. In eight seasons with Texas, Bell hit .293 with 499 RBIs.

But he was especially sensational with the leather. Bell won six consecutive Gold Gloves with the Rangers and made four of his five All-Star appearances in a Texas uniform.

"I loved playing in Texas; it was great," Bell told Jesse Sanchez of MLB.com in 2002. "The time I spent in Arlington was a lot of fun. It's hot, but I don't mind the heat because you can cool down quickly if you have to."

Bell had most of his best statistical years in Texas. In December 1978 the Rangers made somewhat of a risky trade, sending one of their most popular players in team history, Toby Harrah, to the Indians for Bell.

It proved to be a great move for Texas, as Bell played in all 162 games in '79, collecting 200 hits and 101 RBIs. The following year he hit a career-best .329.

Bell was a hot commodity in trade rumors for several years. In '83, for example, the Rangers rejected a trade with Detroit that could have brought Kirk Gibson and Howard Johnson to Texas for Bell. By the time the Rangers were finally willing to part with Bell, several knee injuries and depreciating numbers had greatly reduced his perceived trade value.

Following his 18-year career as a player, Bell stayed in baseball, coaching with the Reds and Indians and eventually becoming a big-league manager with Detroit and Colorado. Bell, who turned 60 in August 2011, also watched two of his sons, David and Mike, reach the major league level. As of 2011, he was serving as the director of operations for the Chicago White Sox's minor league system.

51 Jim Bibby Throws First No-Hitter in Rangers History

When Jim Bibby died in February 2010 after a battle with bone cancer, many of the obituaries in newspaper sports sections across the country focused primarily on the hard-throwing right-hander's tenure with Pittsburgh toward the tail end of his career. In the Steel City, he helped the "We are Family" Pirates to the 1979 World Series title, going 12–4 with a 2.81 ERA and starting two games in the Fall Classic.

One year later, he was even better, as Bibby went 19–6 for the Pirates, appeared in the All-Star Game, and finished third in the National League Cy Young Award balloting. In five seasons with Pittsburgh, Bibby went 50–32 with a 3.53 ERA.

The Really Good and Really Bad of Jim Bibby

While Jim Bibby's most significant accomplishment in a Rangers uniform was probably the no-hitter he tossed against Oakland in 1973, he was also quite memorable in 1974, as well, when the Rangers went 84–76 and finished second in the American League West.

Both Bibby and fellow pitcher Ferguson Jenkins started a club-record 41 games in 1974, with Jenkins winning 25 and Bibby picking up 19 wins. In those 19 victories, Bibby was dominant, holding opponents to a .194 batting average and compiling a sparkling 2.50 ERA.

When Bibby was good, he was often awesome. The opposite was also true.

Bibby set a club record that still stands in 1974 with 19 losses. In those 19 setbacks, his ERA was 9.23.

Bibby's control problems plagued him again early in 1975, as he went 2–6 with a 5.00 ERA. The Rangers finally lost patience and dealt him, along with Jackie Brown and Rick Waits, to Cleveland for future Hall of Famer Gaylord Perry, who was feuding with then–Indians manager Frank Robinson.

Long before he played on a big-time winner, however, Bibby first made a name for himself and generated national headlines while playing on one of the worst teams in Texas Rangers history. The 1973 Rangers went 57–105, featured the worst team ERA in the American League, allowed 225 more runs than they scored (also worst in the league), and drew only 686,085 fans to old Arlington Stadium for the entire season.

In the midst of that absolutely miserable season, James Blair Bibby provided a spectacular memory for a franchise in desperate need of feel-good moments. On July 30, 1973, Bibby took the mound on a cold night in Oakland and allowed six walks while throwing 148 pitches. He struck out 13 batters and did not allow a single hit against an Oakland team that would go on to win the World Series.

"Man, it was cold out there when the game started, and I thought I was gonna freeze my [butt] off," Bibby said on the Rangers' postgame radio show, as quoted by Mike Shropshire in the book *Seasons in Hell*. "But I bet I lost 10 pounds by the time it was over. But I am gonna get it all back in the clubhouse with some of that good cold beer, and I'm ready for it now."

Bibby certainly created a clubhouse happy hour with his remarkable performance.

The Rangers had acquired the imposing, 6'5" flamethrower on June 6, 1973, in a trade with the St. Louis Cardinals for Mike Nagy and John Wockenfuss. He'd originally been signed by the New York Mets as an undrafted free agent in 1965, but his pro career was delayed when he spent two years serving in Vietnam.

When he returned to the U.S. in 1968 he worked his way through the Mets' farm system and was eventually dealt to the St. Louis Cardinals in 1971. Bibby, who featured a 95 mph fastball but sometimes struggled mightily with his control, made his major league debut with the Cardinals in 1972. But after Bibby began the 1973 season with an 0–2 record and a 9.56 ERA, then–Rangers manager Whitey Herzog encouraged Texas management to make a trade for the extremely talented 235-pounder.

Herzog had been the Mets' director of player development prior to becoming the Rangers' manager and took a liking to Bibby. "I had him for five years in the minors," Herzog said shortly after Texas acquired Bibby. "With the exception of Nolan Ryan, he throws harder than anybody in this league."

Less than two months after the trade, Bibby was staked to an early lead in Oakland after Jeff Burroughs hit a grand slam off of the Athletics' Vida Blue in the top of the first inning. Bibby took the hill in the bottom of the first and was so dominant in retiring Bert Campaneris, Bill North, and Sal Bando that Rangers pitching coach Cha-Cha Estrada turned to Herzog and said: "Bibby's got it tonight. They won't touch him."

They didn't. The A's only managed a couple of hard hits on the night, as Bibby's fastball was extraordinary. After Reggie Jackson struck out on a 3–2 pitch for the second out of the ninth inning, Jackson told the media in the postgame clubhouse: "That was the fastest pitch I ever saw. Actually I didn't see it. I just heard it."

Inside the visitors' clubhouse after the game, then–Rangers owner Bob Short walked up to Bibby, hugged him, and handed him a bonus check for $5,000. That was a pretty sizeable chunk of money, considering Bibby's base salary with the Rangers for the 1973 season was reported at $15,000.

52 Nolan Ryan Teaches Robin Ventura a Lesson

When the dust had finally settled after the Rangers' 5–2 victory over the Chicago White Sox on August 4, 1993, at Arlington Stadium, slender, baby-faced Chicago third baseman Robin Ventura stood before the media in the visiting clubhouse and did his best to save face and preserve some masculinity.

"He [Nolan Ryan] gave me a couple of noogies on my head, and that's about all," Ventura said of the most famous bench-clearing brawl in Rangers history...at least until the Rougned Odor–Jose Bautista brawl in 2016. "If you know the game, it's no secret what he was doing. If you don't think he did it on purpose, you don't know the game."

Duh, Boy Wonder. Of course he did it on purpose.

Ryan drilled Ventura just above the right elbow with a fastball in the third inning before a crowd of 32,312 at the old stadium. One inning earlier, White Sox starter Alex Fernandez had plunked

Nolan Ryan holds the Chicago White Sox third baseman Robin Ventura in a headlock while punching him after Ventura charged the mound in an August 1993 game. (AP Images)

Rangers slugger Juan Gonzalez—the fourth Texas player to be hit by a Chicago pitcher in three games to that point in the season.

What did Ventura, who had singled off Ryan in the first inning to give the Sox a 1–0 lead, expect? Something over the heart of the plate? Something fat? Something he could hit?

"I think [Ryan] should have been thrown out of the game," then–White Sox manager Gene Lamont said after his extended on-the-field tirade that included cursing umpires, fans, and foes in the aftermath of the fight. "He hit Robin, and he was the one throwing the punches. He should have been ejected too. Robin thought he was throwing at him, and he did exactly what he should do. It's strange that that was the only pitch that got away from him all night."

Gene, Gene, Gene…. "Don't mess with Texas," is much more than an advertising campaign. It was a way of life when "Big Tex" played for the Rangers.

The division-leading White Sox tested the Rangers' resolve by plunking a couple of players. The 46-year-old Ryan retaliated by hitting a Chicago hitter in the meaty part of the arm above the elbow. The 26-year-old Ventura, after taking three steps toward first base, decided to charge the mound.

The rest is video/YouTube history. Ventura hesitated, then threw down his helmet, ran toward the mound, and ducked his head—probably hoping that teammates would arrive quickly.

Ryan calmly tossed his glove aside, grabbed the youngster in a headlock, like Ventura was a steer charging a rodeo cowboy, and began pummeling him. Ryan landed five punches on the top of Ventura's ducked head and then pasted him with an uppercut to the chin. By the time Ryan landed his best punch, both benches had cleared and raced toward the confrontation.

Ryan was still swinging when a mass of humanity from both benches descended upon him.

"I've had a couple of confrontations in my career, but nothing of that nature," Ryan said after the game. "All I know is I was on the bottom of the pile, and it felt like their whole team was on top of me. In that situation, you're totally at the mercy of your teammates."

Ryan's teammates protected him, and only Texas coach Mickey Hatcher left the field with blood streaming down his face. He had a butterfly bandage on the wound in the clubhouse.

Ventura and the incensed Lamont, who blew a gasket when Ryan was not tossed from the game, were both ejected.

Meanwhile, Ryan buttoned up his jersey after the fight and pitched magnificently the rest of the night. He faced 13 batters and

Bo Knows—and Respects—Nolan

Two of the most famous photographs in Rangers history—still available in reputable memorabilia stores everywhere—involve Nolan Ryan in confrontations against Bo Jackson's teams, first with the Kansas City Royals and then the Chicago White Sox.

Long after those confrontations, it has sometimes been misrepresented that Ryan and Jackson were involved in a personal altercation. Nothing could be further from the truth. Both superstars have always maintained a tremendous respect for each other, dating back to when Jackson first bloodied Ryan's face and jersey.

On September 8, 1990, at Arlington Stadium, Jackson, while playing for Kansas City, smacked a wicked one-hopper back to the mound. It nailed Ryan on the lip, smattering blood everywhere.

The Rangers' trainer came to the mound, but Ryan sent him away with a fierce glare and kept pitching. Ryan, 43 at the time, took stitches between innings but continued to pitch another six innings, continually wiping blood on his sleeve. He had to change jerseys three times between innings.

Impressed by Ryan's grit, Jackson later asked for one of the jerseys as a souvenir. Ryan sent him a clean one, autographed with a personal message to Jackson.

A few years later, after Jackson had landed with the White Sox, Chicago's Robin Ventura charged the mound after Ryan hit him with a fastball in the third inning. Not surprisingly, the extremely athletic Jackson was one of the first players to reach the mound when the dugouts cleared.

Ryan ended up at the bottom of the pileup that followed, but protecting him, according to some sources, was none other than fellow Nike spokesman Bo Jackson.

recorded 14 outs following the fight. He even avenged the charging of the mound immediately by picking off Craig Grebeck, who had gone to first base to run for Ventura when things calmed down.

Ryan worked seven innings and gave up just two runs on three hits. It was his longest outing of the year and easily his feistiest. He made the final start of his glorious career less than two months later against Seattle on September 22. But the fight on August 4 added yet another heroic chapter to Ryan's glorious story. And Ventura is in line to take a beating from Ryan again in 2012 as the new White Sox manager prepares his rebuilding team to take the Rangers executive's two-time defending American League champions.

"Ryan's six-punch KO of Ventura was a thing of beauty," wrote the late Neil Hohlfeld in the *Houston Chronicle*. "A middle-aged legend met a 26-year-old upstart head-on and provided all middle-aged men with yet another reason to love Nolan."

53 The First Rangers All-Star: Toby Harrah

In 1966 the Philadelphia Phillies signed Sissonville, West Virginia, native Colbert Dale "Toby" Harrah as a second baseman. Harrah was honored, but he considered blowing off professional baseball altogether.

"I wasn't even sure I wanted to go to spring training," Harrah told *Sports Illustrated's* Bruce Anderson in 1982. "I had a girlfriend at home. My high school coach told me, 'Go down there and give it all you've got for one month. If you want to come home [after that], come home.' I went."

Wise decision for Harrah. And the yet-to-be relocated Rangers.

The fiery, hustling Harrah was picked up by the Washington Senators after one year in the Phillies organization, and in 1971 he jumped from Double A to the major leagues, becoming Washington's starting shortstop at age 22. One year later, he made the move with the franchise to Texas, where he became the first Rangers player to be selected to play in the All-Star Game in 1972.

He missed that game because of an injury, but he was selected to the All-Star team again in 1975 and 1976. He was also the

Frank Howard: The Franchise's Marquee Name When It Moved

As a member of the Rangers, Frank "Hondo" Howard (nicknamed Hondo by teammates after a John Wayne movie) hit .244 with nine home runs in 95 games before his contract was sold to the Detroit Tigers.

That's it. So, why is he even worth mentioning in a book about the most important names to know in Rangers history?

When the team moved from Washington to Arlington in 1972, Howard was the biggest man (he was listed at 6'7" and had once been drafted by an NBA team) and the biggest name (aside from manager Ted Williams) on the team.

With the Senators, the powerful Howard became known as "the Washington Monument" and "the Capital Punisher." In 1969 he hit a career-high 48 homers. And as recently as 1970, the corner outfielder had captured two-thirds of the Triple Crown, blasting 44 homers with 126 RBIs to finish fifth in the American League MVP balloting.

When the ballclub moved to Arlington, Howard gave team officials a well-known name to promote. He didn't waste any time in making his presence known in the Lone Star State. On April 21, 1972, in the first Rangers game ever to be played at Arlington Stadium, Howard homered in the first inning of a 7–6 win over the Angels in front of a crowd of 20,105.

Unfortunately, the Ohio-born Howard, who was 35 when making his debut for the Rangers, didn't do too much else the rest of the year with Texas. The team sold him to Detroit rather unceremoniously in August 1972.

Nevertheless, Howard still ranks prominently in the Rangers' franchise record book. Howard, who had been an All-American in baseball and basketball at Ohio State, began his major league career with the Dodgers in 1958. But his most productive years (1965–72) were with the Senators/Rangers franchise.

Howard's 246 homers with the Senators/Rangers ranked third all-time in franchise history as of 2011, behind only Juan Gonzalez and Rafael Palmeiro. Overall, he hit 382 career home runs, the eighth-most by a right-handed hitter, when he played his last major league game with the Tigers in 1973.

Rangers Player of the Year in 1975, when he hit .293 with 20 home runs and a career-high 93 RBIs. And Harrah seemed to have a knack for dramatic and/or unusual achievements.

In 1976, for example, Harrah played a complete doubleheader without handling a chance in the field, a major league record. One year later, he moved to third base and hit a career-high 27 homers. One of those homers was an inside-the-park round tripper off New York Yankees pitcher Ken Clay. On the next pitch, Rangers second baseman Bump Wills duplicated the inside-the-park feat.

Harrah's numbers slipped to .229 with 12 homers and 59 RBIs in 1978, and he was traded to Cleveland on December 8, 1978, for All-Star third baseman Buddy Bell. That was the first of two trades in team history in which the Rangers dealt one future major league manager for another. The other was Lee Mazzilli for Bucky Dent.

Harrah acknowledged that he was initially excited about the trade because he sometimes felt unappreciated in Arlington, especially by the local media. As Mike Hargrove, Harrah's teammate in Texas and later in Cleveland, once said: "Every day you could open the paper [in Dallas or Fort Worth] and read about how bad Toby was. The treatment he received from the press was terrible."

The treatment he received from the media and fans in Cleveland, however, quickly made him appreciate his first seven years in Arlington. Some writers labeled the Harrah-for-Bell trade as Cleveland's worst in almost two decades, while fans constantly hollered, "Buddy would've had that one," whenever Harrah missed a ground ball.

"I think it hurt Toby," Cleveland center fielder Rick Manning said. "The fans didn't appreciate him, particularly when Texas came to town. He wasn't relaxed."

He enjoyed some good years with the Indians nonetheless, including 1982, when Harrah played in 162 games, scored 100 runs, and hit for a .304 average.

After playing 88 games for the Yankees in 1984, Harrah returned to the Rangers in 1985 and had one more solid year at second base, hitting .270 with nine homers, 44 RBIs, and 113 walks. He was the last of the Senators and original Rangers to still be playing.

Harrah retired after the 1986 season and went on to manage at Triple A Oklahoma City in 1987–88 before joining the Rangers' coaching staff in 1989. He managed the team for 76 games at the end of the 1992 season and later became the Detroit Tigers' minor league hitting instructor. In 2009 Harrah was inducted into the Rangers Hall of Fame.

"I was so proud to wear the Texas Rangers uniform," Harrah said when he was inducted, as reported by T.R. Sullivan of MLB. com. "I didn't play for stats, I played to win and to compete and play against the best players in the world. Some were my teammates. It's an honor. This is great news for me, my wife, and my family. Coming from Washington, being an original Texas Ranger, makes it even more special to me. I've always been a Texas Ranger at heart and always will be."

54 Jeff Burroughs: The First MVP in Arlington

Following the Rangers' historic run to the 2010 World Series, the team's first breakout star in Texas, Jeff Burroughs, showed up at spring training in Surprise, Arizona, and spoke about how much he enjoyed watching "his team" reach the Fall Classic for the first time. A couple of weeks later, Burroughs and Charlie Hough threw out the ceremonial first pitch before a sold-out crowd on Opening Day 2011 at Rangers Ballpark in Arlington.

Burroughs, the team's first American League MVP in 1974, threw the first pitch to 2010 MVP Josh Hamilton.

"As we recognize the Rangers' 40th season in Texas, we felt that the first-pitch ceremony should reflect the history of the club," Rangers CEO and president Nolan Ryan said. "Jeff Burroughs was the first great offensive star for the Rangers in the 1970s, and Charlie Hough was the club's ace throughout the 1980s. It is very appropriate that they take part in the Opening Day activities."

Burroughs was moved by the recognition, the positive response of the fans, and the opportunity to represent the defending American League champions on Opening Day in Arlington.

"This is where it began for me," Burroughs told the *Fort Worth Star-Telegram*. "When we made the move from Washington to Texas, I went. I made a lot of friends in Texas and got to know a lot of people. I consider this my home team, actually. It was quite exciting."

It was great for Rangers fans to hear those warm words from Burroughs. They rarely heard them when Burroughs played in Arlington.

When Burroughs spoke publicly as a player for the Rangers from 1972 to 1976, he often complained about how much he detested hitting in the prevailing south winds of old Arlington Stadium. After hitting a game-winning home run in Milwaukee in 1973, for example, Burroughs told Lou Chapman of the *Milwaukee Journal*: "That home run? Just another long out in Texas.... That wind in Arlington has turned me into a singles hitter."

In response, former *Fort Worth Star-Telegram* beat writer Mike Shropshire wrote in his book *Seasons in Hell*, "Bitch, bitch, bitch. The Texas press had heard it all before [from Burroughs]. Lou Chapman, though, was taking it all down."

Despite his disdain for the winds in Arlington, Burroughs was much more than a singles hitter for the Rangers. He was the No. 1 overall pick in the 1969 draft by the Washington Senators, and after playing mostly in the minor leagues from 1969 to 1972, Burroughs started the 1973 season in Arlington, enjoying a breakout season that put the 22-year-old on the baseball map. Burroughs hit .279 and slugged 30 homers in '73. But the best was yet to come.

In the Rangers' breakout season of 1974, Burroughs was the offensive star, hitting .301 for the season with 25 homers, a league-best 118 RBIs, 91 walks (third best in the league), and a .504 slugging percentage. Thanks to those phenomenal numbers and the Rangers winning 27 more games than the previous year, Burroughs won the 1974 American League MVP, beating out the Oakland trio of Joe Rudi, Sal Bando, and Reggie Jackson and Rangers teammate Fergie Jenkins.

Unfortunately for the Rangers and Burroughs, things took a dramatic turn for the worse in 1975. The team went 79–83, 19 games back of first-place Oakland, and Burroughs' batting average fell to .226, although he did manage to hit 29 homers.

The following year was even less productive, as the Rangers dropped to 76–86 and Burroughs hit just 18 homers with a .237 batting average. The following off-season, Texas dealt its onetime superstar to the Atlanta Braves in a blockbuster trade that sent pitchers Adrian Devine, Roger Moret, and Carl Morton and outfielders Ken Henderson and Dave May to Texas.

Burroughs returned to top form in Atlanta, bouncing back with a pair of strong seasons in 1977 and 1978. Overall, he spent four seasons in Atlanta before ending his career with one season in Seattle, three in Oakland, and one more in Toronto. In 16 seasons, Burroughs amassed 1,443 hits, 240 homers, 882 RBIs, and a career batting average of .261.

Burroughs returned to the national spotlight in the early 1990s, as he coached his son, Sean, and a youth team from Long Beach to the 1992 and '93 Little League World Series. Sean Burroughs was selected ninth overall in the 1998 draft, turned down an opportunity to play collegiate baseball at USC, and signed with the San

Diego Padres. He advanced through the Padres' system quickly, reaching the major leagues at 21. The Padres hoped Burroughs would become a power hitter like his father, but he never did. He was released by the Mariners in 2007 but returned to the major leagues in 2011 with the Diamondbacks, the same year his father returned to Arlington for a memorable first-pitch ceremony.

55 Wetteland Finishes Career Strong in Texas

One of the better winter free-agent signings in team history came in December 1996 when the Rangers and then–general manager Doug Melvin inked reigning World Series MVP and former Yankees closer John Wetteland to a four-year, $23 million contract.

Wetteland eventually became the Rangers' all-time leader with 150 saves from 1997 to 2000. He averaged 38 saves per year with Texas and posted a 20–12 record with a 2.95 ERA in 248 relief appearances. He was inducted into the Rangers Hall of Fame in 2005.

Under any circumstances, Wetteland's Texas numbers were outstanding. But considering how bad the Rangers' bullpen had been before he arrived, Texas fans typically viewed him as an out-of-this-world addition.

In 1996 the Rangers won the American League West and advanced to the playoffs for the first time in franchise history. But they might have gone all the way to the World Series if they had possessed a closer like Wetteland. The '96 Rangers endured a major league–high 11 losses after leading with three outs to play and had a total of 16 blown saves.

Texas' closer in '96, Mike Henneman, produced 31 saves but also had a 5.79 ERA with an 0–7 record.

Meanwhile, Wetteland converted 43 of 47 save opportunities during the 1996 regular season and then went 7-for-7 in the play-offs, including both opportunities against Texas in the ALDS. He saved all four World Series victories against the Braves and was later presented the Rolaids Relief Man Award.

Wetteland had initially wanted to stay with the Yankees, but New York deemed him expendable because team officials believed Mariano Rivera was ready for the closer's role. The Yankees were obviously correct in that assessment, but Wetteland was a long way from being washed up, and the Rangers were giddy about signing the righty with the 95 mph fastball.

"Somebody said this is as big as when Nolan Ryan came aboard," Melvin said when announcing the signing of Wetteland. "We feel this is the final piece of a puzzle to get us to the next level. There is no doubt in my mind we have the best closer in baseball today."

He pitched well for a '97 team that didn't make the playoffs and was at his best the following two playoff seasons. He helped Texas win the 1998 and 1999 American League West titles, with 42 and 43 saves, respectively, while being named to the All-Star team in both seasons.

"The time I spent [in Texas] was probably the most enjoyable time in my career," said Wetteland when he was inducted into the Rangers Hall of Fame. "That had a lot to do with the people that are here. There are always wonderful people here.

"My wife [Michelle] and I, we have always been enamored with Texas. It's been an absolute joy to be here. The quality of people you find here is really amazing.... I think that's why you find a lot of athletes making their homes here. To play for four years and have such a response from the fans exemplifies the type of connection that can be made with the people here, and I really appreciate it."

Wetteland, who debuted with the Dodgers in 1989 and also pitched with Montreal before joining the Yankees in 1995, retired on top in 2000. He was only 33 years old when he left the game as a player.

In his 12 major league seasons, Wetteland recorded 330 saves with a career ERA of 2.93. Wetteland once again put on a major league uniform in 2006 when he was hired as bullpen coach of the Washington Nationals. He also served as the Mariners' bullpen coach in 2009–10.

56 The Wild and Wonderful Bobby Witt

During parts of 11 seasons with the Rangers (1986–92 and 1995–98) and throughout his 16-year career in the major leagues, Robert Andrew "Bobby" Witt was Forrest Gump's kind of pitcher. Like life and a box of chocolates, you just never knew what to expect next from Witt, the third overall pick in the 1985 amateur draft.

When Witt was on, he could be astonishingly good. When he was bad, however, he could be dreadfully dismal.

And the variation didn't necessarily go from start to start. Sometimes, Witt could go from marvelous to miserable or from dreary to dazzling in the span of one inning to another. Or from one batter to the next.

Take, for example, the second start of Witt's career in 1986 against Milwaukee. The hard-throwing Witt, who played college baseball at Oklahoma, threw five innings of no-hit ball and struck out 10. But he also walked eight, threw four wild pitches, and surrendered two runs before he had to be pulled by manager Bobby Valentine despite the fact that he still had a no-hitter.

That defined his rookie season. And, for the most part, his career.

"I wasn't going to finesse you," Witt told ESPN baseball research specialist Mark Simon. "My thought process was to go out there and let it go. At 100 pitches, I was just getting loose."

Witt remains one of the most prominent names in the Rangers' pitching record books...in both good categories and bad.

Witt ranks third in Rangers history in most victories with 104, and he holds the team record for most consecutive wins with 12 in 1990. He also shares the record for most successive complete games (nine) with Fergie Jenkins and Gaylord Perry. On the other hand, Witt holds the records for most walks in a season (143 in 1986), most wild pitches in a season (22 in '86), and most starts beginning a career without a complete game (55 from 1986 to 1987).

The personable Witt had pitched for the 1984 U.S. Olympic Team and made his debut with Texas in 1986 after pitching only 35 innings in the minors. In his first two seasons, the raw flamethrower with an upper-90s fastball led the American League in both strike-outs per nine innings (9.93 and 10.07) and walks (143 and 140). He was 19–19 in his first two seasons, but his ERA was above 5.00.

In 1988 Witt started horribly, and he was 0–5 with a 7.68 ERA when he was demoted to Triple A Oklahoma City. When he returned in July, however, he completed his first nine starts and 12 overall, posting a 2.93 ERA. He later tied Rangers records for most strikeouts in a game with 14 in July 1986 and most walks in a game with nine in April 1987 (a dubious feat Witt accomplished three times in a Rangers uniform).

Witt's best season was in 1990, when he recorded 17 wins—including 12 straight from late June to early September—and finished with a 3.36 ERA. He ranked second in the American League behind teammate Nolan Ryan with 221 strikeouts.

After an injury-plagued 1991 season, he was traded in August 1992, along with reliever Jeff Russell and outfielder Ruben Sierra, to Oakland in exchange for Jose Canseco.

Witt was an ironman on the Athletics' staff, making 57 starts in 1993 and 1994 while leading the club with 10 complete games. Following a brief stint with the Marlins, Witt was dealt back to the Rangers in August 1995, where he would go 28–24 the next two seasons.

He finished his career with stints in St. Louis, Tampa Bay, Cleveland, and Arizona, winning a World Series title with the Diamondbacks in 2001.

While Witt's overall career numbers (142–157 record with a 4.83 ERA and 1,955 strikeouts) will never earn him a spot in the Hall of Fame, his bat is in Cooperstown. On June 30, 1997, Witt became the first American League pitcher since the designated hitter rule came into effect to hit a home run, going deep at Dodger Stadium against Ismael Valdes.

57 Gaylord Perry: A Few Tricks Up His Sleeve

In late August 1973 Cleveland pitcher Gaylord Perry, who'd long been accused by opposing managers and players of doctoring baseballs and throwing a spitball—or greaseball—pitched a gem against the Tigers, blanking Detroit with an array of pitches that darted and dropped.

Afterward, Detroit manager Billy Martin gave the reporters plenty of juicy commentary, informing them that he had ordered his pitchers to throw spitters the last two innings.

"The umpires are making a mockery of the game by not stopping Perry," Martin said. "Everyone knows he does it, but nobody does anything about it. We're going to keep on doing it every time he pitches against us." Martin also referred to Major League Baseball commissioner Bowie Kuhn and American League president Joe Cronin as "gutless." Cronin suspended Martin for three days, but the Tigers fired him before he could serve it. A week later, Martin was hired as manager of the Rangers.

In the spring of 1974 Perry and Bob Sudyk released a book titled *Me and the Spitter, An Autobiographical Confession*. Perry told numerous tales of confrontations with angry hitters and umpires, admitting that he "tried everything on the old apple, but salt and pepper and chocolate sauce topping." But he also wrote that he was finished with greaseballs: "I'm reformed now. I'm a pure law-abiding citizen."

Nobody bought Perry's "clean pitching" prose, and the accusations continued throughout the rest of his career—a career that took him to the Martin-managed Rangers. On June 13, 1975, Perry was dealt to Texas for pitchers Jim Bibby, Jackie Brown, and Rick Waits, and $150,000.

His new manager had a major change of heart regarding Perry: "I realize how wrong I was," Martin said. "I'd like to get on the record immediately as saying Gaylord does nothing illegal."

While the best years of Perry's 22-year Hall of Fame career were behind him by the time he landed in Texas, he improved his résumé with the Rangers. Perry went 12–8 with a 3.03 ERA for Texas the rest of '75, joining Fergie Jenkins at the top of the rotation.

Jenkins moved to Boston the next season, and Perry became the staff ace, going 15–14 with a 3.24 ERA. Though he was 38 years old entering the 1977 season, Texas protected Perry in the expansion draft, with owner Brad Corbett pointing out that, "Gaylord's value to this team is much more than just as a pitcher."

In 1977 Perry rewarded the Rangers by going 15–12 in Texas' 94-win season. In February 1978, however, Texas sent Perry to San Diego for Dave Tomlin and $125,000. Like the Indians three years earlier, the Rangers needed the money, including the savings from Perry's $200,000 contract.

It was a mistake. Perry went 21–6 with the Padres in '78 and 12–11 in '79.

In August 1979 Corbett acknowledged publicly that trading Perry was the biggest mistake he made in baseball and said that he had promised Perry a front-office position at the end of his career. Later that month, Perry informed the Padres that he wanted to be traded, preferably back to Texas. In February 1980 Perry returned to Texas, where he had the best ERA on the staff (3.43), despite going only 6–9. On August 24 Perry was sent to the Yankees for pitcher Ken Clay, giving him another shot at the postseason.

Perry finished his career with brief stints in Atlanta and Seattle. Overall, he won 314 games and struck out 3,524 hitters (575 as a member of the Rangers), becoming the first pitcher in history to win the Cy Young Award in both leagues. Perry retired after the 1983 season and was elected to the Hall of Fame in 1991, along with Jenkins, his former Rangers teammate.

58 Chuck Morgan: The Public Address Voice of the Rangers

Unlike many of the Rangers' players, coaches, and front-office personnel, Chuck Morgan can walk into virtually any restaurant, grocery store, or gas station in the Dallas–Fort Worth area anonymously, without concern of being delayed, deferred, or altogether detained by admiring fans.

At least until Morgan opens his mouth. Then all bets are off.

In baseball circles, the personable and upbeat Morgan may possess the Metroplex's most familiar, friendly, and flourishing voice. Except for a one-year hiatus in 2002 when he worked in Kansas City, Morgan has been the public address announcer of the Rangers since 1983.

You can debate whether Jim Sundberg or Pudge Rodriguez was the greatest catcher in Rangers history. Ditto in terms of the quintessential power-hitting outfielder: Juan Gonzalez or Josh Hamilton. You can even debate the greatest on-air announcers in Rangers history, deciding between Eric Nadel and the late Mark Holtz.

But there is no dispute regarding the official in-game voice of the Rangers. Morgan is the man. He is Texas' classy commentator, the Rangers' version of the late, great Bob Sheppard—P.A. voice of the Yankees from 1951 to 2007. Yet Morgan's delivery is distinctively Southern, more down-home, and much more friendly than formal. In many ways, he is as forthcoming and exhilarating as the great Mel Allen, longtime host of *This Week in Baseball*.

Above all else, Morgan is uniquely attached and bonded to the Rangers' organization. Fans may not recognize the face, but those who have occupied the seats in Arlington on a handful of occasions or a few thousand times definitely know the voice.

"I can be standing in line at the grocery store talking to the checkout person," Morgan says, "and someone behind me might say, 'Hey I recognize that voice. You are the guy at the Rangers game, right?' It happens all the time. But I will never grow tired of it. I hope I will be known as the in-game 'voice of the Rangers' for a long, long time. That is a good thing to be known for."

Morgan is much more than the public address voice of the Rangers. His official title is vice president, in-park entertainment. In that capacity, he is essentially responsible for everything a fan sees or hears when he/she enters Rangers Ballpark in Arlington.

When the Rangers added a monstrous video board in right field in 2011, Morgan oversaw the installation and implementation of the new graphics. When players want to change their walk-up song prior to at-bats, they contact Morgan. When highlights are shown or presentations are held between innings or prior to games, Morgan oversees it all.

For the most part, though, Morgan is known to baseball fans in Texas as the golden, booming voice of the franchise. But the Rangers weren't the first organization to notice Morgan's multiple talents.

Morgan—whose birth name is actually Chuck Gulledge—was raised in Southern Illinois, which is closer to Nashville than Chicago, and he received his start in radio when he was 14. Morgan initially dreamed of playing major league baseball, but when he was playing in the Pony Leagues in Southern Illinois, he was propositioned by a friend about handling the public address announcements at a Little League game.

"I'd already caught the radio fever when I was playing in a Pony League at 14," Morgan recalled. "There was a guy who'd played earlier who was doing the P.A. for the Little League games. The guy said, 'I have a date tonight, do you want to take over for me?' He told me he would give me a couple of packs of baseball cards to do it.

"That was my first assignment and my first 'paycheck.' So, around 14 or 15, I knew I could do the P.A. and some radio. Even when I would be playing wiffle ball games with friends, I'd be announcing my best Harry Caray impersonation, announcing every move, and bringing guys up to the plate."

Morgan started college at Southern Illinois University, but he decided to train under the bright lights of Nashville instead of finishing his degree. He worked as a disc jockey at a country radio station and served as an announcer for the Grand Ole Opry for eight years. He also hosted an all-night trucking show and made appearances on the popular TV show *Hee Haw.*

In 1978 Morgan's career path forever changed when his friend Larry Schmittou, the vice president of marketing with the Nashville Sounds minor league baseball team, asked him to join the team as its field announcer. Five years later, Schmittou was hired by the Rangers, and Morgan was asked to move to Arlington to become the voice of the team.

"All I'd ever done for Larry in Nashville was the public address for the Sounds," Morgan said. "I knew I would have to do more than just the P.A. to make a living. I thought about it for a while and asked him what else I would be doing. He put me in sales. I knew I probably should have stayed in Nashville because I had so many things going for me, but I loved baseball, so I decided to give it a try. I joined the Rangers in February of 1983."

The rest is Rangers history. Morgan worked his 2,000th game in Arlington in 2008, and he estimates that he worked 2,600 home games before he was treated to three World Series games in 2010 and three more in 2011.

"Finally being able to do the World Series was very rewarding," says Morgan, who has two grown sons, Kelly and Rhett, who both played baseball past high school. "But that was the icing on the cake of what I do. When I was growing up and going to games at old Sportsman's Park in St. Louis, it was always a special thing. Even in late September, if the Cardinals were out of the race, it was still a major league baseball game, and I was so excited to be there.

"Someone cared about how I felt about those games, and the atmosphere was so exciting to me. I try to approach every day at the ballpark with that kind of mentality. It doesn't matter if the Rangers are leading the West by 10 or if they are behind by 20. You have to take care of the experience of going to a major league baseball game. Make it special. Make it meaningful and fun. My job is to help make memories for the kid making his first game and to protect the beauty of the game for the grandfather who is accompanying him. I always think about it being someone's first game, and I always hope it is special for them. That is something I keep in mind. It's something that inspires me."

59 The Sweet-Swinging Al Oliver

From his home in Portsmouth, Ohio, Al Oliver jumps aggressively on the question like he once pounced on belt-high, heart-of-the-plate fastballs when ahead in the count.

"There's no question that my single-most-meaningful event in professional baseball came as a member of the Pirates on the '71 team that won the World Series," said Oliver, who turned 70 on October 14, 2016. "But aside from that, I'd say my very best years in baseball—including the way I played in the field—came in Texas. I loved my time in Texas. I loved the environment, I loved the atmosphere, and I really loved the fans in Texas.

"Texas was a really underrated place to play. We had some very good teams when I was there. We deserved a lot more national attention and respect."

Ditto for Oliver, the left-handed–hitting, sweet-swinging, line drive–producing, and eternally optimistic character of the Rangers' clubhouse from 1978 to 1981. Oliver produced Hall of Fame credentials in 18 full seasons in the major leagues, retiring as a career .303 hitter with 2,743 hits in 2,368 games.

In four particularly prolific seasons in Texas, Oliver hit a combined .319 in a ballpark (Arlington Stadium) that was widely viewed as unfriendly toward hitters because of the swirling winds that often stymied fly balls. Because of his ability to stay on top of the ball and spray frozen ropes to all fields, Oliver was largely unaffected by the winds.

Average-wise, his best year in Arlington was 1978, when he hit .324, second in the American League behind only Rod Carew. In terms of overall raw numbers, however, it's hard to top the 1980 season when Oliver played in 163 games, generating 209 hits, 117 RBIs, 43 doubles, and a .480 slugging percentage.

"Al was an amazing line-drive hitter," recalls former *Fort Worth Star-Telegram* columnist and Rangers beat writer Jim Reeves. "Al was also the president of his own fan club. It was almost as fun to talk to him as it was to watch him at the plate because he was so entertaining. To say Al was supremely confident in his abilities is a major understatement."

Reeves recalls one season when Oliver was off to an exceptionally blistering start. Three or four weeks into the season, with his average hovering near .500, Reeves jokingly asked Oliver if he thought he could maintain that pace for the entire season. Remember, no one had hit .400 for an entire season since Ted Williams in 1941, and Reeves fully expected Oliver to laugh at the question.

"He didn't laugh," Reeves recalled. "He paused for a moment, thought about it very seriously, and said, 'Hitting .500 for the full season would be tough.' Even then he didn't rule it out. That was just Al being Al. He believed he could do anything."

Not in a cocky or egotistical way, though. In a 1980 article in *Sports Illustrated*, former Rangers second baseman Bump Wills told reporter Steve Wulf that there wasn't a single player in the clubhouse who didn't like Oliver.

"He's like Ali," Wills said. "He doesn't come off as being egotistical because you know he can back his words up. Once, when he was going 0-for-23 or something, I tried to catch him off guard and make him say something negative. I said, 'Hey, what's happening?' He turned to me and said, 'Not me, that's for sure—but I will be.'"

Another prime example of his perpetually confident outlook at the plate—in addition to the vanity license plates on his vehicle that read, "AL HITS"—came following a rare strikeout in a 1979 spring training game. When he returned to the dugout, Oliver's teammates were purposely quiet, staring at him peculiarly.

"I hope you all saw that," Oliver told his teammates, "because you won't be seeing it very much this season."

He was right. Oliver struck out only 34 times in 538 plate appearances in '79. As Wills contended, it ain't bragging if you can back it up.

Oliver's positive perspective on baseball and life is ultimately a result of his choices in the most tumultuous times. His mother died when he was 11, and on the day he was called up to the major leagues—September 14, 1968—his father, Al Sr., passed away. His younger siblings did not handle the deaths well, and Al often served as a counselor to his pregnant teenage sister and his severely depressed younger brother immediately following their father's death.

Al, on the other hand, stayed upbeat in the midst of trials—a trait that has essentially been the theme of his life.

He was part of some great Pittsburgh teams from 1968 to 1977, where he was an integral part of an offense known as the "Pittsburgh Lumber Company" and helped the Pirates win one World Series and five National League East titles. Throughout his tenure in Pittsburgh, however, Oliver typically seemed to be overshadowed by fan favorites such as Roberto Clemente, Willie Stargell, and Dave Parker.

So, when he was part of a convoluted, four-team trade in December 1977—which, among many other things, brought Oliver, Nelson Norman, and Jon Matlack to Texas and shipped Bert Blyleven to Pittsburgh and Tom Grieve to the Mets—Oliver was intrigued about the possibility of becoming a star in Arlington.

He did just that, hitting line shots in all directions and playing every outfield position with Texas, where he flashed the great glove work that first earned him the nickname "Scoop" as a first baseman in Pittsburgh.

Al Oliver's Defining Day in Detroit

In the midst of watching Al Oliver hit for at least a .300 average over the course of nine consecutive major league seasons, former Rangers manager Pat Corrales once surmised that unlike most every other player who celebrated each hit, "A bad day for Al is when he goes 1-for-4."

While accumulating 2,743 hits, 1,326 RBIs, 219 home runs, and 529 doubles in 18 seasons, Oliver certainly had plenty of memorable days at the plate. But one day—August 17, 1980, at Tigers Stadium—was particularly grand. Oliver established an American League record with 21 total bases in the doubleheader, ripping four homers, a double, and a triple.

Coincidentally, he'd almost asked Corrales for the day off because some hometown friends from Portsmouth, Ohio, had kept him awake too long the night before.

"I had a suite in Detroit, and we sat around and talked and laughed for hours upon hours," Oliver said. "Some were drinking, but most of the guys weren't. We were high on life. I stayed up late that night and broke my own rule about kicking everybody out of my room by midnight. When I got to the ballpark, I felt terrible, and I almost—and this would have been very uncharacteristic of me—went to Pat to ask him for a day off.

"Thankfully I didn't. I'm convinced that the reason I had the day I did was I was so relaxed at the plate. I couldn't overswing because I was too tired. I sometimes wondered after that day if I should deprive myself of sleep more often."

To add to the significance of those two games for Oliver, it was Al Kaline Day in Detroit.

"It was a dream-come-true kind of day," Oliver said. "One other thing I remember is that I hit a foul ball that missed being a home run by maybe a foot. So it would have been five homers. That was also the first time in my career that I received a standing ovation from an opposing crowd. What a great memory."

"I wish I had 25 Al Olivers on this ballclub," Rangers manager Pat Corrales said in 1980. "No, take that back. Thirteen Al Olivers and 12 Buddy Bells. I'd need some right-handers."

Inexplicably, the Rangers traded him on March 31, 1982—to the Montreal Expos for Larry Parrish and Dave Hostetler. Oliver says he'd hoped to retire in Texas, but instead he spent the final four seasons bouncing from Montreal to San Francisco and on to the Phillies, Dodgers, and Blue Jays. Oliver says he really doesn't count the last two years of his career, although he is proud of delivering two game-winning hits in the 1985 ALCS for Toronto and hitting .375 for the series.

Today Oliver is—fittingly—a motivational speaker, who operates by the slogan, "Life's a hit. Don't strike out." In his travels across the country to speak to grade schools, high schools, colleges, businesses, and so forth, Oliver is often asked about why he has been overlooked by the Hall of Fame in Cooperstown.

"My best friend is a dentist in Columbus [Ohio], and he says me playing in Texas was like being in exile because so few people knew what was going on in Arlington," Oliver says. "I'll say this [about the Hall of Fame]: If Texas had been then where they are now—a legitimate contender that had been to the World Series—and I was there doing the same things that I did back then, it would have helped get me a great deal in getting into the Hall.

"I know the numbers are there for the Hall. But I firmly believe now that I will never go. I don't know why. You'll have to ask the voters. Some people say that if I had played other places, then I would be in, but I don't worry about that. I may never make it to Cooperstown, but I wouldn't give up my memories of Arlington. My hope is that those fans who saw me down there still appreciate and remember me."

They do. After all, Al Oliver is virtually impossible to forget.

60 Respect the Work of the Beat Writers...Like Jim Reeves

Shortly after making the transition from Rangers beat writer to sports columnist for the *Fort Worth Star-Telegram* in 1987, Jim Reeves—known to practically everyone in media circles as "Revo"—sat down to have dinner at home with his wife and three boys one late-spring evening.

As the Reeves family enjoyed the meal, Revo's youngest son suddenly realized something was amiss. It was baseball season. The Rangers were at home. And his father was sitting at the family dinner table.

"He looked up and said, 'Dad, have you retired?'" Revo recalled with a laugh. "That gives you an indication of how difficult being a baseball beat writer can be on families. Unfortunately, it cost me my first marriage. Being a beat writer is a very difficult job. It is a day-in and day-out grind...kind of like what the players go through. But the difference is that they get paid—even back then—an enormous amount of money. When they have a problem, they can throw money at it. If they need to spend time with their wife, they bring her on the road trips. Writers don't have the same luxury."

Not hardly. Sportswriters are generally low paid, and although the concept of hanging out with ballplayers and traveling across the country to watch the Rangers play 162 times a year may initially sound like pure bliss for a baseball aficionado, the daily drudgery can be far more grueling than glamorous.

Players in the midst of slumps don't typically like to talk about their struggles. Managers can be extremely condescending during tough stretches. Editors can be patronizing in good times or bad. Fans rarely side with the media when conflicts arise. Deadlines, particularly on the West Coast trips, can be nerve-racking. And the late-night hours can drive anyone insane.

Despite those demands—and many others—the Rangers beat has been manned by some of the best baseball writers in the country. Back in the early and mid-1970s, the *Star-Telegram* featured an afternoon and a morning newspaper, and Dallas was a two-newspaper town with the *Morning News* and *Times Herald.*

Those four papers produced phenomenal beat writers, such as current radio talk show host and *Star-Telegram* columnist Randy Galloway; Tim Kurkjian, now of ESPN's *Baseball Tonight*; Phil Rogers, now of the *Chicago Tribune*; current *Orange County Register* Page 2 columnist Randy Youngman; the *Philadelphia Daily News'* Paul Hagen; Tracy Ringolsby, a recipient of the Baseball Hall of Fame's J.G. Taylor Spink Award; and many other talented writers and reporters.

The newspaper business has changed dramatically since the Rangers moved to Arlington in 1972, as many papers across the country, including the *Dallas Times-Herald*, shut their presses a good many years ago. Likewise, the mediums in which fans receive their news have undergone striking changes, especially with the advance of technology.

Nowadays, beat writers like Jeff Wilson of the *Star-Telegram* and Evan Grant of the *Morning News* are expected to Tweet, blog, file video for the website, and also provide daily newspaper content, which is sometimes somewhat of an afterthought. Because of the technological advances, some of the nation's best and hardest-working beat writers no longer are employed by newspapers. Three exceptionally hardworking Rangers beat writer who fits that description is T.R. Sullivan of MLB.com, one of the most knowledgeable reporters on all things Rangers.

From this viewpoint, however, the very best of the best as a Rangers beat writer was Reeves, who combined excellent reporting skills with an exceptionally entertaining and colorful writing style.

Revo took over the beat in '76, working 11 full seasons before transitioning to a columnist in '87. Even after that, he was a regular on the beat, working pregame and postgame radio for KRLD and covering numerous games as a columnist.

For the most part, it was a labor of love, and Revo lists Jim Sundberg, Buddy Bell, Larry Parrish, Mickey Rivers, and Nolan Ryan as some of his favorite players to work with through the years, while managers such as Johnny Oates and Don Zimmer and coach Jackie Moore were some of his favorite men who occupied the dugout.

During his long tenure with the *Star-Telegram*, Revo covered some terrible Texas teams, with only a smattering of good ones and a select few outstanding clubs. After watching so much mediocre baseball for so many years, Reeves was particularly pleased that he was—at long last—able to cover the Rangers in the World Series in 2010 and 2011 as part of ESPNDallas.com. Contrary to what some players, managers, and fans may think, every writer enjoys covering a winner.

The stories are better. The interviews are more enjoyable. And it makes the job far more satisfying.

"I was trying to look up one of the columnists for the *Star-Telegram* [early in 2011], and my tag was still online as a columnist," Reeves said. "The description of me read: 'Jim Reeves, who hopes to hang on long enough to see the Rangers win a World Series.' I didn't quite make it long enough at the newspaper to see the Rangers in the World Series, but I was able to see it and cover it for ESPNDallas.com. It was fantastic.

"One of the things I made sure to do after they beat the Yankees [in the 2010 ALCS] was to get out on the field during the celebration and just soak it all in. I did that after the game, and then I wandered into the clubhouse just to get the smell of champagne in my nostrils. I gave Jim Sundberg a hug and gave Nolan a hug. It was a fantastic experience, and I am very grateful to have lived long enough to have seen it."

True to form, nobody painted a more vivid picture—especially from a historical perspective—of how the championship seasons unfolded than Reeves.

61 The Rangers' Lone Star State Supremacy

The Texas Rangers and Houston Astros first met in interleague play on June 8, 2001, as part of MLB's interleague play, which was designed to promote some of the natural rivalries across the country. From 2001 to 2012, the teams played six times annually—three games in Arlington and three times in Houston—and the squad that won the most games each year (or won the tie-breaker in an event of a season spit) was presented with the Silver Boot Trophy, a 30-inch tall, size-15 cowboy boot cast in silver, complete with a custom, handmade spur.

The Rangers won the boot in nine of the first 12 years, but the series really wasn't much of a rivalry—at least in the opinion of the players—until more recent years. The Astros, who were members of the National League from 1962 to 2012, were required by Commissioner Bud Selig to join the AL West in 2013, leaving both the AL West and the NL Central with the same number of teams as the other divisions.

In the first four years following that move, the Rangers essentially used that boot to kick the Astros around.

In the first year as division opponents, Texas went 17–2 against a woeful Houston team that suffered a franchise-worst 51–111 record in 2013 (the Astros' third consecutive year with 106 losses or more).

The Astros' young players began showing progress the following year, as Houston went 70–92 in 2014. Houston also won the season series against the injury-riddled Rangers for the first time since 2006, going 11–8 against Texas.

But the rivalry really began to intensify in 2015, when the Rangers overcame an eight-game deficit in the AL West to pass the Astros and win the division. Houston seemed to be in control of the division for much of the year, but the Astros could consistently beat Texas, which won the season series 13–6.

Additionally, Texas' Rougned Odor and Houston catcher Hank Conger were at the center of a bench-clearing shove-fest at Minute Maid Park on July 18, 2015, in which Astros manager A.J. Hinch shoved Prince Fielder. Enraged, Rangers manager Jeff Bannister bumped into Hinch and pointed in his face, as he yelled, "Don't touch my guy!" At the trade deadline later that month, left-handed starter Cole Hamels used his no-trade clause to block a move that would have sent him from Philadelphia to Houston and instead accepted a trade to Texas.

Hamels played a huge role in helping Texas pass Houston to win the title. In mid-September, for example, Hamels started the opening game of a key four-game series in Arlington.

The Rangers entered the series 1.5 games behind Houston for the AL West lead, but Texas swept Houston and the Astros left town trailing by 2.5 games. The Rangers later clinched the 2015 AL West Division title, while the Astros entered the 2015 playoffs as a wild-card team.

In 2016, the Astros began the year as the overwhelming favorite to win the West, and they probably would have if they had been able to handle the Rangers. Texas went 15–4 against Houston in '16. In the first four years of being division rivals, Texas went 53–23 against the Astros.

"It's alive," Texas manager Jeff Banister said of the rivalry in September 2016, as reported by Jean-Jacques Taylor of ESPN.

com. "It may mean a little more to me than some: I'm a Texas kid. Growing up in Houston and getting to manage the Texas Rangers, for me, you're asking a guy who probably has a little more invested in this than some."

"I don't know that both clubs have been at this level ever before at the same time," Rangers general manager Jon Daniels added. "When it matters to both teams, that's when it's really fun."

62 Eddie Chiles: A Mad and Memorable Majority Owner

During his fabulously successful business career, Eddie Chiles had become a firm believer in the power of setting goals and documenting progression toward those objectives. Chiles, a hard-charging self-made millionaire, lived an inspiring, rags-to-riches story that was made possible, he said, due to his understanding of success principles, such as regularly writing down his goals.

Chiles had worked as a merchant seaman and as an oilfield roustabout before earning a degree in petroleum engineering from the University of Oklahoma. He later pioneered a method of acidizing wells to increase production and founded the Western Company of North America in 1939 with two trucks and three employees. With Chiles providing visionary direction, the company survived some lean times and hit its stride in the 1960s and '70s, growing into a $500 million–a-year business with more than 5,000 employees.

Chiles built his business with simple formulas for success. He figured he could apply those same formulas to the Texas Rangers.

Upon hiring Don Zimmer to manage the 1981 Rangers, for example, Chiles explained to the longtime major league player, coach, and manager that his oil business employees began each week by forecasting their productions. He expected Zimmer and the Rangers players to do the same, writing down their expected number of wins, hits, pitching totals, fielding percentages, and so forth for the week.

While that did not go over particularly well in the Rangers clubhouse, the mandatory goal-setting day the following year was even more peculiar.

"Early in 1982 Chiles locked down Arlington Stadium with armed guards on an off-day to keep media out and sequestered the players for a management seminar stressing individual and group goals," former *Fort Worth Star-Telegram* beat writer and sports columnist Jim Reeves recalled. "When writers asked one of the guards if his gun was loaded, he answered, 'Sure, it's loaded. It wouldn't do any good if it wasn't.' Writers dubbed the whole thing as, 'Fort Arlington.'"

Unfortunately, the goal-setting seminar was an exercise in futility. The '82 Rangers went 64–98, and although Chiles had been quoted in a magazine article that it was not his style to fire an executive just because the company was going through tough times, Chiles fired general manager Eddie Robinson 18 days after the quote was published.

Chiles ultimately appointed himself as general manager, accepting the advice of the media, who said he couldn't do any worse than Robinson. Chiles also made headlines later in '82 when he first said Zimmer's job wasn't in jeopardy. Four days later he fired Zimmer, but he asked the manager to stay on for a few days until a replacement was found.

Zimmer stayed on for four days. And Chiles wondered aloud why he was receiving criticism for making such a request.

"When he bought the team, he had vowed to stay out of baseball operations," Reeves said. "But he couldn't help himself. He was quite the character."

The Sales of the Team That Didn't Happen, and What Might Have Been

When the bottom fell out of the oil market in the late 1980s, Eddie Chiles' Western Company of North America took a tremendous tumble. Western's revenues, which peaked in 1981 at $725.7 million, plunged to $176.5 million in 1987, and Chiles was reluctantly forced to find a buyer for the Rangers.

One deal that fell apart involved a group led by members of the wealthy Mack family, which operates a large real-estate-development business based in Rochelle Park, New Jersey, and Tampa Bay–based automobile dealer Frank Morsani.

Chiles initially agreed to sell his controlling interest in the Rangers for $80 million in August 1988. But when it became clear that Morsani planned to purchase the team and move it to Tampa Bay, Chiles announced to a major league ownership meeting in Montreal that he was voting against the sale, and he urged other owners to do the same. The sale was not approved, and Chiles eventually sold 58 percent interest in the Rangers to a group headed by George W. Bush in March 1989.

That worked out well for the Rangers and their fans in North Texas. But it probably could have been so much better for the team if another deal had been approved by Major League Baseball.

Edward L. Gaylord, a billionaire businessman and philanthropist who expanded the *Daily Oklahoman* newspaper he inherited from his father into a business empire that included Nashville's Opryland, twice attempted to turn his minority ownership in the Rangers into a majority ownership. He had agreed in principle to purchase Chiles' majority interest in the team, but he was blocked by Major League Baseball for fear of what the Rangers could become when combined with Gaylord's media empire.

Gaylord Entertainment was known initially in North Texas for its ties to Fort Worth–based KTVT/Channel 11, which it had owned since 1963. Since that station also televised Rangers games, baseball owners—led by Jerry Reinsdorf, chairman of baseball's joint ownership committee at the time—opposed Gaylord's bid because they did not want another team owned by a broadcasting company.

Translation: owners didn't want the Rangers, with the help of a possible superstation like KTVT could have become, to develop into the equivalent of the Chicago Cubs (WGN) and the Atlanta Braves (WTBS), bolstering the financial coffers of the club and making the Rangers a nationally known franchise.

"I have been informed by the Major League Baseball ownership committee this afternoon that they have reached a recommendation that the transaction between myself and Mr. Gaylord not be approved in accordance with the guidelines for the transfer of controlling interest that were adopted by baseball in 1988," Chiles said in late January 1989.

Gaylord was worth about $2 billion when he died in 2003, so it's at least interesting to ponder the possibilities of what might have been—and what resources he could have poured into the team—if the sale of the team had happened as Chiles and Gaylord had twice approved.

Indeed, he was. Chiles went from regional businessman to national lightning rod in the late 1970s when he began speaking out against big government policies and procedures on radio commercials in which he proclaimed, "I'm Eddie Chiles, and I'm mad." The commercials were broadcast on 650 stations in 14 states where Western had operations and generated almost a million bumper stickers reading, "I'm mad too, Eddie." Chiles typically ended the commercials with the tagline: "If you don't own an oil well, get one."

After Brad Corbett announced he was selling the Rangers because they were dogs on the field and off, Chiles invested $4 million of his money to purchase majority ownership in the team. Chiles, who was almost 70 years old when he made the purchase in 1980, announced that he would not be making any ludicrous deals like the 10-year, $2.9 million contract outfielder Richie Zisk had signed under the previous regime.

"I bought the club as a general civic duty," Chiles told *Time* magazine in a 1980 article. "We have to improve the quality of life here."

While Chiles made some dubious mistakes as owner of the Rangers, he also made some wise moves. Chiles instilled corporate discipline to the team's front office, and in September 1984, he made 36-year-old Tom Grieve the youngest general manager in baseball. He also gave Grieve plenty of flexibility, and the Rangers were especially aggressive in scouting, signing, and developing Latin American players like Juan Gonzalez and Ivan Rodriguez under scouting director Sandy Johnson.

Under Chiles' leadership, the Rangers made numerous upgrades to Arlington Stadium and purchased the facility from the city of Arlington in 1987. Before mounting losses in his oil business led Chiles to sell his 58 percent interest in the Rangers to a group headed by George W. Bush Jr. in March 1989, Chiles approved probably the most important off-season acquisition in Rangers history when Texas signed Nolan Ryan to a one-year, $2 million contract.

Chiles said selling his share of the Rangers was "like losing a member of the family" but that younger ownership would be good for the team. He initially continued as the team's chairman, but his health soon became an issue. He suffered a stroke in 1992 and died in his sleep in August 1993. He was 83.

63 Arlington Stadium: A Slice of Hell in the Metroplex

The site for the facility that would eventually become the first home of the Texas Rangers was chosen because it was situated in a natural bowl, saving millions of dollars in construction costs in the early 1960s. Because of its geographical location, the playing surface of Turnpike Stadium—the original name of the facility— was significantly below the surrounding parking lots.

In other words, the playing surface was a little closer to hell than most other ballparks, which definitely seemed appropriate given what transpired during most of the 22 seasons in which Arlington Stadium served as the home of the Rangers.

"Calling it a 'hellhole' seems pretty fitting," said former Rangers outfielder Al Oliver, who hit at least .300 in each of his four seasons with Texas (1978–81). "For one, it was a terrible hitter's park. I was fortunate with my style of hitting, and I was successful there because I hit low line drives. But anybody who had any elevation on the ball hated that stadium because the wind would knock down so many home runs. My old teammate, Richie Zisk [1978–80 with the Rangers] really despised Arlington Stadium."

So did many other hitters. And managers. And fans.

There really wasn't much to love—or even like—about the old stadium. It had opened as a minor league stadium in 1965, and it was often a major headache for team executives, players, and fans until it was demolished in 1994.

Instead of the brick-and-mortar façade of the Rangers' current home, Arlington Stadium resembled a rusted erector set. Seats and suites were added over the years, but the ballpark never really lost its minor league feel. It was a strange combination of red seats, blue bleachers, and suites down the first-base line that seemed woefully

Arlington Stadium Was "Nacho" Ordinary Facility

While Arlington Stadium certainly wasn't fan-friendly in its amenities, it did produce some memorable contributions to the sports world and did possess a few interesting features.

The old ballpark gave baseball fans a taste of Tex-Mex, as the Rangers were the first franchise in all of sports to ever serve ballpark nachos. In 1976 Frank Liberto, CEO of Ricos Products Company, conceived a new concession menu item that consisted of fried tortillas covered in soft, gooey, neon-colored cheese. In 1977 Liberto began marketing and selling his creation—ballpark nachos—to fans at Arlington Stadium. Nachos are now a staple at most every stadium nationwide.

Another popular Arlington Stadium original that has gone nationwide is the "dot races."

The original main scoreboard for the stadium was located above the left-field bleachers and featured an outline of the state of Texas on the far right-hand side of the horizontal, 200'-by-60' board. It was a far cry from the exploding scoreboard at Comiskey Park in Chicago or the animated four-story scoreboard at the Houston Astrodome, but at least it was distinctive.

That scoreboard, however, was removed in the mid-1980s and replaced by state-of-the-art video boards and massive billboards that stretched across the entire length of the outfield bleachers from foul pole to foul pole. In addition to the advertising revenue the billboards added, the hope was that the wrap-around boards would cut down on the winds that traditionally made the stadium unfriendly to power hitters.

"Those billboards certainly didn't make Arlington Stadium a hitter-friendly park," said radio announcer Eric Nadel. "Maybe it became slightly less inhospitable toward home run hitters, but it was never hitter-friendly."

The new scoreboards were, however, a hit with the fans because of the creation of the dot races.

Chuck Morgan, who had come to Texas from Nashville to serve as the Rangers' VP of In-Park Entertainment, began talking with *Fort Worth Star-Telegram* beat writer Jim Reeves about ways to utilize the new scoreboard and entertain the fans. Their creation has stood the test of time, and it is still a prominent attraction at Rangers Ballpark in Arlington.

"We did something like that in Nashville [in the minor leagues], where we had two lights that chased each other across the board," Morgan recalled. "Jim Reeves and I were talking about it one day, and he had seen something similar in Oklahoma City. This was about 1986, and we decided to do something like that on the scoreboard here. It took a few months to design something that I thought would work on the video board at old Arlington Stadium. It was a combination of our two ideas, and I designed it for the video board. The fans really seemed to get into it."

Another hit with the hometown fans involves the playing of "Cotton-Eyed Joe," as opposed to "Take Me Out to the Ballgame" during the seventh-inning stretch.

out of place. As longtime Rangers beat writer T.R. Sullivan so aptly described, "it ended up looking like a child's creation out of Play-Doh."

The concourses were narrow, making it miserable to move around or purchase concession items on the few nights when the Rangers did attract a large crowd; chain-linked fences surrounded the facility, giving it a schoolyard look; and the outfield bleachers, made entirely of aluminum and metal, reverberated sound and reflected the scorching sun, adding to the overall sauna effect of the facility.

"The heat factor is always brought up as one of the negatives of playing for the Rangers, and if it was me as a player, it would probably factor into my contract decision on whether I'd want to sign or re-sign with the Rangers," said longtime Rangers radio announcer Eric Nadel. "Even as an announcer, I sometimes feel worn down by the excessive heat after a long summertime homestand. But as tough as things are now in the summertime, they were so much worse in the old ballpark. The sun stayed in the old ballpark a lot longer than it does now. The players aren't in the direct sunlight as much anymore. The old stadium was awful. I can remember when the game-time temperatures were in excess of 110, and it didn't drop under 100 until after the sun was completely down."

To combat the excessive heat, the Rangers became the first major league team to consistently schedule all games—even Sunday games—at night once the summer began. But even 7:00 PM and 7:30 PM games didn't keep players from baking in the sun. The searing temperatures did keep fans and free agents away, however. On so many sultry August nights the original capacity of the stadium—10,600—would have been more than enough.

Turnpike Stadium, which was built at its original capacity for $1.9 million, opened in 1965 and served primarily as the home of the Texas League's Dallas–Fort Worth Spurs, although the University of Texas-Arlington played its football games in the venue during the early 1970s. The first expansion of the facility raised seating capacity to just over 20,000.

When Arlington mayor Tom Vandergriff lured the Senators from Washington to North Texas in 1972, capacity at Arlington Stadium was hastily increased to 35,000. In the late 1970s a plaza deck was built on top of the stands behind home plate, raising capacity to just over 41,000.

But that capacity was rarely needed. The Rangers never hosted an All-Star Game or a playoff game at Arlington Stadium.

64 The Bobby Valentine Years in Texas

When Bobby Valentine was dismissed by the Rangers on July 9, 1992, he'd won more games (581) than any other manager in the team's history. On the other hand, the then-41-year-old Valentine also held the dubious distinction of managing more games (1,186) with one team without winning a division title, pennant, or World Series than any other manager in major league history.

In other words, Valentine was not shocked when the axe finally fell, ending an eight-season association with the ballclub. When George W. Bush, the Rangers' managing general partner at the time, made the official announcement at a press conference, the typically personable Valentine was in attendance...and was unusually upbeat for a man who had just been canned.

"I'm not ready to move away from this team right now with my heart, my mind, or my talent," Valentine said. "We might stay here and watch them win the World Series."

Or maybe not. The Rangers, who were 45–41 and 6½ games out of first place in the American League West when Valentine was fired, took a turn for the worst and finished the '92 season at 77–85 overall, 19 games behind the Oakland Athletics. In fairness to Valentine, the A's were the predominant story throughout much of his tenure in Texas, which began three days after Valentine's 35th birthday when he replaced Doug Rader as manager on May 16, 1985.

Oakland dominated the division during much of the latter half of the Valentine era in Texas, winning the division four times in five years and reaching the World Series three times. The Twins also came out of the American League West to win two World Series during that span (1987 and 1991).

"The American League West produced some really good teams during Bobby's tenure [in Texas]," recalled Tom Grieve. "But that doesn't detract from some of the things he did in Texas. I've never met anyone like Bobby. I've never met anyone who had passion for everything he did like Bobby. He could've been the CEO of a *Fortune 500* company, but it just happened that baseball was his passion. We had some decent teams while he was here, and a lot of that was due to his passion.

"I played for Ted Williams, Whitey Herzog, Joe Torre, etc., but I never met anyone who knows the game better than Bobby Valentine. He could teach hitting, pitching, and fielding at the highest level. If there was an SAT for baseball, he'd score a 1600. He's the most brilliant baseball person I've ever met, and what he did for our team is underrated in Rangers history."

He was undoubtedly one of the more loquacious, entertaining, and engaging managers in Rangers history. Especially in his younger days, he looked a little like Frankie Avalon, and he was always quite comfortable in front of the camera.

Valentine possessed a gift for gab and was never reluctant to speak his mind…even when it might have been wiser to keep his mouth shut. Valentine frequently questioned umpires and yelled at opposing players from the dugout. His passion sometimes came across as cockiness, and his competitiveness often drew the ire of other players and managers.

Fans and baseball people either loved Bobby V. or they loathed him. There weren't a lot of people in the middle.

"I can understand why some people don't like me," Valentine told *Sports Illustrated's* Leigh Montville in an April 1992 article. "I think I'm misunderstood sometimes. I'm loud. I say things. I do more things than a lot of managers do, so that means there are more things that people can decide not to like. I smile a lot. It drives some people crazy. I understand that. You see somebody

*Former manager
Bobby Valentine
holds the Rangers
franchise record
for both wins and
losses, posting a
581–605 mark
over eight seasons.*
(Ronald C. Modra/
Sports Imagery/Getty
Images)

who smiles a lot.... Steve Garvey always was smiling. People hated him for it. I just smile."

For the most part, Rangers fans had plenty of reasons to smile back at Valentine. He was extremely active in the community on many levels and was typically accessible and open to the fans. And while he wasn't immediately successful in Arlington—his first team finished the 1985 season by going 53–76—Valentine generated plenty of excitement in 1986, as the Rangers went 87–75 to finish five games behind the California Angels in the American League West. That team, which included 10 rookies at one time or another, led the division for 47 days.

Doug Rader: Memorable for All the Wrong Reasons

After losing 98 games in 1982, Texas owner Eddie Chiles and general manager Joe Klein interviewed several candidates for the vacant position, including future legendary manager Jim Leyland and former Houston Astros Gold Glove–winning third baseman Doug Rader.

The Rangers chose Rader. Rangers fans are still shaking their heads in disbelief.

Leyland led Pittsburgh to three National League East titles in the early 1990s, guided the Marlins to the World Series crown in 1997, and helped Detroit win the American League pennant in 2006.

Rader managed less than two and a half seasons in Texas, compiling a 155–200 record. He didn't win many friends, either.

"Doug Rader's entire two-plus years as manager were strange, from his clashes with umpires, opposing players, media, and his own players," wrote longtime Rangers beat writer T.R. Sullivan. "He also crashed his car into the same tree every day in spring training."

At least he hit something with consistency...something his players rarely did. During one spring when the Rangers were struggling to score runs, Rader picked up a drunk off the street, put him in uniform, and introduced him to the players as one of the finest hitting instructors in the game.

"This poor guy was so hungover, he hadn't shaved in weeks, he smelled horribly, he had peed in his pants, he had thrown up on himself," former Rangers coach Rich Donnelly told ESPN's Tim Kurkjian, a former beat writer with *The Dallas Morning News.* "He came out with a fungo bat and said, 'Okay, you grab this thing, and you swing it like this.' It was absolutely ridiculous. But Mickey [Rivers] said, 'That's right. We need to listen to this guy. He knows what he's talking about.' Everyone cracked up. We cleaned him up, gave him something to eat, dropped him back downtown in a Rangers uniform."

Rader did have a sense of humor. But it was no match for his temper.

The 1983 Rangers started well and were in first place at the All-Star break. The collapse began right after the break.

"In Kansas City, after losing a fourth straight game, Rader became enraged," wrote Peter Gammons in a 1989 *Sports Illustrated* article. "When a writer asked a question, Rader crushed an unopened beer can with one hand, smashed a steel door with his fist, and slapped his clothes rack so hard that his pants flew across the room and landed atop a reporter's head. Everyone was so intimidated that the pants stayed on the reporter's head until the interview session ended. Afterward, Rader told Donnelly, 'I'm walking back.'"

It was a six-mile trip from Royals Stadium to the hotel. Before beginning the hike, Rader took off his boots and handed them to Donnelly, saying, "I've got to punish myself." By the time he reached the hotel, his bare feet were badly blistered.

His players grew accustomed to "the Red Rooster's" verbal blisterings. Rader criticized Rangers veterans Jim Sundberg and Buddy Bell. At the end of the 1983 season, Texas traded Sundberg, arguably the most popular player in team history at that point, to Milwaukee for Ned Yost. Rader said he needed a different kind of player behind the plate.

He got it in Yost, who hit .182 in 1984 and stopped just 17 percent of opposing runners' stolen-base attempts. Meanwhile, the Rangers went 69–92, and Rader did more damage behind the scenes.

"Tom Henke and Dave Stewart, who would blossom into October heroes for the Blue Jays and A's, withered under Doug Rader's harsh managing," wrote former Rangers beat writer Phil Rogers. "Henke, like former first-round pick Jeff Kunkel, was reduced to tears in the dugout by Rader's screaming. Stewart and Rader almost came to blows in the spring of 1985 when Rader wanted Stewart to quit fooling around with the forkball, the pitch he would use to win 20 games four years in a row with the A's."

Rader also feuded with the media, responding to one writer's questions with the same two-word expletive for 12 straight days. "It got to the point where they expected me to act like an ass, and I did," Rader told Gammons. "When I was finally fired, I was actually relieved."

So were Rangers fans. Rader was fired in May 1985 after leading the Rangers to a 9–23 start. He later managed three years with the Angels, displaying a slightly calmer demeanor. But the results were similar: he started off really well in the first year in 1989, began to slide in the second, and was fired during the 1991 season.

He never managed again. Thankfully.

The lineup in 1986 was hardly "Murderer's Row," as Scott Fletcher and Gary Ward were the only everyday players to hit .300 or higher. But the pitching staff was filled with promising young-sters like 20-year-old Edwin Correa, 23-year-old Jose Guzman, 22-year-old Bobby Witt, 21-year-old Mitch Williams, and 24-year-old Jeff Russell.

The star of the farm system, 20-year-old outfielder Ruben Sierra, also made his debut in '86. Shortly thereafter, Valentine began listening to Berlitz cassettes in his car to learn Spanish so that he could communicate directly with Sierra. Later in his career with the Rangers, Valentine was rarely without his book of Spanish idioms and his book of 501 Spanish verbs so that he could talk to the numer-ous Latin American players on his roster such as Rafael Palmeiro and Juan Gonzalez. He genuinely reached out to many of his players.

Valentine was also the manager of the Rangers during some special nights with Nolan Ryan: strikeout No. 5,000, no-hitters Nos. 6 and 7, and victory No. 300. And while he never won a divi-sion title, he did guide the Rangers to three consecutive winning seasons (1989–91) for only the second time in the franchise's history. He left with a winning record in '92, as well.

"[Valentine] is a good man, he's a good manager," George W. Bush said at the press conference on the day Valentine was fired. "He's done a lot for this community. But having said that, we were concerned about the 1992 pennant race getting away from us."

In hindsight, that was only expedited by Valentine's release. In the big picture of the ballclub's history, Bobby V. should probably be remembered far more favorably than apathetically by Rangers fans. Quite frankly, there's not much doubt that he was the greatest manager in Rangers history over an extended time, before Johnny Oates. Valentine will return to Arlington in 2012—albeit as a visitor—as the new manager of the Boston Red Sox.

65 Read and Subscribe to the *Newberg Report*

At the Dallas-based law firm Vincent Lopez Serafino Jenevein, P.C., Jamison D. Newberg answers to the titles of "attorney" and "shareholder." At home, he responds to "Dad" to his two kids or to various affectionate terms from his wife, Ginger, whom he first met while the two were attending the University of Texas in the late 1980s.

But it is in another role—the hobby that has made him a household name among so many Rangers fans throughout the Metroplex—where Jamey Newberg's title is less clearly defined. Since 1998 the personable lawyer and passionate baseball fan has penned an email notes package on the Rangers and the franchise's entire farm system called the *Newberg Report.*

It started innocently, as Newberg, an admitted lifelong statistics junkie and box score scrutinizer, posted regular minor league personnel updates on *The Dallas Morning News'* Rangers message board. At the time, Newberg was intrigued by the story of Canadian-born pitcher Jeff Zimmerman, who'd played at TCU, in an independent league, and even in France before being acquired by Texas in 1998. Newberg, who obtained most of his information from newspaper reports across the country and publications such as *Baseball America*, encouraged fellow forum readers to keep an eye on Zimmerman, as well as another undrafted free agent in the farm system, outfielder Rubén Mateo.

Before the start of the '98 season, *The Morning News'* website was briefly taken offline for upgrading, and a handful of Newberg's message-board buddies sent him personal emails requesting continued information of the Rangers' top prospects. Newberg obliged and began sending out detailed information and thought-provoking observations to a handful of people, probably no more than six to 10, including his own longtime friends.

"Word of mouth grew from that point, and their coworkers and neighbors soon came on board," recalled Newberg. "By the end of '98 someone tipped off Mike Rhyner (co-host of *The Hardline* on 1310 KTCK-AM, The Ticket). He and I started corresponding. At the beginning of the '99 season, I was driving home from work the first day after the minor league openers. That afternoon [Rhyner] read directly from my report. I had no clue he was going to do that. They had good feedback, and they did a segment of my stuff every day. I even had a theme song, and I actually came on air from time to time if we made trades or called somebody up. The mailing list grew by the dozens every day because of that. That's how it all started."

It's since taken on a life of its own. Newberg also does an outstanding bound edition at the end of each year, which is a "must-have" for Rangers die-hards. According to Newberg, each season is chronicled in the book, "in daily, exhaustive, emotional detail."

Newberg is highly respected by many members of the Rangers' front office personnel and is featured regularly on the Rangers' website. Media following the Rangers rely heavily on his minor league expertise, and *The Dallas Observer* ranked him as one of the "50 Most Powerful People in Metroplex Sports" four consecutive years. Then, in 2011, he was named the best local sports columnist by the *Dallas Observer.*

But don't dare refer to Newberg as a "sports journalist." Don't confuse him with an aspiring baseball scout or farm director, either. According to Newberg, his title in regard to his newsletter should be far less formal.

"I'm just another big-time fan providing a service for fellow fans," Newberg says. "That's all."

With all due respect to his humility, if Newberg is "just another fan," then Nolan Ryan was "just another pitcher" for the Rangers, or the 2011 loss in Game 6 of the World Series was "just another setback."

Newberg is a five-tool Rangers fan, who first began attending games at old Arlington Stadium in 1976. The former Hillcrest High School shortstop and pitcher attempted to walk on twice at UT and thought he came relatively close to making the Longhorns' roster once. So, he knows the game. He also loves it with a boyish passion, while studying, examining, and dissecting it as if he were writing his dissertation on the Rangers' farm system.

"You can tell that he really cares about the Rangers and the players he discusses," said longtime Rangers television color commentator and former player and general manager Tom Grieve. "As time has gone on, he's really become a trusted source where Rangers fans can get information on how players are progressing through the minors and a lot more. He is really good in his evaluations."

Cases in point: Zimmerman and Mateo, the two players Newberg encouraged his forum followers to watch. Zimmerman played Single A and Double A ball in 1998, started in Triple A in 1999, and made it to the major leagues early in 1999, where he was so sensational as a reliever that he made the All-Star team in '99. He went 9–3 with a 2.36 ERA in '99 as a middle reliever and saved 28 games in 2001 while compiling a 2.40 ERA. Injuries ended his career prematurely, but Zimmerman was, as predicted by Newberg, someone to watch.

To a lesser degree, so was Mateo, who also debuted for the Rangers in '99. The outfielder would go on to play six major league seasons for the Rangers, Reds, Pirates, and Royals.

Newberg critiques players without being overly critical. That's one of the ways he distinguishes himself from most sports journalists. Another way is that he acknowledges he is totally biased in his observations. He's a proud Rangers lifer, and he takes an optimistic outlook whenever the situation warrants it.

Even after extremely difficult times for the team—like being eliminated from the playoffs in 2015 and '16 by the Blue Jays—Newberg possesses an ability to make Rangers' fans appreciate the ballclub and to paint a perspective on the big picture of the franchise and life as a baseball fanatic.

"The Rangers are a true passion of mine," Newberg says. "My kids are into baseball, and my wife has become a fan, too. So it's a family affair, as well. I don't sleep a lot, but I don't regret that, either. I really have had fun with this, and even if I wasn't doing this report, I'd watch every game with the passion and interest that I do now. I write from a fan's perspective because I am a fan."

Actually, he's Superfan, the informant of fans. He's just far too humble to put that title on his business card.

66 Trade for Burkett Bolsters First Playoff Run

Virtually every professional team has its fair share of terrific trades and terrible ones that positively and negatively shape the history of the organization. But very rarely can one team claim both a wonderful and woeful exchange regarding the same player in back-to-back seasons.

Such is the case, however, in regard to the Rangers and right-handed pitcher John Burkett.

The first trade for Burkett was one of the more fruitless deals in Rangers history. The second was critical in ending more than two decades of playoff-less futility.

It was all a matter of timing. Really bad and exceptionally good timing.

On December 24, 1994, rookie Rangers general manager Doug Melvin, who'd been on the job for only a couple of months, traded prospects Rich Aurilia and Desi Wilson to the Giants for Burkett. While Wilson played only one major league season, Aurilia became a 15-year veteran and an All-Star shortstop for the Giants.

Meanwhile, Burkett did absolutely nothing for the Rangers. When the 232-day major league strike in 1994–95 came to an end on April 2, 1995, the Rangers made a financial decision regarding the top of their pitching rotation: keep Kenny Rogers as the No. 1 starter and release Burkett.

"We couldn't keep both because of their salaries," former Rangers manager Johnny Oates said. "We decided to go with Kenny because he was a left-hander, and he had been in our organization for years."

On April 7, 1995—less than four months after trading for him—the Rangers granted Burkett free agency. He signed with the Florida Marlins, and Melvin received nothing but a valuable lesson. He later acknowledged he didn't know what he had parted with when he traded Aurilia.

"I didn't know Rich Aurilia," Melvin said. "I saw him in the fall league, but I only saw him a couple of games. The reports were that he had a chance to hit, but they weren't sure he was going to be an everyday shortstop. I think people thought he might have been an extra player, a utility player. He was better than what the reports said."

That experience taught Melvin to rely on his eyes more than his reports. But the general manager made up for that mistake on August 8, 1996, when Texas, holding a two-game lead in the American League West, traded right-handers Ryan Dempster and Rick Helling to the Marlins for Burkett, who'd gone 14–14 with Florida in '95.

The trade didn't generate much national attention, as Burkett was only 6–10 with the Marlins in '96. But until the 2010 Rangers traded with Seattle for Cliff Lee, the Burkett deal in '96 could have been considered the most important summertime pitching acquisition in the franchise history.

Burkett went 5–2 down the stretch with the Rangers, including a masterful performance on September 21 to lead Texas to a 7–1 win over the Angels that was—at that point—the most important victory in franchise history. Entering that game, Texas had lost nine of its last 10, and its lead in the American League West had diminished from nine games to one.

Vosberg Did More Than "Handcuff" Hitters for Mid-1990s Rangers

In 1996, left-handed reliever Ed Vosberg played a significant role in helping the Rangers reach the postseason for the first time in team history. Unfortunately for Vosberg, that's not how he first made national headlines as a major leaguer.

After an extended minor league career that began with the Padres' organization in 1983, Vosberg made his first significant and extended impact at the major league level with the 1995 Rangers, appearing in 44 games and going 5–5 with four saves. But he did more than close a few games in '95. He also closed a deal in the parking lot for which he was arrested.

When the Rangers played host to the 1995 All-Star Game, Vosberg invited his brother from Phoenix to attend the game. To cover his brother's travel expenses, Vosberg decided to scalp some tickets to the All-Star Game. Unknowingly, Vosberg cut a deal with an undercover cop.

As a result, Vosberg, who was making $125,000 at the time, was arrested for scalping six tickets outside the Ballpark in Arlington.

"I made a mistake," Vosberg said. "No one's more embarrassed about it than I am."

Vosberg bounced back from the embarrassment to go 1–1 with a 3.27 ERA in '96, picking up eight saves in 44 innings to help lead the Rangers to the postseason for the first time. In mid-August 1997 he was traded by the Rangers to the Marlins for Rick Helling.

Burkett's gem stopped the bleeding, and the 31-year-old went on to outpitch the Yankees' David Cone in the first game of the 1996 ALDS in New York. Burkett pitched a complete-game 10-hitter in the Rangers' 6–2 victory.

The '96 deal for Burkett, who won 32 game with Texas from 1996 to 1999, looked even better on August 12, 1997, when the Rangers reclaimed Helling in a trade with the Marlins for Ed Vosberg. The Rangers were out of the race in '97, and Vosberg, a left-handed reclamation project, was viewed as a valuable bullpen piece to Florida, which was making a wild-card run. The Marlins eventually won the '97 World Series, with Vosberg pitching in 17 games.

Helling's return to Texas was huge for the Rangers. He won 20 games in 1998, leading Texas back to the playoffs. He remained a key member of the Texas rotation through 2001.

67 The Very Expensive Alex Rodriguez Experiment

We had to put this somewhere. So, why not here, at No. 67? Representative of the $67 million the Rangers agreed to pay Alex Rodriguez just to unload him to the Yankees in February 2004.

Of course, that wasn't the original plan. Let's rewind a couple of months.

For a few weeks in November and December 2003, the Rangers and Boston Red Sox negotiated a possible trade that would have sent Rodriguez, the high-profile slugging shortstop, to Boston for a package that included Manny Ramirez and cash.

It didn't proceed as planned, however, as the Major League Baseball Players' Association rejected proposed changes to A-Rod's world-famous (or notorious), 10-year, $252 million contract.

A couple of weeks later, in an attempt to smooth hard feelings between the star and the ballclub, Rodriguez was named Texas' team captain—at agent Scott Boras' suggestion—during a five-hour meeting with owner Tom Hicks, general manager John Hart, and manager Buck Showalter in New York, where team officials had gathered to support Rodriguez as he accepted the American League MVP Award at the New York Baseball Writers' Dinner.

The captain thing didn't work out as planned, either.

A couple of weeks later, A-Rod was back in New York. Full-time. In mid-February 2004 the Rangers ended the A-Rod era in Arlington, pulling the string on a blockbuster trade that sent their temporary captain to the Big Apple for Alfonso Soriano and a player to be named later, who turned out to be talented infield prospect Joaquin Arias, whom the Yankees coveted. The Rangers chose Arias from a pool of five players that included another top infield prospect in the Yankees' system. Some guy named Robinson Cano.

Like virtually everything else regarding Rodriguez's tenure as a Ranger, that didn't work out for Texas. Cano became a star for the Yankees. Arias played a total of 91 games for the Rangers before being dealt to the Mets in 2010.

"We thought we could build a championship-caliber team with Alex," Rangers owner Tom Hicks said on the day the Rodriguez-to-the-Yankees deal was completed. "We tried everything we could to win. We brought in some expensive players, but for a lot of reasons it didn't work."

Hicks and the Rangers shocked the baseball world on December 11, 2000, when A-Rod signed the most lucrative contract in professional sports history. It was widely ridiculed by baseball executives across the country, and Hicks was mocked for handcuffing the

In December 2000 the Rangers signed slugging shortstop Alex Rodriguez to a 10-year, $252 million contract. In three seasons in Texas, Rodriguez led the American League in home runs each year. But the Rangers, unable to build a competitive roster around Rodriguez's salary, finished last in the American League West all three seasons. Rodriguez was traded to the New York Yankees before the 2004 season. (AP Images)

organization. Meanwhile, Rodriguez, who was labeled by many media members as "Mr. Two-Fifty-Two," felt immense pressure to prove his worth.

"He felt it," former Rangers catcher Bill Haselman told *Sports Illustrated's* Selena Roberts. "He had the mentality of somebody trying to hit a three-run homer with nobody on base."

Richie Zisk: The Other 10-Year Deal that Didn't Go As Planned

Spanish American philosopher, essayist, poet, and novelist George Santayana (1863–1952) is credited with the aphorism that states, "The one who does not remember history is bound to live through it again."

Apparently, Tom Hicks wasn't a student of Santayana's teachings.

In December 2000 Hicks signed Alex Rodriguez to a 10-year, $252 million contract that rocked the baseball world. It wasn't actually unchartered waters in Rangers history.

A couple of decades earlier, Texas owner Brad Corbett was convinced that a right-handed power hitter was all that the Rangers needed to win the pennant. The 1977 Rangers had gone 94–68 but finished eight games behind Kansas City in the American League West. In November 1977 Corbett opened his checkbook and offered free agent Richie Zisk a 10-year deal reportedly worth $2,955,000. While that's not staggering by today's standards, it was the second-most-lucrative contract in baseball history at that point.

Zisk lasted three years with the Rangers (1978–80). He produced some good numbers, too. But he couldn't put Texas over the top. In fact, the Rangers' record with Zisk grew worse each season before he was traded away.

Just like A-Rod a couple decades later. One major difference was that A-Rod came from Seattle to Texas. Zisk went from Texas to Seattle, where he ended his career in 1983.

Zisk began his career in Pittsburgh, where he replaced Roberto Clemente in right field in 1973 and finished ninth in the National League Rookie of the Year balloting. From 1973 to 1976 Zisk averaged .302 with 17 homers, but he said he felt underappreciated compared to more popular Pirates, like Willie Stargell and Dave Parker. He welcomed a trade to the Chicago White Sox after the 1976 season, producing a monster year in the Windy City with 30 homers and 101 RBIs in 1977.

Among other moves, Texas added Zisk and his former teammate in Pittsburgh, Al Oliver, to the lineup for the 1978 season.

"The Rangers lost [the American League West] by eight games [in '77]," Zisk said at spring training in 1978, "and there's no question that we've made up the difference."

It didn't work out that way. As a member of the Rangers, Zisk hit .262 twice and .290 in 1980, averaging 20 homers and 75 RBIs. Good numbers, but compared to the '77 season he had with the White Sox, they were disappointing.

"One man can't win a pennant," Zisk told *Sports Illustrated* after he was traded to Seattle. "A lot was expected of me, but we didn't put it together as a team. I got into some bad habits in Texas, where the wind blew in from right center. I started trying to pull the ball too much, which isn't my natural style at all. It's been fun to rediscover the things I can do with a bat."

In Seattle, Zisk hit .311 as a designated hitter in 1981, setting a Mariners record with homers in five straight games and earning American League Comeback Player of the Year honors. After multiple knee operations and a wrist injury, he retired after 1983.

Nevertheless, Rodriguez performed admirably. In 2001 he led the American League in home runs (52) and runs scored (133). A year later, he led the majors with 57 homers, 142 RBIs, and 389 total bases. And in '03 he won the American League MVP, leading the league with 47 homers, 124 runs scored, and a .600 slugging percentage. He also won his second straight Gold Glove. In three seasons with the Rangers, he hit .305 with 156 home runs and 395 RBIs.

But in three seasons, the Rangers finished last in the American League West each year, a combined 99 games out of first, with an overall three-year record of 216–270.

"It's not Alex's fault we finished last the three years he was here," Hicks said.

Added Hart: "Alex didn't do anything other than go play his heart out. He is a very special player and very special kid."

Unfortunately, Hart and Co. did not surround A-Rod with many other "special" players. While the Rangers featured some exceptional young players, such as Michael Young, Mark Teixeira, Hank Blalock, and Laynce Nix, Hart's maneuvers were less than magnificent. He traded for outfielder Carl Everett and pitcher John Rocker at his first winter meetings with the Rangers following the 2001 season and signed starting pitcher Chan Ho Park as the team's big free-agent acquisition.

Those moves—like the entire A-Rod era in Texas—simply didn't work out as planned.

68 The Bitter Collapse of 2012 Just Short of the Finish Line

On the night of June 30, 2012, Josh Hamilton launched his 25th homer of the season to propel rookie Martin Perez to his first win before 46,711 fans at Rangers Ballpark in Arlington. On that night, the Rangers became the first team in the majors to reach 50 wins, improving to 21 games over .500 and extending their AL West Division lead to 6.5 games over the Angels and 13.0 over the A's.

After playing 33 playoff games in 2010 and '11 and representing the American League in consecutive World Series, Texas again looked to be destined for a triumphant postseason run. And there was a legitimate hope among Rangers fans that the third time could, indeed, be the charm for the best team in baseball.

Rest assured, no one could have projected then that the Rangers would nosedive while the A's would thrive. But that's exactly what happened as the calendar flipped to July. The Rangers limped through July, going 9–14, scoring a league-worst 81 runs, and tying a club record for fewest wins in a month.

The team rebounded in August and early September, and the Rangers held a five-game lead over the red-hot A's in the AL West with just nine regular season games remaining. That's when the bottom dropped out. Texas lost seven of its final nine regular-season games, including the final three in Oakland. In the final game, the A's overcame a four-run deficit to win 12–5 in a comeback that was punctuated by Hamilton's dropped fly ball on a routine play in centerfield.

Oakland moved into first place for the first time all year on the final day of the season. As a result, the Rangers were forced to play in the AL Wild Card Game against Baltimore. The Rangers lost the game 5–1 as the offense went silent.

"It's kind of shocking," TBS broadcaster and Hall of Fame pitcher Dennis Eckersley told MLB.com's T.R. Sullivan. "Texas was supposed to be the best team in baseball most of the season. At the All-Star break, I was picking Texas...last week, I was picking Texas. I think they are as shocked as anybody."

Perhaps the most shocking aspect was the dreadful performance of Hamilton. The former AL MVP, who had been so good early in the 2012 season, was awful down the stretch.

Hamilton saw eight pitches in the Wild Card game. He swung at six and watched the other two for strikes, going 0-for-4 and striking out twice. He was also booed during that loss. The Wild Card game only continued a trend, as Hamilton struck out in 18 of his last 39 at-bats.

"It sucked, didn't it?" Hamilton said. "It was a disappointing year."

It soon became more disappointing for Rangers fans regarding Hamilton.

Hamilton agreed to a five-year, $125 million deal with the Angels. Then, in February, Hamilton disparaged the local fans. "There are true baseball fans in Texas, but it's not a true baseball town," said Hamilton in a television interview. "They're supportive, but they also got a little spoiled at the same time pretty quickly. You think about three to four years ago [before two straight World Series appearances in 2010 and 2011]. It's like, come on man, are you happier there again?"

69 Julio Franco: A Unique Stance and the 1991 Batting Title

During 23 major league seasons, Julio Franco played for eight teams, collected 2,586 hits, delivered 1,194 RBIs, and stepped into the batter's box with his distinctive stance 9,731 times. Franco also played professionally in Mexico, Korea, and Japan, producing at the plate no matter what uniform he wore.

In all those seasons, however, one year stands out as most meaningful—1991. Ironically, the batting title he won that season playing for the Rangers had little to do with what made the year so special.

"I had just won the batting title, and I was at the peak of my career, but I still wasn't happy," Franco told Chuck Johnson of *USA TODAY* in 2004. "There was something missing in my life. I come from a Christian background, and my brother said to me [on a trip home to the Dominican Republic in late December 1991], 'Why don't you go to church?' My mother reminded me that we always used to go to church. So I went to church, and that night I found out what I was missing in my life. After I gave myself to the Lord, everything started changing."

Until that time, Franco's reputation was rather tainted. He broke into the major leagues in 1982 with Philadelphia and was soon traded to Cleveland with four other players in a deal for Von Hayes. With the Tribe (1983–88), Franco compiled outstanding offensive numbers, finishing second in the Rookie of the Year Award balloting in '83 and winning a Silver Slugger Award in '88.

But Franco struggled at shortstop, leading the league in errors in 1984 and '85. He also was deemed somewhat of a malcontent in the clubhouse, where he earned scorn for, among other things, bringing a Rottweiler and a snake. During his first six-year tenure with the Indians, Franco also failed to show up for games twice, once during a road trip to New York and again following a pregame dispute with his wife. He also earned Dominican jail time for carrying a gun in his automobile.

His moodiness made the Indians willing to trade him to the Rangers on December 6, 1988, as Texas general manager Tom Grieve shipped first baseman Pete O'Brien, outfielder Oddibe McDowell, and infielder Jerry Browne to the Indians for Franco, who would play second base in Texas.

Rangers fans quickly learned to love Franco and his highly unusual batting stance—knock-kneed, with his bat wrapped high behind his ear and practically parallel to the ground. The end of the barrel pointed back toward the pitcher, and Franco barely gripped the knob with his left hand, which is why he frequently let go of the bat in his follow-through.

The stance looked strange, but Franco was certainly effective. He hit .316 in '89 and made his first All-Star appearance. In 1990 he hit .296 and was selected as the All-Star Game MVP. And in '91 he was sensational, becoming the first Rangers batting champion by leading the American League with a .341 average. He also produced a career-best 201 hits and 108 runs and made his third straight All-Star appearance. And he became an American citizen in '91.

Still, Franco was viewed skeptically by his own teammates. He often couldn't be found during batting practice because, while his teammates worked in triple-digit heat in Arlington, he'd slip off to a room in the air-conditioned clubhouse to take a nap. Sometimes, he even would go home and sleep. He was labeled as lazy, self-centered, and a number of other negative things until his focus shifted from sleeping to a faith-based awakening.

Franco played only two more seasons with the Rangers (1992 and 1993) and was limited to 35 games because of a knee injury in '92. The Rangers never expected him to return to top form,

Utilizing a highly unorthodox batting stance, Julio becoming the first Rangers batting champion in 1991, leading the American League with a .341 average.
(Ronald C. Modra/Sports Imagery/Getty Images)

and Franco signed with the Chicago White Sox prior to the strike-shortened '94 season.

The Rangers were wrong in their evaluation, as Franco hit .319, blasted 20 homers, and finished eighth in the 1994 American League MVP voting. He would go on to play another 14 seasons, amazing teammates, coaches, and fans with his commitment to staying in shape (he's never been accused of using steroids, not even by Jose Canseco), his penchant for producing big hits, and his mature, Christ-centered approach to life. The moody man of the 1980s and early '90s became a rock of clubhouse stability in the latter half of his career.

"It's a gift from God that I [was able to play until 48]," Franco said. "He's the one that gives me the strength, wisdom, and talent to play this game. I'm just a tool that he uses."

70 Jim Kern: The Great Emu... and a Bit of a "Coo Coo"

It only took one season in Texas for Jim Kern to establish the gold standard for relievers in the Rangers' short history in Arlington. In 1979—his first year in Texas and his finest in a 13-year career in the major leagues—Kern appeared in 71 games, earning 29 saves and compiling a 13–5 record with a sparkling 1.57 ERA in 143 innings. Kern became the first Rangers pitcher to play in the All-Star Game in '79 and was chosen as the Rolaids American League Fireman of the Year.

The hard-throwing, 6'5" Kern gave opposing hitters reason to "fear the beard" long before Brian Wilson and the 2010 San Francisco Giants made outlandish facial hair a key component of a bullpen's overall intimidation factor.

But Kern possessed much more than an overpowering right arm and a wild assortment of whiskers. His fastball made him memorable, but his oddball personality made him unforgettable. His pranks defined him as much as his pitching, and he was as eccentric on and off the field as he was dominant on the mound.

"[Kern] was one of the more interesting characters in the late 1970s and early '80s," said former *Fort Worth Star-Telegram* Rangers beat writer Jim Reeves. "He could be wild in an

Dale "the Horse" Mohorcic Sets Consecutive Appearance Record at 13

After starring at Cleveland State University in the 1970s, it took right-handed pitcher Dale Robert Mohorcic a long time to finally reach the major leagues. He was playing in Canada with the Class A Victoria Mussels of the Northwest League in 1978 when his contract was purchased by the Toronto Blue Jays.

He bounced around the minor leagues for eight years in the Toronto, Pittsburgh, and Texas farm systems before making his major league debut with the Rangers as a 30-year-old reliever in 1986.

Once he made it to "the Show," Mohorcic didn't waste any time in making a major impact. Mohorcic appeared in 58 games for the 1986 Rangers, going 2–4 with seven saves and a sparkling 2.51 ERA. And during one unforgettable stretch from August 6–20, Mohorcic tied Mike Marshall's major league record by appearing in 13 consecutive games.

Rangers manager Bobby Valentine certainly played his part in helping Mohorcic make history. On August 20 at Kansas City, Texas was leading 7–1 with two outs in the ninth as Charlie Hough was pitching a gem. But Valentine allowed Mohorcic to pitch to the final batter of the game in order to tie the record. (He still holds the club record.)

Mohorcic led the Rangers with 16 saves and a 2.99 ERA in 1987 while appearing in 74 games. He underwent elbow surgery in March 1988 and was 0–6 (7.67) in his last 30 appearances when he was traded to the Yankees for Cecilio Guante in August 1988.

intimidating manner on the mound, and he was typically just as wild and wacky in other settings."

Reeves possesses an interesting perspective on that. In addition to covering the team on a daily basis, Reeves and other reporters traveled with the Rangers in those days. On one memorable flight in 1979, Kern confiscated a book Reeves was reading, ripped out the last four pages, and stuffed them into his mouth, chewing them up as he mockingly savored them.

"He was out there," said former Rangers catcher Jim Sundberg, now the team's senior executive vice president. "When I think of [Kern], the first thing that comes to mind is the great season he had in 1979. But his antics aren't far behind. Especially at that time, there was a belief that relievers were a little off the wall. Jim fit that bill. In fact, he may have been one of the primary reasons for that belief."

Kern came to Texas with a well-established reputation for outrageousness. He made his major league debut with Cleveland in 1974 and pitched well for the lowly Indians, serving as Cleveland's All-Star representative in 1977 and '78. But as he did with the Rangers, Kern left some of his most lasting impressions on teammates and fans because of his personality.

Kern says he earned his nickname—"the Great Emu"—in Cleveland one day as he strolled through the team's clubhouse squawking like a crow just as teammates Pat Dobson and Fritz Peterson were attempting to solve a three-letter crossword puzzle clue for the world's largest nonflying bird: *emu.*

The rest is history. But he had other "bird stories" in Cleveland. According to a 2005 story in *The Dallas Morning News* by Ben Shpigel, Kern says he practiced duck calls in front of his locker (to facilitate a trade) and practiced his pellet gun accuracy by shooting pigeons that flew above Cleveland Municipal Stadium. In one particularly accurate season, he says he shot 234.

While the Rangers realized Kern was a bird of a different feather, they hoped he could be the missing piece to the bullpen puzzle. The '78 Rangers won 87 games and finished in second place in the American League West, five games back of Kansas City. One of the weak links of that team had been the bullpen, so Texas placed a priority on adding a couple of relievers in the off-season.

They paid a heavy price, acquiring Kern and infielder Larvell Blanks from Cleveland in exchange for Bobby Bonds and Len Barker, who would win 19 games for Cleveland in 1980 and pitch a perfect game on May 15, 1981. Texas also acquired reliever Sparky Lyle in a 10-player trade with the Yankees that cost the Rangers 1977 first-round draft choice Dave Righetti.

Kern was spectacular in '79, bolstering the Rangers' bullpen in impressive fashion. One year later, Kern and the team took a tumble. Kern battled injuries and struggled with his control in 1980, walking more batters than he struck out and posting a 4.83 ERA. Meanwhile, the Rangers finished fourth in the West, costing manager Pat Corrales his job.

Kern was better in the strike-shortened 1981 season, but he continued to struggle to stay healthy. He was dealt to the Mets after the '81 season in exchange for Doug Flynn and Dan Boitano. Before ever pitching in New York, however, he was sent to the Reds as part of the trade that sent George Foster to the Mets.

Kern was back on top of his game for much of the season, posting a 2.84 ERA for the Reds. But after being dealt to the White Sox in a late-season deal, Kern struggled again. He pitched only one game for Chicago in 1983 and was released after the season. He spent the rest of his career bouncing from the Phillies to the Brewers and finally back to the Indians, where he pitched his last major league game in 1986.

71

The Unforgettable Brad Corbett Ownership Years

Looking back on that era with some 30 years of perspective, former Texas catcher and current team senior executive vice president Jim Sundberg says Brad Corbett—a lightning rod for criticism from fans and media throughout his years as owner of the Rangers (1974–80)—was actually an underappreciated CEO.

"He was a tremendous owner," said Sundberg, whose first stint with the Rangers spanned from 1974 to 1983. "He got a lot of criticism for a lot of things, but I felt like he wasn't deserving of the criticism. He was great for the players, and he did all he could to build a winner."

Al Oliver, a star Texas outfielder from 1978 to 1981, agrees.

"Brad was a great owner, in my opinion," Oliver said. "He treated me and other players with respect. Brad was always looking to improve the team. Always. If he had one fault above all others, it was that he tried too hard. He was always tinkering."

Always wheeling. Always dealing. Always maneuvering. And never allowing a team to jell or for any type of chemistry to truly form.

Those were the trademarks of the Corbett ownership years.

"Brad became a successful businessman by selling one plant here and then buying another one over there," former Rangers general manager Danny O'Brien told *Sports Illustrated's* Kent Hannon in 1978. "It means I have to be, shall we say, very flexible."

Corbett grew up in Queens and worked his way through Wagner College by digging ditches and selling hoagies. He played two seasons of lower minor league ball in North Dakota under an assumed name and dreamed of one day playing in the majors or owning a major league team. He moved to Texas, and in

1968—according to the Rangers' old media guides—parlayed a $300,000 Small Business Administration loan into a plastic-pipe empire.

"I didn't parlay anything," Corbett told *D Magazine's* Tom Stephenson in 1975. "I busted my a—— to get it."

Regardless, Corbett's company, Robintech, was grossing $88 million a year by 1974, when he led a group of Dallas–Fort Worth businessmen who purchased the debt-ridden Rangers from Bob Short, who'd moved the team from Washington to Texas with every intention of selling it. Two days before the start of the 1974 season, Short unloaded the club for $9.5 million and the assumption of more than $1 million in debts to the investors led by Corbett.

Corbett bought his new toy at the onset of free agency. He quickly became known for chasing down fly balls in the outfield during pregame batting practice—often in semibusiness clothes— and chasing after impact players.

"The first time I met Brad Corbett," wrote Gary Cartwright in a 1978 article in *Texas Monthly*, "I thought he was Chuckles the Clown. I thought he ought to trade his three-piece suit for a giant eggplant and try to make it on *Let's Make A Deal*.... He had been off in Florida doing what he loves best—trading players. In his five years as majority stockholder, Corbett has bought, sold, and traded so many players that the Rangers ought to be required to play their home games at Ellis Island.

"Subsidized by Corbett's plastic-pipe empire, the Rangers refuse to abide by the old [ownership rules of baseball]. If they blow a few million on bad deals, Corbett will simply sell some more pipe."

Corbett did his best to bring big-time talent to Texas. In 1977 and '78, for example, he acquired Bert Campaneris, Doyle Alexander, Doc Medich, and Richie Zisk via free agency. At the winter meetings in Hawaii in December 1977, he also master-minded a four-team, 11-player deal that, among other things, brought Oliver and pitcher Jon Matlack to Texas, sent Bert Blyleven to Pittsburgh, and dealt Tom Grieve and Ken Henderson to the Mets.

But when he made transactions, he expected immediate and positive results. Following a 2–1 home loss to Milwaukee in July 1978, Corbett kicked open the clubhouse door and vented: "It's incredible to me that this team—with all its talent—has scored 153 runs less than Kansas City," he shouted erroneously (it was actually

The Bone-Headed 1978 Trade of Dave Righetti

After winning 94 games in 1977 and 87 games in 1978 to finish in second place in the American League West in both years, Rangers owner Brad Corbett was convinced that all Texas needed to win big was a top-notch closer.

Corbett and general manager Eddie Robinson proceeded to make a deal in November 1978 to acquire the Yankees' Sparky Lyle, who'd won the Cy Young Award in 1977 after going 13–5 with 26 saves and had enjoyed a strong season in 1978, going 9–3 with nine saves.

The trade, indeed, helped one team reach the World Series as soon as 1981. Not the Rangers, though. In parts of two seasons with Texas, Lyle was decent, going 8–10 with a 3.84 ERA and 21 saves.

But the young pitcher the Rangers sent to the Yankees as part of that trade, Dave Righetti, was the 1981 Rookie of the Year. He also pitched a no-hitter against the Red Sox on the Fourth of July in 1983, and when he was moved to the bullpen, Righetti saved 31 games in 1984 and 29 in 1985. Then he set a major league record at the time by saving 46 games in 1986, converting 29 of his final 30 save opportunities.

Righetti spent 11 seasons with the Yankees before finishing his career with brief stints with San Francisco, Oakland, the Chicago White Sox, and Toronto. In 16 seasons, he went 82–79 with 252 saves and a 3.46 ERA.

The Rangers also sent outfielder Juan Beniquez, pitcher Mike Griffin, pitcher Paul Mirabella, and outfielder Greg Jemison to the Yankees for Lyle, catcher Mike Heath, pitcher Dave Rajsich, pitcher Larry McCall, and infielder Domingo Ramos.

63 fewer runs). "We're going to have a winner here in Texas—if not this year, then next. It's certainly not because you guys aren't well paid. I'll go broke if I have to. I'll fire till I'm dry."

The quick-tempered Corbett had many emotional outbursts, which sometimes led him to make outlandish comments or to make hasty personnel decisions. Of course, not all the personnel decisions regarding the team were his own. In the spring of '77 Corbett was considering swapping third baseman Toby Harrah for Yankees third baseman Graig Nettles.

One night the phone rang at Corbett's Fort Worth home. On the other end of the line was Yankees general manager Gabe Paul. Thinking he had Brad Sr. on the line, Paul asked if he was ready to pull the trigger on the deal.

"No," said Brad Jr., then 14, who then hung up. That was the end of that.

At least that no-deal worked out for the Rangers. Another one that went down with the Yankees after the '78 season—one that the elder Corbett orchestrated—did not fare well.

According to former beat writer Phil Rogers, the Rangers wanted the Yankees' Sparky Lyle to fill a bullpen void, and the team's scouts coveted Triple A second baseman Damaso Garcia. Corbett put a deal together himself, proudly reporting back to general manager Eddie Robinson that he had gotten everyone the Rangers wanted, including the Hispanic second baseman, Domingo Ramos.

Big mistake. Really big.

While the Rangers certainly fielded some entertaining and competitive teams under Corbett, he began to experience some financial problems away from baseball and with the Rangers— partly because he'd mortgaged the future on free agents and partly because of other bad baseball deals. Early in the 1980 season, he sold his majority stake to Texas oilman Eddie Chiles, ending one memorable ownership era and beginning another.

The Highs and Lows of the Tom Hicks Ownership Years

In May 2009 SportsIllustrated.com ranked the five best and worst owners in the NFL, NBA, NHL, and Major League Baseball. The Rangers were represented prominently, as then-owner Thomas O. Hicks was ranked No. 2 in all of Major League Baseball...on the worst list.

"It's hard to fault Hicks for trying, because he really is," SI.com wrote. "But the stain of signing Alex Rodriguez for $252 million in 2000, then baseball's biggest deal, won't wash away. Then, trading A-Rod to the Yankees for little in return—and agreeing to foot some of the bill—perhaps made it even worse. Beyond that, Hicks made a number of bad signings [Chan Ho Park, Juan Gonzalez, and Rusty Greer for a combined $110 million, for instance] with ridiculously high price tags to match that left Rangers fans scratching their heads. Meanwhile, Texas hasn't made the postseason in nine years and is the only franchise in baseball that hasn't won a playoff series."

To Hicks' critics—and there are many of them—it was appropriate that the Rangers finally shed their "never-won-a-playoff-series" tag the same year (2010) that Hicks filed for Chapter 11 bankruptcy protection and ultimately sold the team to a group led by Chuck Greenberg and Nolan Ryan.

By the end of his ownership tenure with the Rangers (1998–2010), Hicks probably could have alleviated some financial issues by reaching a sponsorship deal with Everlast, the boxing company. He'd certainly become a punching bag for media and fans as they vented over years of Rangers futility and frustration, blaming Hicks for everything from rising ERAs to rising temperatures in Arlington.

In terms of being a lightning rod for criticism, Tom Hicks the Rangers owner had much in common with former Rangers owner George W. Bush as President of the United States.

Hicks obviously deserves his fair share of blame for the Rangers going a decade without making the playoffs and for being downright dismal in many years.

But Hicks doesn't deserve to be Arlington's public enemy No. 1. He essentially did what he vowed to do when he first bought the Rangers from the Bush ownership group in 1998: spend every necessary penny to bring a World Series to town. In his first two years as owner, the Rangers won the American League West, but Texas was swept by the Yankees in the ALDS each year.

"[One of my fondest memories was] the first champagne bath the first year I owned the team [after winning the division]," Hicks told ESPNDallas.com's Richard Durrett in 2010. "That was special. I honestly believed there was a good chance in 1999 that we'd follow up our Stanley Cup [as owner of the Dallas Stars] with a chance to win the World Series. We ran into a buzz saw in the Yankees, and that was probably the best Yankee team in the last 30 years."

To combat that buzz saw, Hicks went for broke, signing A-Rod to a 10-year contract that placed Texas in the national spotlight… for mostly the wrong reasons. Hicks paid as much as $100 million more than other owners had been willing to pay for Rodriguez, dramatically changing the free-agent landscape in one memorable opening of the checkbook.

But equally big mistakes were made by trying to surround Rodriguez with players like Park, an aging Gonzalez, John Rocker, Carl Everett, and so forth.

"I'm convinced that it was Scott Boras who ruined Hicks as an owner," ESPNDallas.com's Jim Reeves wrote. "Tom never recovered from the Alex Rodriguez/Chan Ho Park debacles. Hicks had never had anyone pick his pocket like Boras did, and it hurt. From that point on, as much as Tom gave lip service to winning, it was always about the money."

From this perspective, Hicks' biggest mistakes came in hiring front-office personnel. He fired former general manager Doug Melvin and arranged a disastrous union between John Hart as general manager and Grady Fuson as Hart's assistant. Hart had built the Cleveland Indians into a playoff powerhouse in the 1990s with shrewd and successful moves. In Texas, however, his moves often seemed more scatterbrained than mindful.

After the 2002 season, for example, the Rangers chose not to re-sign catcher Ivan Rodriguez. Instead, Hart chose to trade prospect Travis Hafner for catcher Einar Diaz. Moves like that wrecked the Rangers during Hicks' ownership years.

To his credit, Hicks did hire Jon Daniels to replace Hart as general manager, and he endorsed Daniels' commitment to developing the farm system, rebuilding with youth, drafting, and signing top prospects and sticking to the plan that carried Texas to the 2010 World Series. Hicks also hired Nolan Ryan as president, hired Ron Washington as manager, and made a number of other positive decisions for which he often receives no credit.

Perhaps that's because so many Rangers fans are still having so much fun blaming him for past blunders. It may still be more in vogue to pound the Hicks punching bag than to ever pat him on the back.

The 2004 Fighting Showalters: A Sliver of Hope

In the midst of some extremely bleak times, the 2004 Rangers shone like a beacon in the darkest of nights, giving long-suffering Texas fans at least a momentary lapse from their new millennium misery.

In a span of nine seasons from 2000 to 2008, the Rangers endured eight losing years. With the exception of the 2004 season, in which the Rangers went 89–73 and finished third in the American League West, Texas went 600–696 during those other years.

In '04 the Rangers finally gave up on the expensive Alex Rodriguez experiment, sending the superstar to the New York Yankees and making a commitment to make the most of their youngsters.

So, when manager Buck Showalter, in his second season at the helm of the team, led the '04 Rangers to an 18-game improvement from the previous season, it was newsworthy, locally and nationally.

Texas led the American League West in June and July and finished just three games back of the division-champion Anaheim Angels and two games behind second-place Oakland. Texas was not eliminated from playoff contention until the 158th game of the season.

The Baseball Writers Association of America saluted Showalter's tremendous turnaround efforts by choosing him as the American League Manager of the Year for keeping the Rangers in contention throughout the season. Showalter was first on 14 ballots, second on nine, and third on four for 101 points on the 5-3-1 tabulation system. Minnesota's Ron Gardenhire was second with 91 points. Anaheim's Mike Scioscia (31 points) and the Yankees' Joe Torre (18 points) were third and fourth, respectively.

Rangers second baseman Alfonso Soriano, the most recognizable player acquired in the A-Rod trade with New York, also had a great season in '04. He was the All-Star Game MVP in July, and *The Sporting News* named him to its postseason American League All-Star team. Despite not playing after September 16 because of a left hamstring injury, Soriano was the first Rangers second baseman to be named to the *TSN* team since Julio Franco received the honor in 1991. Soriano hit .280 with 28 home runs and 91 RBIs in 2004.

But the real story of the '04 season was how Showalter molded the youngsters on the Rangers roster—players like shortstop Michael Young, first baseman Mark Teixeira, third baseman Hank Blalock, outfielder David Dellucci, outfielder Laynce Nix, outfielder Kevin Mench, pitcher Ryan Drese, pitcher R.A. Dickey,

2005 Rangers Blast Eight Homers in a Game...Twice

Despite finishing the year with a losing record, the bashing 2005 Rangers led the American League with 260 homers. Two games from that season, in particular, epitomized the explosiveness of the "Power Rangers."

On May 21 David Dellucci led off the interleague game against the Houston Astros with a home run. Mark Teixeira hit a three-run blast to highlight a four-homer second, and the Rangers set a club record with eight blasts in an 18–3 win at Rangers Ballpark in Arlington.

Dellucci added another homer in the third, and Rod Barajas, Hank Blalock, Laynce Nix, Richard Hidalgo, and Kevin Mench also homered in the barrage of bombs.

"Eight-homer games don't happen very often," said Dellucci, who went 3-for-4. "We got a fast start, and they were just coming in bunches."

About a month later, they came in bunches again, as the Rangers matched their club record with eight homers again in an 18–5 home win over the Angels. Mench hit three homers, Teixeira added two, and Alfonso Soriano, Blalock, and Dellucci hit one each on June 30.

Ironically, Chris Young was the Rangers' winning pitcher in both eight-homer, 18-run afternoon games in Arlington.

and pitcher Francisco Cordero—into winners. Soriano, Young, Blalock, Cordero, and 39-year-old veteran starter Kenny Rogers all made the American League All-Star team in '04.

"There's definitely something to build on," Young said immediately after the conclusion of the '04 season. "Right now, we all need some time to recharge our batteries. But we're looking forward to next year because we know we've got a chance to be a better team than we were this year. It's a little disappointing that we didn't get to the playoffs. But this is the most fun I've had playing baseball in the major leagues. This is why I play baseball, to be in situations like I was in this year. When spring training rolls around, we're going to have a great deal of optimism."

Unfortunately, the optimism didn't translate into improved productivity on the field. After going 72–90 in 2002 and 71–91 in '03, the 2004 season was a mere oasis in a wasteland that nearly covered an entire decade. In 2005 Texas went 79–83, followed by an 80–82 record in '06 and a 75–87 record in '07. From 2000 to 2008, the Rangers produced just one winning season, which is why '04 was so memorable for so long.

74 Blown Lead against Brewers Costs 1981 Rangers Shot

In 1981 the executive board of the Major League Baseball Players Association voted unanimously to strike on May 29 due to the unresolved issue of free-agent compensation.

Owners had already lost at the bargaining table and in the courts regarding the free-agency draft, but they hoped for at least some small consolation. They had been demanding compensation for losing a free-agent player to another team.

When they lost a player to free agency, the owners wanted a player who was selected from the signing team's roster (not including 12 "protected" players). But the players maintained that any form of compensation would undermine the value of free agency. As negotiations continued, the players agreed to extend the strike deadline from the end of May to June 12.

That was significant for the Rangers. Texas started the season decently, compiling a 19–16 record on May 20. The following day the Rangers began an exceptional streak, winning five in a row and 14 of the next 19. The red-hot Rangers were 33–21 after beating Milwaukee on June 10, pulling within one game of American League West–leading Oakland.

"It wasn't a great Rangers team in 1981, but they played really well in stretches," former beat writer Jim Reeves recalled. "They had some decent pitching, and they had Fergie Jenkins on the hill [on June 11]."

Playing in Milwaukee, Texas jumped out to a 3–1 lead over the Brewers. If they had maintained that lead, the Rangers would have made the playoffs. But the Brewers rallied for a 6–3 win, giving Texas a 33–22 record when the strike started. Oakland lost on June 10 to drop to 37–23.

Because of scheduling quirks, the A's played five more games than the Rangers. Oakland had a .617 winning percentage and a 1½-game lead on Texas, which had a .600 winning percentage, when the strike started. If Texas had won on June 11, the Rangers would have been 34–21, which would have amounted to a .618 winning percentage. That would have given the Rangers first place by a percentage point when the strike began on June 12.

The strike forced the cancellation of 713 total games in the middle of the regular season. On July 31, a compromise was reached, and baseball resumed on August 9 with the All-Star Game in Cleveland.

Due to the two-month strike, owners tried to create an equitable solution. On August 6 the owners decided to split the 1981 season into two halves, with the first-place teams from each half in each division meeting in a best-of-five divisional playoff series. The four survivors would then move on to the two best-of-five League Championship Series. It was the first time that Major League Baseball had used a split-season format since 1892.

In the American League West, Kansas City won the second half with a 30–23 record. Oakland finished second at 27–22, and the Rangers were third at 24–26. So, the A's met the Royals in the first round of the playoffs despite the fact that the Rangers had a better overall record (57–48) than Kansas City (50–53) for the season.

Oakland swept Kansas City in the first round 3–0 before being swept by the Yankees 3–0 in the league championship series. The Dodgers beat the Yankees 4–2 in the World Series. After the 1981 season, the Rangers would not post another winning record for another five seasons.

Early Rangers Promotions: Milking It for Every Fan

During their first two years in Arlington, the Rangers lost 205 games and typically played the least entertaining brand of baseball in all of the major leagues. As a result, Arlington Stadium on game nights often resembled Mount Rushmore: a few familiar, solemn faces overlooking the uniformed "park Rangers."

Texas often played its early 1970s home games before vast sections of empty rows and seats. The Rangers drew less than 700,000 fans in each of their first two seasons in Texas.

Since team officials couldn't entice locals to Arlington Stadium by giving them high-quality baseball, they tried to attract fans by giving away T-shirts, trinkets, caps, and collectibles. And cheap, low-quality baseball gear for kids. And a bunch of other Rangers-branded rubbish.

Bob Short, the owner of the team when the franchise moved from Washington to Texas, originally envisioned overflowing, standing-room-only crowds in North Texas. Instead, he quickly learned to celebrate those nights when the turnstile count hit 10,000.

His "Short-sighted" solution to the lack of butts in seats: get 'em with giveaways.

"Every night was Something Night at the ballpark," wrote Mike Shropshire in the book *Seasons in Hell*. "Bat Night—they staged about five of those. Ball Night. Cap Night. T-shirt Night. Rangers Keychain Night. Rangers Calendar Night. Yes, and even Rangers Panty Hose (guaranteed to yield fewer runs than the home team) Night."

Bat Night was always particularly entertaining in the old stadium. Eventually, team officials—after answering numerous complaints from parents—provided kids 12 and under with bat coupons that were redeemable at local grocery stores. This literally prevented numerous headaches.

But in the old days, every kid was actually presented with a wooden, Little League–sized bat upon entering Arlington Stadium.

Most of those bats were dinged up before ever making it onto the area's youth diamonds, as thousands of kids typically banged their bats—constantly—against the metal aisles and aluminum seats of the outfield bleachers. The decibel level during a Rangers rally on Bat Night rivaled a flyover of a squadron of fighter jets… during an outdoor, heavy metal rock concert…in the midst of a thunderstorm.

The Rangers also had plenty of memorable promotional nights that didn't involve giveaways. In the early '70s, for example, Short's director of special events, Oscar Molomont, concocted the idea for Hot Pants Night, which involved a contest open to any female who could squeeze into the tiniest, tightest pants in an effort to display the best-looking butt in the stadium on that particular night.

In the '80s, Rangers marketing vice president Larry Schmittou devised Las Vegas Night. A drawing was held, and the winning fan earned a trip to Las Vegas. The stipulation was that he/she had to leave that night, directly from Arlington Stadium.

Perhaps the most entertaining and wholesome promotion of the old Rangers was Farm & Ranch Night, which was always held between games during scheduled doubleheaders. Players from both teams competed against each other—on the playing field—in rural-oriented activities such as egg tossing, cow milking, and hog calling. And back in the 1970s, the players really seemed to enjoy it.

"We loved Farm & Ranch Night," said former Texas outfielder Tom Grieve, who is now the team's television color analyst. "I don't know if you could get the players nowadays to participate anymore, but we looked forward to it. I won the egg-tossing contest one time with [former infielder] Leo Cardenas. I will never forget [former pitcher] Jackie Brown winning the cow-milking contest and [former catcher] Kenny Suarez doing the hog-calling contest. It was a blast. That was one day when the players had as much fun with the promotion as the fans did."

76 The Brew and the Brawl: One Unforgettable 1974 Night

In the ensuing decades since the June 4, 1974, "10-Cent Beer Night" in Cleveland's old cavernous Municipal Stadium on the shores of Lake Erie—also known as "the Mistake by the Lake"—hundreds of major and minor league teams have unveiled thousands of promotions designed to place butts in seats.

Some have been outlandish and off-the-wall. Many have misfired. And a few have been downright dismal.

But few—with the possible exception of the 1979 Disco Demolition Night at Chicago's Comiskey Park—have been more dangerous and ultimately dim-witted than beer for a dime in Cleveland for the Rangers-Indians game. The only restriction initially placed on customers was that they were limited to six cups of beer per trip to the concession stand.

Sixty cents for six eight-ounce cups of beer and absolutely no restrictions on the number of return visits fans could make. Oh, and one other really stupid oversight…nobody thought to contact the Cleveland Police Department about sending a few extra officers to the stadium for crowd control.

If the entire idea wasn't bad enough, Indians officials—as demand increased during the game and concession workers were no longer able to keep kegs full and flowing—allowed fans to line up behind the outfield fences to have their cups filled directly from Stroh's company trucks.

"The promotion achieved critical mass at that moment, as weaving, hooting queues of people refilled via industrial spigot," wrote Chicago-based freelance writer Paul Jackson in a 2008 article for ESPN.com's Page 2.

No wonder things spiraled so completely out of control. The night started with firecrackers being set off in the stands and thrown into the bullpen, featured a midgame array of streakers and drunkards parading onto the field, and ended with the Indians forfeiting after both teams emptied the benches and brandished their bats to help teammates escape the riotous crowds, who'd stormed the field in the ninth inning equipped with parts of stadium seats they had destroyed and were using as weapons.

So, what was the Indians' inspiration for this terrifically bad idea? How did they decide to ensure binge drinking at the ballpark and a demolition of drunks in the parking lots afterward?

Well, research shows that the Indians conceived this ridiculously sorry scheme from...*your Texas Rangers*. If there was any team more desperate for fan support than the Rangers in '74, it was the lowly Indians. Twenty years earlier—on September 12, 1954—86,563 fans piled into Municipal Stadium to see the Indians-Yankees matchup in what was the largest crowd ever to see a baseball game at that time.

By 1974, however, the Indians needed an average of seven home games to attract 86,000 fans to the Mistake by the Lake, as 85 percent of the seats inside the stadium went unsold for home games. On one particularly dismal night in mid-May, only 4,234 fans showed to watch the Indians beat the Red Sox.

So, when the Rangers successfully marketed a 10-Cent Beer Night in Arlington, the Indians front office took notice.

Adding to the intrigue of the Indians' version of drunkenfest was the retaliation factor. In the Rangers' 3–0 win over Cleveland on May 29, 1974, in Arlington, beer cups—some of them full—were tossed onto the Indians when the game was interrupted by a brawl following a major dispute between Indians pitcher Milt Wilcox and Rangers infielder Lenny Randle. Cleveland players complained afterward about the way they were treated by the Texas fans.

That turned out to be nothing more than a schoolyard scuffle compared to what transpired in Cleveland less than a week later as 25,134 people—more than double the average crowd that season—arrived to take advantage of free-flowing suds at dramatically discounted prices.

"Through deliberate coordination or spontaneous groupthink, hundreds of fans showed up with pockets full of firecrackers," wrote Paul Jackson. "Anonymous explosions peppered the stands from the first pitch, lending the game a war-zone ambiance that would seem increasingly appropriate. Though it is not clear whether this impromptu celebration cost anyone a finger or hand, an uneasy *je ne sais quoi* settled into the stadium along with clouds of exploded gunpowder and marijuana smoke.

"The Rangers took the lead in the top of the second inning on a home run by designated hitter Tom Grieve. Just a few pitches later, a heavyset woman sitting near first base jumped the wall, ran to the Indians' on-deck circle, and bared her enormous, unhindered breasts to appreciative applause from the beer-goggled teenagers who made up the stadium's primary demographic that night. She then attempted—unsuccessfully—to kiss umpire crew chief Nestor Chylak, who was not in a kissing mood."

To the inebriated crowd's delight, streaking and exhibitionism continued throughout much of the game, including the naked man who slid into second base in the fourth inning. Aside from the empty gallon of wine tossed at Rangers rookie first baseman Mike Hargrove—it narrowly missed his head—most of the shenanigans, such as the contingent of fans who attempted to remove the padding from the left-field wall, were relatively harmless for the majority of the game, as the Rangers built a 5–3 lead heading into the bottom of the ninth.

The mood of the crowd turned from mischievous to malicious in the bottom of the ninth after the Indians tied the score at 5–5 and had the potential winning run, Rusty Torres, at second.

Be Careful in Pursuit of Foul Balls

According to the Rawlings website, one dozen official major league baseballs could be purchased in the summer of 2011 for $191.99, which amounts to about $16 per ball. Keep that in mind if you're ever tempted to lunge, lean, or leap in an effort to catch a foul ball or home run at Rangers Ballpark in Arlington. The ball simply isn't worth the risk.

In the summer of 2010 and again in 2011, fans fell over the railings at the ballpark in efforts to catch baseballs. Tyler Morris, a firefighter from Lake Cities Fire Department near Dallas, fell 30 feet from the club level to the lower seating bowl during a game on July 6, 2010. Morris, who was sitting in the front row of Section 235, was reaching for a foul ball that had sailed over his head and caromed back toward the field. He survived the fall.

Shannon Stone, a 39-year-old firefighter from Brownwood, was not so fortunate. With his six-year-old son, Cooper, at his side above the scoreboard along the left-field wall, Stone reached out to catch a ball tossed toward him by Rangers outfielder Josh Hamilton on July 7, 2011. Stone had requested the ball from Hamilton and reached too far for it, tumbling over a railing. He fell 20 feet head first onto concrete below. He survived the fall long enough to ask about his son. Moments later, Stone suffered a fatal heart attack.

After Stone's death, the Rangers announced plans to raise the height of railings on the first row of every level to 42". Previously, the rails measured 30 inches high on the club level. The left-field–area rails measured 34", and the upper home run porch in right field was already at 42". All of those heights were already above building code requirements, but the Rangers felt the need to do everything possible to prevent another fall.

In August 2011 the Rangers also announced they would recognize Stone by erecting a full-sized bronze sculpture depicting the late Rangers fan. Hamilton said he also altered how he handles flipping balls in the stands. He still does it, but he won't throw them in high places or to fans near railings.

In an extremely emotional moment on September 30, 2011— prior to the opening game of the ALDS against Tampa Bay—Cooper Stone and his mother, Jenny, returned to the Ballpark where Cooper

threw the ceremonial first pitch to Hamilton. There weren't many dry
eyes in the stadium when Hamilton hugged Cooper and his mom.

"We want to once again thank Nolan Ryan and the Texas
Rangers," Jenny Stone said in a statement. "They have turned a
difficult return to The Ballpark into a once-in-a-lifetime experience for
Cooper. Nothing could be more exciting for a boy than throwing out
the first pitch to his favorite player. We are glad and grateful to be
here to see the Rangers start their march to the World Series."

On April 11, 1994, at the Rangers' first official game at their new
ballpark, 26-year-old Hollye Minter was posing for a photo on the
upper-deck railing in right field after the game when she fell about
35 feet. Minter, who suffered a broken arm, two broken ribs, and
fractures to bones in her neck, sued the Rangers, the city of Arlington,
a Dallas architectural firm, and a Washington, D.C., architect for
$200,000 after the incident.

But keep in mind that such incidents are not merely a problem at
Rangers Ballpark in Arlington. For example:

- On September 17, 2003, a fan fell to his death from the
right-field wall while attending a Giants game at Pac Bell
Park in San Francisco.
- On June, 26, 2009, a man fell out of the upper deck during a
Cardinals-Twins game at Busch Stadium in St. Louis.
- On May 24, 2011, a 27-year-old man died three days after
falling about 20 feet and striking his head on concrete during
the seventh inning of a Rockies game at Coors Field in
Denver.

At that moment, yet another fan leapt onto the field—again, it
might have been nice to have a uniformed cop or two protecting
the field—and flipped off the cap of Rangers outfielder and 1974
American League MVP Jeff Burroughs, who'd already had several
fans run up to him in an attempt to shake his hand the previous
inning. Stunned, Burroughs quickly turned to confront the fan and
stumbled.

From his sunken perspective in the dugout, the not-so-mild-
mannered manager of the Rangers, Billy Martin, couldn't tell

whether Burroughs had gone to the ground under attack or simply as a result of tripping. But Martin—being Billy Martin—followed his instincts. He grabbed a fungo bat and led his reserves, ala Mel Gibson in the movie *Braveheart*, sprinting toward combat in right-center field.

When they reached Burroughs, the Rangers' rescue troops found him unharmed. But the battle charge had transformed the drunken fans into combative warriors as well. Texas players and coaches quickly found themselves surrounded by as many as 200 beer-guzzlers-gone-bad. Martin later said he noticed that many within the mob had chains, knives, and clubs fashioned from pieces of stadium seats.

Indians manager Ken Aspromonte quickly assessed the situation from his dugout and determined that Martin looked as stunned and hopeless as George Custer must have been at the Battle of the Little Bighorn. With Indians fans playing the part of Crazy Horse, Sitting Bull, and so forth, Aspromonte ordered his players to storm the field in an attempt to rescue the Rangers.

Several hand-to-hand combats ensued between players and fans, but the combined forces of the Indians and Rangers with their bats eventually forced the fans to retreat beyond the battle lines and foul lines and back into the stands. Given an opening, both teams escaped into the safety of their clubhouses and locked the doors.

Chylak, the crew chief who'd rejected the kiss of a big-bosomed flasher earlier in the game, finally awarded the Rangers a forfeit victory when a hunting knife landed in the grass behind his leg.

"Fu—— animals," Chylak said after the field was cleared by late-arriving Cleveland police officers. "You just can't pull back a pack of animals. When uncontrolled beasts are out there, you gotta do something. I saw two guys with knives, and I got hit with a chair."

In the end, Cleveland relief pitcher Tom Hilgendorf was also hit in the head with a folding chair, nine fans were arrested, and the Indians' front office announced that for the three future 10-Cent

Beer Nights that had already been planned, fans would be limited to four cups apiece per night. No exceptions. American League president Lee MacPhail took exception to that and took things a step further, announcing that all promotional events were canceled, pending league review.

As for the rest of the story, Hargrove, who was involved in one fistfight during the melee, returned to Cleveland as a player in 1979 and served as the Indians' manager from 1991 to 1999. He led the Indians to the World Series in '95 and again in '97, and throughout his time as the skipper in Cleveland he kept a picture from 10-Cent Beer Night on the wall of his office.

77 The Memorable Mick "the Quick" Rivers

After spending the first 10 years of his major league career on the West Coast with the California Angels and then on the East Coast with the New York Yankees, John Milton "Mickey" Rivers landed in the perfect place to finish his career: Texas.

When the Rangers traded for Rivers in 1979, they desperately needed a center fielder who could cover plenty of ground. Rivers fit that description.

Meanwhile, Rivers desperately needed a place to call home that didn't feature pari-mutuel betting. Texas in the late 1970s and early '80s fit that.

For the most part, Rivers and the Rangers worked out well for each other for the last five and one-half years of his memorable career.

Practically everything that Rivers did on the baseball diamond throughout his career—from his painfully slow walk to the plate prior to at-bats to his off-the-wall quotes after games—was extraordinary. Unfortunately for Rivers, his trips to the race tracks were also unforgettable for all the wrong reasons.

In his prime, Rivers, who stole 70 bases for the Angels in 1975, could run like a horse. His weakness was betting on them.

During his first three years with the Yankees (1976–78), Rivers played a huge role in leading New York to three consecutive World Series appearances, including championships in '77 and '78. As the Yankees' leadoff man, he hit .312 in '76 and .326 in '77, finishing third in the American League MVP balloting behind Thurman Munson and George Brett in his first year in the Bronx.

But Rivers couldn't stay away from the race tracks. To cover his gambling debts, Rivers frequently asked Yankees management for pay advances. When the Yankees refused, Rivers often pouted. Or failed to hustle. Or threatened not to even play.

"We had to trade him; we had to get him out of the New York environment," former Yankees owner George Steinbrenner told *Sports Illustrated's* Henry Hecht in 1980. "He's just a sweet, sweet kid, but…."

With the Rangers in third place (4½ games out in the American League West) on August 1, 1979, Texas sent Oscar Gamble and Amos Lewis and two players to be named later (future major leaguers Ray Fontenot and Gene Nelson) to the Yankees for Rivers and minor leaguers Bob Polinsky, Neal Mersch, and Mark Softy.

While none of the other players Texas received ever made it to the major league level, Rivers thrived in Arlington, hitting .300 in 58 games to close out the 1979 season and hitting a team-best .333 in 1980 when the Rangers featured four .300 hitters (Rivers, Buddy Bell, Al Oliver, and Rusty Staub) and finished second in the American League with a .284 team batting average. Rivers' 165 singles in 1980 is still a club record.

Rivers, who was born in Miami, even seemed to prosper in the Texas heat.

The Mendoza Line's Ties to Texas

While there are varying accounts regarding the precise origins of the now well-known baseball term "the Mendoza Line," it most likely was conceived in the Seattle Mariners clubhouse in 1980.

The Mendoza Line references a .200 batting average and essentially separates poor hitting from the truly atrocious averages. When a regular hitter in the lineup falls below a .200 batting average—sinking under the Mendoza Line into the realm of the buck-something batting average—he is often considered to be well on his way back to the minors or out of baseball altogether.

The namesake for the term is Mario Mendoza, a slick-fielding middle infielder from Chihuahua, Mexico, who began his major league career with the Pirates in 1974. In five seasons in Pittsburgh, Mendoza hit .204 before being traded to the Mariners. Mendoza hit .198 in 148 games with Seattle in 1979 and a career-best .245 in 1980.

According to a 2010 interview with Dave Seminara of the *St. Louis Post-Dispatch*, Mendoza says his place in history was the result of two Seattle teammates, Tom Paciorek and Bruce Bochte.

"[Paciorek and Bochte] were giving George Brett a hard time [in 1980] because he had a slow start that year, so they told him, 'Hey, man, you're going to sink down below the Mendoza Line if you're not careful,'" Mendoza said. "And then Brett mentioned it to Chris Berman from ESPN, and eventually it spread and became a part of the game."

Berman deflected credit back to Brett, telling Seminara: "Mario Mendoza—it's all George Brett. We used it all the time in those 1980s *SportsCenters*. It was just a humorous way to describe how someone was hitting."

The Rangers connection comes into play after that 1980 season. Mendoza was traded to the Rangers, along with Rick Honeycutt, Willie Horton, Larry Cox, and Leon Roberts for Richie Zisk, Jerry Don Gleaton, Ken Clay, Rick Auerbach, Brian Allard, and Steve Finch on December 12, 1980.

In his first season with the Rangers, Mendoza hit .231 in 88 games. The following year, however, he fell well below the Mendoza Line, batting .118 in 12 games. He finished his nine-year career with a .215 batting average.

"I was brought up in Florida, so there isn't much difference between playing there and playing here [in Texas]," he said shortly after the trade from New York. "The climax are about the same."

Yes, he said "climax." He had an unforgettable way with words that New York media loved, prompting them to compare him to Yogi Berra. In the Big Apple, Rivers had plenty of Yogi-like head scratchers, such as: "Me and George [Steinbrenner] and Billy [Martin] are two of a kind."

But he also was not afraid to stir the pot in the clubhouse in New York, especially in regards to Reggie Jackson. When Jackson said he had an IQ of 160, Rivers responded: "Out of what, a thousand?"

And in July 1977 Rivers made this comment about Jackson's full name, which is Reginald Martinez Jackson: "No wonder you're all mixed up. You got a white man's first name, a Spanish man's second name, and a black man's third name."

Rivers continued to produce memorable quotes in Texas, such as this one in 1984: "We'll do all right if we can capitalize on our mistakes."

His production began to fade in 1981, and injuries reduced his playing time dramatically in '82. He finished his major league career with solid seasons in 1983 and '84, although injuries hampered him in those seasons as well. Prior to the 1985 season, the Rangers released Rivers, and he did not play in the majors again.

78 Bert Blyleven's Brief but Rather Brilliant Tenure in Texas

In 2011 Bert Blyleven finally was inducted into the Baseball Hall of Fame, an honor that was probably long overdue for the right-hander with a magnificent curveball and a memorable personality. With his inclusion into baseball's most exclusive club, the free-spirited Blyleven became the fifth Hall of Famer to have played with the Rangers.

All five of them—Blyleven, Gaylord Perry, Ferguson Jenkins, Nolan Ryan, and Rich Gossage—are former pitchers who played short stints of their terrific careers with Texas. From a Rangers perspective, the short length of Blyleven's time with Texas is the most baffling among the Hall of Fame fivesome. It's also probably the most disappointing.

For the most part, Ryan, Gossage, Perry, and Jenkins played the majority of their time with the Rangers in the latter stages of their careers. Not so with Blyleven. He arrived in Arlington in his prime. The 25-year-old was extremely happy about coming to Texas from Minnesota, where he'd felt underpaid and underappreciated. He pitched exceptionally well for the Rangers and registered the franchise's second no-hitter in September 1977.

He could have been the anchor of the Rangers' staff for many years, as he played 14 more seasons following 1977. But inexplicably, the Rangers dealt Blyleven at the winter meetings in December 1977. Blyleven went on to help Pittsburgh get to the 1979 World Series title and helped lead Minnesota to the '87 world championship. What could have been....

"[Blyleven] was a pitcher you loved to have on your team," Tom Grieve told T.R. Sullivan of MLB.com. "He would pitch nine

Jon Matlack: Not the "Met" Results the Rangers Had Hoped For

During much of the early and mid-1970s, Jon Matlack was an outstanding pitcher on some terrific New York Mets staffs that also featured Tom Seaver and Jerry Koosman. He was the 1972 Rookie of the Year, pitched one of the finest postseason games in Mets history in the 1973 NLCS, and was the winning pitcher and co-MVP in the 1975 All-Star Game.

When he was traded to the Rangers in December 1977 in a four-team exchange that involved Texas, Atlanta, Pittsburgh, and the Mets, the Rangers had high hopes that Matlack would enjoy similarly stellar results.

He did. Unfortunately for Texas, though, it was for only one season.

Matlack was terrific for Texas in his debut season in Arlington, going 15–13 with 18 complete games and 270 innings pitched. His 2.78 ERA in 1978 ranked second among American League starters behind only the Yankees' Ron Guidry.

But he had elbow surgery in 1979, when he went 5–4 with a 4.13 ERA in 13 starts. He was never quite the same afterward.

After the 1981 strike, in which he served on the negotiating committee and as the Rangers' player rep, his pitching role changed. In 1982 he was used as a starter and a reliever, while he was mostly used out of the bullpen in 1983.

Later, he says, some speculated that there were hard feelings from ownership about his role in the 1981 strike. He was released by the Rangers following the 1983 season with a career record of 125–126 (82–81 for the Mets, 43–45 with the Rangers) and three All-Star appearances.

"I had a lot of fun for a while with a lot of good people and thoroughly enjoyed it," Matlack told *New York Newsday* in 2008. "Could it have been different, better? There's every possibility, but I was very pleased to take part in it."

Matlack, who was 33 when he retired from baseball, initially tried commercial real estate and raising horses in Texas. But by 1988, he was back in baseball, hired as a pitching coach for the Padres' rookie league team. In 2011 Matlack was the minor league pitching coordinator for the Detroit Tigers, and he was hired by the Astros after the season.

innings with dominating stuff, a No. 1 starter and a great guy. As a teammate he was the ultimate guy to have on the team."

Blyleven, who was known as a clubhouse prankster, became part of the Rangers' team after spending the first six and a half years (1970–76) with the Twins. He wanted out of Minnesota and had requested a trade in December 1975. When that didn't happen, he talked openly about becoming a free agent following the '76 season. Before that happened, the Twins and Rangers reached a deal.

Texas owner Brad Corbett worked out a four-year, $700,000 contract with Blyleven, and the Rangers acquired him and infielder Danny Thompson on June 1, 1976, for infielders Mike Cubbage and Roy Smalley, pitchers Jim Gideon and Bill Singer, and $250,000 in cash. Blyleven was ecstatic about the change of scenery.

"Mr. Corbett gave me the security and the salary I thought I deserved," Blyleven said at the time. "It was quite a change."

Blyleven went only 9–11 in 24 starts with Texas in the second half of '76. But he compiled a 2.76 ERA and tossed six shutouts, which is tied for the most in club history. In 1977 he went 14–12 with a 2.72 ERA in 30 starts, even though he missed much of September because of a groin injury.

Blyleven was attempting to return from that injury after two weeks off when he took the mound on September 22, 1977, at Anaheim Stadium. Against the Angels, he walked one, struck out seven, and didn't allow a hit, becoming the second Ranger to throw a no-hitter.

"In the eighth inning, he tweaked that groin but stayed in the game," catcher Jim Sundberg recalled. "He finished the no-hitter and didn't pitch again the rest of the season. He was traded after that. He went from being hurt, to pitching a no-hitter, to being hurt again, to being traded."

The 1977 Rangers won 94 games, but Corbett believed his team needed more offense. At the ensuing winter meetings in

Honolulu, Blyleven was part of a four-team trade that involved the Rangers, Pirates, Braves, and Mets. Among other moves, Blyleven landed in Pittsburgh, while the Rangers acquired pitcher Jon Matlack from the Mets and outfielder Al Oliver and infielder Nelson Norman from the Pirates.

79 Roger Moret and the Most Bizarre Clubhouse Scene

During the 1976 winter meetings, Texas parted ways with slugging outfielder Jeff Burroughs, who'd been drafted with the first overall pick in 1969 by the Senators and won the 1974 American League MVP in Texas but had complained to anyone who'd listen about how much he hated playing in the swirling Arlington Stadium winds.

The Rangers sent Burroughs to Atlanta in exchange for Adrian Devine, Carl Morton, Ken Henderson, Dave May, Roger Moret, and $250,000 in cash. Morton was the 1970 National League Rookie of the Year and had three 15-plus win seasons in Atlanta. Devine, a native Texan born in Galveston, was another key pitching acquisition, as he would go 11–6 with a 3.58 ERA in '77 for Texas. May was a promising offensive piece of the trade, as he was an All-Star with Milwaukee in 1973.

Moret, a slender left-handed pitcher, was essentially the throw-in of the deal, but for reasons other than baseball, he may have left the most lasting impression on the clubhouse in team history.

"It was one of the most bizarre things I'd ever seen in a baseball clubhouse," recalled former Rangers beat writer and *Fort Worth Star-Telegram* columnist Jim Reeves. "I forever have the image in my mind of Roger in a catatonic trance holding his shower shoe [out in front of him]. A lot of strange things had already happened to the Rangers since moving to Arlington, but that event may have taken the cake in a category all its own."

Although he struggled in his one season with the Braves (1976), the Puerto Rican–born Moret enjoyed two stellar years in Boston, sandwiched around a mediocre one. Overall, he went 41–18 with the Red Sox from 1973 to 1975, leading the American League in winning percentage in two seasons.

He fell out of favor in Boston because he'd been involved in an automobile accident in the wee hours of the morning on a day he was scheduled to pitch in 1975. He also did not pitch particularly well in the 1975 World Series, as Boston was beaten by Cincinnati. As a Rangers trivia note, Moret was traded by the Red Sox to Atlanta on December 12, 1975, for future Texas pitching coach Tom House.

For the Rangers in 1977, Moret was solid, going 3–3 with a 3.73 ERA in 18 games, eight of them as a starter. His season was ended prematurely due to surgery to repair circulation problems in his pitching arm. But he was part of the Rangers' overall pitching plans when he showed up at training camp in 1978. That's also when Reeves first noticed Moret acting strangely.

"He'd come to me and said that he wanted to go home, home to Puerto Rico," Reeves said. "I told him to talk to [general manager] Eddie Robinson. It was also in that spring training that he had slapped or hit another pitcher on the roster. Maybe I should have suspected something then."

Nobody could have anticipated what happened on April 12, 1978, though. With an especially large media contingent at the ballpark to cover Detroit pitcher Mark "the Bird" Fydrich's matchup against Texas' Jon Matlack, Reeves arrived early in the Rangers' clubhouse to gather pregame notes. He immediately noticed something was amiss.

"Everybody was tiptoeing around the clubhouse, looking funny," Reeves said. "Finally, someone pointed to Moret, who

"Roger Reference" in *Fever Pitch* Is All Wrong

It's not unusual for Hollywood producers and directors to use artistic/poetic license in movies based on true stories. Sometimes, distortions of facts are necessary to expedite real-life stories in an effort to keep movies as brief as possible.

Other times, Hollywood just seems to stretch the truth for the heck of it. That seemed to be the case in the 2005 movie *Fever Pitch*. Directors Peter Farrelly and Bobby Farrelly really reached in the romantic comedy that is set in Boston and centered around one fan's lifelong love affair with the Red Sox and his attempt to have a relationship with a woman who cares nothing about baseball.

The 20th Century Fox movie, which stars Drew Barrymore and Jimmy Fallon, features actual footage of the Red Sox's historic 2004 season in which Boston won the World Series for the first time in 86 years. It also features some action shots of the Rangers at Fenway Park.

But it includes at least one major factual blunder that a true Rangers fan will likely notice.

During one scene at Fenway Park, Lindsey (played by Barrymore) brings several Red Sox–related books to the ballpark and shows them to Ben (played by Fallon). She is doing her best to learn about Ben's world and his fascination with the Sox. But she mispronounces Carl Yastrzemski's name and makes light of the "Curse of the Bambino."

Immediately, Ben and the season-ticket holders around him begin citing painful examples of how the curse has caused the Red Sox to often lose in excruciating form. They mention Bucky Dent, Bill Buckner, and several other specific players. They also mention Roger Moret, who pitched with the Red Sox from 1973 to 1975, leading the American League in winning percentage in two seasons. But the reference to Moret is all wrong.

While discussing the Curse of the Bambino, one fan says to the group: "Remember the time Roger Moret went catatonic? The grounds crew had to carry him out in a wheelbarrow."

Not true. Not even close.

Moret went catatonic in Arlington. As a member of the Rangers. In 1978, after he had spent a season with Atlanta and then with Texas. And they wheeled him out of the stadium in an ambulance.

was standing in front of his locker. He was frozen—like a statue—holding his shower shoe. It was so spooky that none of the players wanted to be in the clubhouse. Even Matlack went into the dugout to watch batting practice because he didn't want to stay in there. The Rangers called for the team doctor, and he kept giving Moret injections of tranquilizers.

"Later, we found out they gave him enough to bring down a horse, but they could not get him out of this catatonic trance."

At one point, Rangers infielder Toby Harrah had stood within inches of Moret's face, trying to make him move and pull him out of the trance. As Harrah finally backed away, Moret took two or three hops forward until the shower shoe almost poked Harrah in the face, but he did not come out of the trance.

When the game started, most of the media left the clubhouse for the press box, but Reeves stayed behind, slipping into the equipment manager's office to continue his watch. When Moret finally came out of the trance—some five hours after he'd slipped into it at 4:00 PM—he slapped Eddie Robinson in the face.

"Finally, they backed an ambulance up to the door to take him to a psychiatric hospital," Reeves said. "They weren't sure how Moret would respond to being taken to the hospital. [Owner] Brad Corbett and Robinson got into the ambulance and covered up the side windows of the ambulance with their suit coats. I walked around and looked through the windshield in the front of the ambulance to see him get loaded up. Moret was calm, and he went on to the [Arlington Neuropsychiatric Center]. It was crazy."

No official diagnosis was released, but Moret returned to the Rangers for several appearances in late May and the first half of June. In his last appearance in the majors (June 16, 1978), Moret started against the Blue Jays and lasted 1⅔ innings, giving up six hits and four earned runs.

He made a couple of other comeback attempts and was invited to spring training in 1979 with the Rangers and in 1980 with

Cleveland but never again pitched in the majors. In 1981–82 Moret played in the Mexican League. According to several sources, he now lives in Guayama, Puerto Rico, his birthplace.

80 The Claw and Antler Craze of 2010

In addition to all they accomplished in the postseason, the 2010 Rangers were probably the most cohesive, fun-loving, and harmonious group—at least to that point—ever assembled in Arlington.

The team bonded early and exhibited tremendous chemistry. Whether you watched them once or 162 times, it was obvious that the 2010 Rangers liked each other and truly loved playing together.

"We had a very unique team chemistry," former pitcher Tommy Hunter said. "You can't fake that. I've been on a lot of teams at different levels, but that [2010] team had so much fun playing together and rooting for each other. I could give you so many examples of how much fun we had together."

Perhaps the best involves the claw and antler hand signals that began at spring training and became galvanizing symbols of the Rangers' unity and frivolity.

"It's one small thing that we do that kind of builds some camaraderie," then–third baseman Michael Young said during the 2010 season, as reported by Stephen Hawkins of the Associated Press. "It started early, and we've been doing it ever since."

The "claw" hand signal was introduced by utility infielder Esteban German at spring training in 2009. German said players in the Dominican Winter League used the claw—fingers slightly curled with an arm extended in a rising swoop—as kind of a long-distance high-five between players in the dugout and those who had done something positive on the field.

But it didn't catch on in '09. Perhaps that Rangers team didn't have enough camaraderie. It also didn't produce enough wins (the '09 Rangers went 87–75 but finished 10 games out of first place) to completely captivate the community.

In 2010, however, everything came together in a perfect storm. After a somewhat slow start (Texas was 11–12 in April), the Rangers caught fire in June. So did the claw hand signal, which German had re-introduced in Surprise, Arizona, in spring training.

Manager Ron Washington said he first started to notice the claw early in the regular season when Vladimir Guerrero and Elvis Andrus were particularly hot and kept flashing the sign. It was most popular among the Latin players early in the season, but then Hamilton started doing it. And Young. And virtually everyone else.

While the claw symbolized a good play or a base hit, the antlers emerged a little later in the season. Hamilton and Cruz had often talked in previous years about running like a deer when going from first to third, beating out an infield hit, or hustling to make something happen in the field or on the base paths. Hamilton even hung a 10-point buck, which he had shot with a bow and arrow, above his locker (and next to Cruz's) in the Rangers clubhouse.

At some point during the season—there are several versions of the origins of the antlers hand sign, performed by holding both hands open above the ears to imitate a deer—players began using both the claw and antlers in salutes to each other.

But the phenomenon didn't truly take on a life of its own until Rangers equipment manager Richard "Hoggy" Price asked Cruz and Guerrero for permission to make claw/antler T-shirts for the entire team. Price then took some Nike shirts to an Arlington firm, Visual Impact, whose in-house artist, William Early, created the renowned designs. Visual Impact initially screened 60 T-shirts, to be used under the jerseys, for team members.

Rangers Fans Clamor for Claw and Antler Gear

The final pitch of the 2010 World Series had been thrown by San Francisco reliever Brian Wilson long ago. Nelson Cruz had swung and missed, ending Game 5 and kick-starting a triumphant celebration by the Giants' players, coaches, and family members on the field of Rangers Ballpark in Arlington.

Interviews followed. Then trophy presentations. And more interviews.

But even after the loss, many dejected Rangers fans did not merely shuffle silently into the parking lots. They stayed in their seats for a while and chanted: "Let's go Rangers." Then they made their way into the concourses and stood in line at the memorabilia shops for more World Series merchandise.

"Usually people go home [after their team loses]. They're bummed," Howard Smith, Major League Baseball's senior vice president for licensing, told Barry Shlachter of the *Fort Worth Star-Telegram*. "[But after Game 5], fans were 20, 30 deep in line buying shirts. I've never before seen anything like this. Unbelievable."

It was just the final snapshot of the unbelievable T-shirt phenomenon of 2010. The Rangers sold plenty of Josh Hamilton, Michael Young, Ian Kinsler, Cliff Lee, C.J. Wilson, and other replica jersey T-shirts in 2010, but the one wardrobe item that many fans deemed as "must-have" featured a sketched "hand" on the front and a deer's head with two more human hands above the deer on the back.

The sketches on the T-shirt represented the "claw" and "antlers" hand signals that unified the Rangers and their fans throughout the 2010 regular season and postseason. By early November 2010, more than 360,000 claw and antler T-shirts had been sold.

"It was the biggest-selling T-shirt the entire year for Major League Baseball," Smith said following the World Series. "We've never done anything like that."

In fact, the Rangers moved more logo gear than the Giants, even though they lost the World Series.

"Sales [in October 2010] eclipsed [the 2009 World Series between] Yankees and Phillies," Smith added.

The claw and antler T-shirt continued to be a hot-selling item throughout Christmas 2010 and into the 2011 season.

After the team was presented with its undershirts, Emily Jones of FOX Sports did a TV spot about the players' new shirts during a game, creating a buzz that translated into more media coverage and demand from fans.

The entrepreneurial Price secured rights to the shirt and negotiated a deal with the ballclub. But it took several weeks to receive approval from Major League Baseball to produce and sell the claw/antler shirts.

The first order, placed in August, was for 1,800. When retail preorders reached 1,200, the organization knew it had a winner. And as it became more obvious that the Rangers were destined to win the American League West, everybody who entered Rangers Ballpark at Arlington seemed to be inflicted with claw and antler fever.

Chuck Morgan and his video staff introduced the "Deer Cam," which showed fans giving the sign before the eighth inning, the "Claw Cam" before the bottom of the eighth, and deer montages on the video screens. Fans began attaching antlers to brooms and helmets, and a parade around the field was organized.

The dot race acknowledged the craze when one of the dots sported a pair of horns. Facebook pages, such as "The Claw and Antler Nation" and the "Claw and Antlers Republic," received thousands of Likes. Even a song was made, titled, "Do the Claw."

Virtually every player joined the act, as well. Bengie Molina flashed the antlers after a couple of extra-base hits. Pitcher C.J. Wilson sported the antlers after a spectacular defensive play against the Yankees, where Wilson fielded a high chopper on the run and dove into first base to barely beat Derek Jeter, who had to hurdle over Wilson to avoid stepping on him.

"There is nothing like it when something like this happens naturally," former Rangers CEO Chuck Greenberg told William Wilkerson of the *Dallas Morning News*. "The fact that this came from the players, the fans adopted it, and it wasn't a bunch of marketing people sitting around coming up with the idea…makes it the best thing going. It's a true grassroots idea. It's as pure as can be."

The following year, which produced even better regular-season and postseason records, the claw and antler craze fizzled. Some Rangers players started the year by performing the gestures, but it didn't continue. Instead, the Rangers began using another hand gesture—eventually identified as a "ducks on a pond." But because the players didn't really elaborate on its origins or its meaning, most of the fans viewed it more as a "lame duck."

81 Jose Canseco: Big Name, Big Gaffes along the Way

In a news conference prior to his first game as a Ranger in September 1992, 28-year-old media magnet Jose Canseco stood on baseball's biggest stage—Yankee Stadium—before a multitude of reporters and made a bold prediction about the long-term impact of the trade that delivered him from first-place Oakland to fourth-place Texas.

"[The trade represents] a shift in power," Canseco said prior to a game between the Rangers and Yankees. "Texas is a team of the future. In my opinion, Oakland is definitely going to cut back. They're just going to field a team next year, not be a serious contender."

In hindsight, Canseco was at least partially correct. The A's held on to win the American League West in '92, their fourth division title in five years. But the franchise that won the World Series in 1989 and made it to three straight Fall Classics from 1988 to 1990, took a tremendous tumble in 1993—just as Canseco predicted—falling to dead last in the American League West.

Unfortunately for Rangers fans, the second half of Canseco's prognostication did not go completely as planned. While Texas did improve to second place in the 1993 American League West standings, it didn't have much to do with anything Canseco brought to the ballclub that year.

And despite a productive, strike-ended 1994 season, Canseco's tenure in Texas will forever be remembered less for the handful of highlight-reel homers he produced, especially in 1994, and more for the embarrassing bloopers he produced with the team and the incriminating steroid accusations he detailed in tell-all tweets and scandalous books after his playing career ended.

Meanwhile, the Rangers didn't actually become a "team of the future"—winning three division titles in four years—until they had made the high-profile Canseco part of their past. Nevertheless, the trade that brought him to Texas, along with the blunders and bombs he generated, did thrust the Rangers into the national spotlight.

The trade, orchestrated by Texas general manager Tom Grieve and Oakland counterpart Sandy Alderson, was a head-turner for many reasons, beginning with the fact that it happened two hours before the midnight eastern trading deadline on August 31, 1992. It had to be done before midnight or the players the A's acquired from the Rangers—All-Star outfielder Ruben Sierra, starting pitcher Bobby Witt, and reliever Jeff Russell—would not have been eligible for the postseason roster.

Canseco had to be called back from the on-deck circle by manager Tony La Russa, who notified the star slugger of the trade. Witt and Russell were pulled from the Rangers' bench to be notified in the clubhouse in Kansas City. Sierra was informed at home, where he was recovering from the chicken pox.

On the surface, the Rangers appeared to give up a boatload to land Canseco, who still had three years left on his contract. But the reality was that all three Rangers were eligible for free agency at the end of the year, and Sierra had already rejected a five-year, $25 million extension from Texas because he wanted a contract equal to the one Bobby Bonilla had signed with the Mets. Just as Canseco had predicted, the A's, who were only interested in making one more serious postseason push with their current roster, weren't concerned with signing long-term deals with free agents.

"Sandy wanted to improve his pitching, particularly his bullpen behind Dennis Eckersley, with the playoffs in mind," Grieve told Jamey Newberg of NewbergReport.com. "He didn't bring Canseco's name up until talks got serious. But I always felt that, even if just in the back of his mind, moving Canseco was what he wanted to do all along."

All the players involved cleared waivers, and the deal was completed. Sierra, Witt, and Russell helped the A's reach the postseason, where Oakland lost to Toronto in the ALCS, despite the fact that Sierra hit .333 and led the A's with seven RBIs in six postseason games.

Canseco didn't do much for Texas to close the '92 season, but he made major headlines in the spring of '93. On May 26 in Cleveland, Canseco drifted under a deep fly ball in right field hit by the Indians' Carlos Martinez. But he lost sight of the ball, which hit him on top of the head and bounced over the fence for a home run.

"I was trying to give him the benefit of the doubt," said then-Rangers center fielder David Hulse, who raced over to Canseco, "and I said, 'Jose, did that hit you on the head?' And he goes, 'No, it deflected off my glove.' I fell out right then and just started laughing."

The play was later named the greatest blooper in the history of *This Week in Baseball* and is still a YouTube favorite. Three days later, however, nobody with the Rangers was laughing when Canseco convinced manager Kevin Kennedy to allow him to pitch in a lopsided losing effort in Boston. Canseco blew out his arm that afternoon, requiring Tommy John surgery that ended his season.

On May 26, 1993, Rangers right fielder Jose Canseco lost sight of a deep fly ball off the bat of Cleveland's Carlos Martinez. The ball bounced off of Canseco's head, then over the fence for a home run. (Ron Kuntz Collection/Diamond Images/ Getty Images)

Canseco redeemed himself in 1994 when he helped open The Ballpark in Arlington with a 31-homer, 90-RBI season in just 111 games in the strike-shortened season, landing American League Comeback Player of the Year honors. His 480' homer that season ranked as the ballpark's longest until 2010, when Josh Hamilton launched a 490' blast against Houston. Canseco also helped the Rangers draw more than 2.5 million fans in '94, third-most among American League teams.

The following off-season, however, new Rangers general manager Doug Melvin made his first trade, sending Canseco to Boston for center fielder Otis Nixon and third-base prospect Luis Ortiz, ending the Canseco era in Arlington.

82 2010–11 and 2016 Rangers Choose Celebratory Beverages Wisely

Even before the short fly ball off the bat of Oakland infielder Cliff Pennington settled into the glove of Rangers outfielder Nelson Cruz, third baseman Michael Young began hopping in anticipation, inching toward the mound where the postgame celebration would start.

It was late in the afternoon on September 25, 2010, and the Rangers, holding an eight-game lead over the Athletics in the American League West at the start of the day, needed just one more out to clinch the franchise's first division title in 11 years.

Here's Rangers radio announcer Eric Nadel's call of that final out:

"The pitch. Swung on, high pop up to short left field. [Elvis] Andrus going out, Cruz coming on. Cruz with the call. He makes the catch. And the Rangers are champions of the American League

West! They are streaming to the mound to mob Neftali Feliz, who has just set a major league record for saves by a rookie. The Rangers have beaten the A's 4–3. The West Division race is over!"

The celebration that ensued was crazy. It began near the mound and continued into the clubhouse. And it was especially sweet for Young, who was playing in his 1,502nd game for the Rangers on that day in Oakland. Only Cardinals outfielder Randy Winn had played more games in the majors among active players without ever being in the postseason in his career than Young.

In the Rangers' clubhouse at Oakland–Alameda County Coliseum, players sprayed champagne on each other, drank beer, smoked cigars, and danced in delight. But they saved the big tub of ice to pour over Young, their de facto team captain.

"It's an incredible feeling to see the joy in Mikey's face," second baseman Ian Kinsler told Rangers beat writer T.R. Sullivan of MLB.com.

"I'm so happy because I can see Mike…because he's been here a long time," Cruz said. "I can't imagine what it's like for him."

Young did his best to put it into words that day, saying: "The best feeling in the world, and it's not even close. We've played hard all season long. We deserve it. We know what the ultimate goal is, but this is step one. It's an incredible feeling. The 2010 Texas Rangers are American League West champs. I couldn't be more proud of my teammates."

Unfortunately, all of his teammates didn't participate in that clubhouse celebration. American League MVP Josh Hamilton did not appear in the postgame clubhouse that day because of his well-documented battle with drug and alcohol addiction. In addition to all of his substance-abuse issues prior to joining the Rangers, Hamilton also was the subject of embarrassing photographs in January 2009 during a night of binge drinking in Arizona. Ever since, he had gone to great lengths to avoid alcohol altogether.

The Successful C.J. Wilson Starting Experiment
In 1989 nine-year-old Christopher John Wilson—C.J. for short—signed up for a youth baseball league in his hometown of Huntington Beach, California. His coach decided to try him at third base.

"I was a lefty playing the hot corner," Wilson told *Sports Illustrated's* Franz Lidz in a March 2011 article. "I sucked."

A few years later, Wilson moved to the center of the infield. Almost instantaneously, he was a success on the mound. He found a mentor in former major league pitcher Bud Black, who later became a big-league manager. The first time the two played catch, Black marveled at Wilson's skills: "This kid's got it," Black said.

The pitching experiment obviously worked exceptionally well for Wilson, the Rangers' fifth-round pick in 2001. He made it in the majors for good in 2005 as a starting pitcher. But after six extremely rough starts, his 0–5 record and 12.05 ERA necessitated a change of scenery.

The then-25-year-old moved to the bullpen, where he steadily began gaining confidence and added to his overall repertoire of pitches. During the first five years of his career, Wilson excelled at virtually every role in the bullpen.

In 2009, for example, he compiled a 2.81 ERA and 84 strikeouts in almost 74 innings of work, proving he could be effective against hitters on both sides of the plate. During that season, he also began talking to Nolan Ryan about possibly becoming a starting pitcher again. Ryan was impressed by Wilson's passionate plea, and the Rangers gave him an opportunity to start in 2010.

It was a good move. Wilson went 15–8 with a 3.35 ERA and 170 strikeouts in 204 innings in 2010. More impressively, the Rangers were 24–9 in all of his starts, as he played a huge role in leading Texas to its first-ever World Series. He was the second-toughest starter to hit in the American League (.217 batting average against), trailing only Cy Young Award winner Felix Hernandez (.212).

The Rangers made an offer to sign Wilson to a long-term contract following that exceptional first full season as a starter. But ultimately, the front office wanted to see if he could duplicate that kind of success in 2011.

Mission accomplished. Wilson shined as the staff ace, earning his first trip to the All-Star Game by going 9–3 with a 3.20 ERA in the first half of the 2011 season. He also cut down dramatically on his walks in 2011 (74 total in the regular season) after leading the American League with 93 walks in 2010.

Wilson finished the 2011 regular season with a 16–7 record and 206 strikeouts. His 2.94 ERA in 2011 was the ninth-lowest in club history and the lowest since Nolan Ryan's 2.91 ERA in 1991. He was far less effective in the postseason, going 0–3 in five starts. On December 8, 2011, Wilson's Rangers career came to an end when the lefty accepted a five-year, $77.5 million offer from the Rangers' American League West rival, the Los Angeles Angels of Anaheim.

In ensuing years, the Rangers tried unsuccessfully to duplicate the reliever-to-starter success of Wilson with Neftali Feliz and Tanner Scheppers.

Then-Rangers starting pitcher C.J. Wilson also skipped the celebration in Oakland. Wilson has said that he voluntarily abstains from alcohol, tobacco, illegal drugs, and promiscuous sex in order to maintain health. Wilson has the words *Straight Edge* tattooed along the length of his torso.

One of the primary strengths of the 2010 Rangers was the team's sense of togetherness. The clubhouse may have been more unified than any other in franchise history to that point. So leaving Hamilton and Wilson out of the initial celebration was bothersome to some of the players and other team personnel.

Equipment manager Richard "Hoggy" Price, along with Wilson, conceived a solution following the division title celebration. When the Rangers won the first two games of the ALDS in Tampa Bay, Price stocked the Rangers' home clubhouse with Canada Dry ginger ale, from the Texas-based Dr Pepper Bottling Company. Unfortunately, the Rays won both games in Arlington, so the ginger ale made the return trip to St. Petersburg, where Texas won its first-ever playoff series by beating the Rays 5–1 on October 12.

As the victorious Rangers celebrated in the clubhouse at Tropicana Field, no alcohol was initially in sight. Everyone—including Hamilton and Wilson—was soaked down in ginger ale.

"It was a really cool thing," Hamilton told Sullivan. "This stuff still burns your eyes, too. But for them to adapt the celebration to this, it really says a lot about our organization."

Young agreed: "It was a great idea," he said. "Josh and C.J. are a big part of our ballclub, and we wanted them to be able to celebrate with us."

Eventually the Rangers broke out the beer and the champagne after beating the Rays, but only after Hamilton and Wilson were properly baptized. Ten days later, when the Rangers won the ALCS on their home field, the ginger ale showers continued on the playing surface of Rangers Ballpark in Arlington.

The following year the ginger ale baths continued after the Rangers won the American League West, the ALDS, and the ALCS.

Interestingly, the ginger ale celebrations returned in 2016. The Rangers, after clinching the American League West title with a 3–0 victory over the Oakland Athletics on September 24, 2016, began their clubhouse celebration with ginger ale for relievers Matt Bush and Jeremy Jeffress. Both players have had a history dealing with alcohol afflictions.

"It just continues to show why I have been able to make things work here in Texas," Bush said, as reported by Sullivan of MLB.com.

83 Mitch Williams: The Wild Ride Began with the Rangers

To watch and listen to him now as a studio analyst on the MLB Network, it's obvious that Mitch Williams has found his niche. On the set, he's typically quick-witted, spontaneous, compelling, and informative, providing a mix of self-deprecating humor and keen insight.

Williams, who turned 47 in November 2011, can be critical regarding players and their performances without being particularly condescending. The grounded father of five is revealing, thoughtful, and mature in his prospective. In other words, he's barely recognizable to the Rangers fans who first witnessed the "Wild Thing" on the major league level in the mid-1980s.

During Williams' 11-year career in the major leagues, he enjoyed an All-Star season in 1989 with the Chicago Cubs, saved a career-best 43 games with the National League champion Philadelphia Phillies in 1993, and sported a sparkling 2.34 ERA in the City of Brotherly Love in 1991.

But Williams also had quite a start to his career with the Rangers. He still holds club records for most appearances in a season by a rookie (80) in 1986 and most appearances in a season (85) in 1987. Williams pitched a career-high 108⅔ innings in '87, going 8–6 with six saves and a 3.23 ERA. One year later, he saved 18 games for the Rangers.

He possibly could have become a Lone Star legend in Texas… if only he had possessed a little more maturity in those days. But Williams, only 21 when he made his debut for the Rangers in '86, desperately needed a change of scenery to grow as a pitcher and a man.

In December 1988 Williams was one of the key pieces involved in a nine-player deal that, among others, brought Rafael Palmeiro and Jamie Moyer to Texas and sent Williams to the Cubs.

Williams helped lead Chicago to the National League East title in 1989, posting 36 saves and a 4–4 record with a 2.76 ERA. Meanwhile, Palmeiro became a fixture at first base for the Rangers.

"That was one of those trades that really worked out for both sides," former Rangers general manager Tom Grieve said.

Besides, Williams had worn out his welcome in Texas. He didn't actually earn his "Wild Thing" nickname until he landed in Chicago and became a fan of flame-throwing pitcher Ricky Vaughn, played by Charlie Sheen in the 1989 movie *Major League*.

But he was plenty wild in Texas. In spring training in 1985, Rangers manager Doug Rader prohibited him from pitching to left-handed batters during practice because he tended to hit so many hitters. Williams said he threw "like a man with his hair on fire."

To which *Sports Illustrated's* Rick Telander replied: "And it's true. He lifts his right knee up toward his head as if trying to douse the flames with his leg, curls his 6'4", 205-pound body ostrich-like around his glove, and unleashes the ball in one of the most out-of-control-looking explosions of vector forces ever seen in the world of high-level sport. After every pitch he careens off to the right of the mound, catching himself with his glove hand before stagger-ing back to an upright position somewhere near the third-base line. Throwing hard is one thing, but Williams looks as though he's trying to destroy his rotator cuff with each fling. The whole wild process scares batters half to death. After narrowly avoiding a Williams scorcher in his ear, Pirate center fielder Andy Van Slyke said, 'If everyone were like him, I wouldn't play.'"

With the Rangers, Williams hit 11 batters in 98 innings in 1986, an average of one plunking per 8.9 innings. But it wasn't the wildness that bothered the Rangers. It was the pouting when he didn't pitch and the me-first attitude.

"He gives off a personality that tees you off," Charlie Hough told Telander. "When you first see him, you have a tendency to hate him."

Added former Rangers reliever Jeff Russell: "I think maturity was the thing he needed. Craig McMurtry pitched unbelievably to earn a save, and Mitch didn't say a word to him because Mitch was upset about not getting into the game. He showered real quick and stormed out."

"A lot of pitchers have been emotional, but there's a difference between being emotional and being a jerk," said former Texas manager Bobby Valentine. "The hang-up in dealing with Mitch is not whether or not he can get the batter out. It's whether it's worth the problem."

Williams obviously matured in the ensuing years, handling blown save opportunities in the 1993 World Series and all the criticism that followed. Like so many others, he's a much different person in his late forties than he was in his young twenties. Nowadays, he's the consummate pro on the MLB Network studio set, far more wily than wild.

84 Rangers, Hamilton March to Triumphant June Tune in 2010

One of the more well-known clichés that has been repeated by generations of ballplayers and managers is that the Major League Baseball season, which begins in early April and typically concludes in early October, is a marathon, not a sprint. While there is certainly a great deal a truth in that statement, don't be entirely misled by the daily babble of clubhouse "coachspeak."

The 14-Game Winning Streak of 1991

The 2010 Rangers used an 11-game winning streak in June to run away from the rest of the American League West. One season later, the 2011 Rangers strung together a 12-game winning streak in July to solidify themselves as serious playoff hopefuls.

But the longest winning streak in Rangers history occurred two decades earlier.

After losing to Boston 5–4 on May 11, 1991, the Rangers dropped to 11–14 overall. On the following day in Beantown, the Rangers pounded out 19 hits en route to a 12–5 victory that kick-started a 14-game winning streak. Kenny Rogers picked up the win while Ruben Sierra drove in four runs, and Geno Petralli three, pulling the Rangers within 4½ games of first place in the American League West.

The win in Boston awakened the Rangers—especially the offense—in a magical way. Texas followed that victory with 13 more in a row. On May 27 Texas won its 14th straight, improving to 25–14 with an 11–4 win over Minnesota. At that point, Texas was in first place, one game ahead of Oakland and three games ahead of the Angels, and only 11 teams in American League history had produced longer winning streaks than Texas.

Furthermore, no team had a longer streak since Kansas City won 16 consecutive in 1977.

The Rangers produced the winning streak without ace Nolan Ryan, who was on the disabled list during the streak.

"Who in spring training would have thought they'd win 10 in row, especially without Nolan Ryan?" Minnesota manager Tom Kelly said prior to the May 27 loss to Texas. "I mean, who would have thought it?"

The streak ended on May 28 in Arlington in a 3–0 loss to the Twins. Minnesota's Scott Erickson went eight innings, scattering seven hits to pick up the win. Jose Guzman pitched well for Texas but suffered the loss.

Texas then dropped 11 of its next 12 games to fall to 26–25. The streaky Rangers then won seven straight.

When the season ended, Texas finished at 85–77 and in third place in the American League West. The Twins eventually won the division, the pennant, and the World Series. The Twins also surpassed the Rangers' winning streak, rolling to 15 straight in early June.

A mad dash over a short stretch of the season can often go a long way toward winning a division crown. Take the historic 2010 Rangers season, for example.

Texas strolled out of the gate through April and May, but when the weather turned particularly warm in June, the Rangers picked up the pace, going from a steady trot to a full-throttle, triumphant tear.

On May 30, 2010, the Rangers, at 26–24, trailed the Oakland A's by a half game in the American League West standings. One magnificent month later—on June 30, 2010—Texas led the West by 4½ games over the Angels, 10 over Oakland, and 14 over Seattle. The Rangers never fell out of first the rest of the way. In fact, they weren't even seriously pushed.

Texas essentially won the division with a spectacular June, going 21–6. The Rangers won 11 straight interleague games against Milwaukee, Florida, Houston, and Pittsburgh, and during one particularly terrific stretch, Texas won 16 out of 18 games from June 8–27. The Rangers were 15 games over .500 in June and just three games over .500 during the entire rest of the season (90–72 overall).

Not only did June make a huge difference in the divisional race; it also was the pivotal month in Josh Hamilton's race to the American League MVP. Hamilton started the season slowly, hitting just .205 in the first 13 games. He increased his average to .281 by the end of May, and once June arrived, Hamilton looked like a man on a mission.

He eliminated his pre-swing toe tap at the beginning of the month and proceeded to hit .454 in June with 31 RBIs, 49 hits, 88 total bases, an .815 slugging percentage, and a .482 on-base percentage, all of which led the majors for the month. He also blasted nine home runs, which led the American League.

Hamilton stayed hot throughout the summer. He hit .384 after the All-Star break, placing the Rangers in position to make their first playoff appearance since 1999. Of course, it wasn't just his play at the plate that made him an MVP in 2010. Hamilton was an exceptional outfielder, playing left and center during the season. He stole eight bases and regularly turned singles into doubles and doubles into triples.

"Anyone who watched him [in 2010] shouldn't take for granted what they saw, especially for about three months," said Rangers television color analyst Tom Grieve. "He was playing at a level as high as the best players in the history of baseball have ever played. He hit over .400 for 330 at-bats. He ran the bases as well as anyone in the league, played Gold Glove–caliber outfield, had one of the best arms in the league, and would score from second base on a ground ball to second to win a game. He won games every way you can win them. The way he played the game for those three months was the best baseball I have ever seen. I've never seen a player play better than that."

Especially in June, when the West and the MVP were essentially won.

85 The Most Unlikely Cycle of Them All: Bengie Molina

One of the anomalies of the Rangers' historic 2010 season was that, despite losing the World Series 4–1 to the San Francisco Giants, Texas catcher Bengie Molina earned a World Series championship ring. Molina had been the Giants' catcher from 2007 until the end of June 2010.

But with the development of then-rookie catcher Buster Posey, the Giants deemed Molina expendable. The Rangers, in dire need of catching help at the time, sent reliever Chris Ray and minor leaguer Michael Main to the Giants on July 1 for Molina. Because

Molina played 61 games for the Giants and 57 regular-season games for the Rangers, San Francisco announced before the World Series that Molina would be receiving a championship ring no matter which team won.

That wasn't the strangest note of the 2010 season regarding Molina, however. The most stunningly bizarre and absurdly improbable moment of 2010 occurred on a rainy, midsummer Friday night in Boston, as Molina—the self-proclaimed "slowest guy in the world"—hit for the cycle. And to add the overall peculiarity of the most unlikely cycle in Rangers history—and maybe in major league history—the rambling, rumbling Molina stumbled coming around first base and tweaked his right quadriceps muscle during his eighth-inning triple.

"This means a lot," Molina told T.R. Sullivan, the Rangers beat reporter for MLB.com. "I'm not a stats guy; everybody who knows me knows that. That's an individual thing, but being one of the slowest guys in the world, and being criticized for it all my career, to be able to do something like that really makes me feel good."

Molina started his historic night with a line-drive single to center in the second inning and then, following an hour rain delay in the third inning, he doubled to right field in the fourth.

With the Rangers trailing 3–2 in the fifth, Red Sox starter Felix Doubrount had a chance to end the inning with the lead when he caught a hard-liner from Josh Hamilton and attempted to convert an inning-ending double play by throwing to second to double off Michael Young. But the wild throw went into center field, keeping the inning alive and allowing Young and Vladimir Guerrero to move to second and third. The Rangers eventually loaded the bases and tied the game, bringing Molina to the plate against reliever Fernando Cabrera with the bases loaded in a 3–3 game.

Molina fell behind 0–2 in the count before hitting a 1–2 pitch into the first row of the center-field bleachers for a grand slam, giving the Rangers a 7–3 lead.

Bengie Molina's Home Run in Game 4 of the 2010 ALCS

The pennant-clinching Game 6 of the 2010 American League Championship at Rangers Ballpark in Arlington was easily the most electrifying, spine-tingling, and tear-inducing moment of the series—and maybe in the history of the franchise—for Texas and its long-suffering fans.

The gutsy performance of Colby Lewis in a 7–2 victory in Game 2, less than 24 hours after blowing a 5–0 lead in the series opener against the Yankees and losing for the 10th consecutive time to New York in the playoffs, may have been the must-win moment of the series for Texas.

And Cliff Lee's 13-strikeout, two-hit gem in an 8–0 victory in Game 3—the first of the series in New York—provided a bold indication to the Rangers and the rest of the country that Texas could, indeed, win a playoff series against the big, bad Yankees.

But if you are looking for one monumental moment in time that effectively turned the entire series and lifted the burden of 14 years of playoff frustration and exasperation against the Yankees, rewind the clock, crank up the DVR, or program the search engine for the top of the sixth inning in Game 4 of the 2010 ALCS. That's the inning that changed history for the Rangers and essentially sent the fat lady to the microphone to begin singing.

Fittingly, it was the chubby man who delivered the crushing blow for Texas.

With the Rangers leading the series 2–1 but trailing the game 3–2, Texas managed to escape a dicey situation in the bottom of the fifth to stay within striking distance. Vladimir Guerrero then led off the top of the sixth against Yankees starter A.J. Burnett with a sharp single to right but was immediately erased on a fielder's choice groundout by Nelson Cruz. With one out and Cruz at first, Ian Kinsler flew out to deep center field. Characteristic of the aggressive nature of Rangers base running all year long, Cruz tagged up and slid headfirst into second base just ahead of Curtis Granderson's throw.

That turned out to be a huge play because, with first base open and the left-handed-hitting David Murphy due up next, Yankees manager Joe Girardi elected to issue the intentional walk to Murphy so that Burnett could face the right-handed-hitting Bengie Molina. Girardi also had the option of going to the bullpen, where reliever Joba Chamberlain was warmed up and ready, but the skipper decided to allow Burnett to face one more batter.

In a fateful example of foreshadowing, the TBS television crew replayed highlights of Molina's past playoff success against the Yankees as New York catcher Francisco Cervelli visited briefly with Burnett prior to the Molina at-bat. In 2005, when he was a member of the Angels, Molina had a monster ALDS against the Yankees, which included three home runs.

As the cameras shifted back to live action, Burnett delivered his first pitch to Molina—a fastball significantly inside. But Molina managed to keep his hands inside the ball and lifted a high, deep drive toward the left-field fence. As soon as it left the bat, the only question was whether it would stay fair.

It did, giving the Rangers a 5–3 lead and completely silencing the crowd of 49,977 inside Yankee Stadium.

"Not a bad job for a fat kid that everyone makes fun of the way he runs," Molina said in the postgame press conference. "[Murphy] kills right-handers, so why not walk him and face me? I haven't been having a great season. I don't think it's a bad move. I think it's the right move that went wrong."

Things continued to go right for the Rangers the rest of the way, as Josh Hamilton homered in the seventh and again in the ninth and Cruz added a two-run shot in the ninth to put Texas up 10–3. Derek Holland also pitched exceptionally well in relief of Tommy Hunter to pick up the win, and by the time Darren Oliver entered the game in the bottom of the ninth to close things out, there were so few Yankees fans left in the stadium that the only noise being made was from the Rangers fans—mostly wives and family members of players.

A full section of Texas fans in the second deck above the third-base dugout could be clearly heard chanting, "Let's go, Rangers!"

The headline on the front page of the *New York Daily News* the following day effectively called the series a lost cause for the Bronx Bummers. Featuring a picture of first baseman Mark Teixeira anguishing in pain (Tex suffered a grade 2 strain of his right hamstring in the fifth inning of the loss), the headline stated, "LAST LEGS: Teixeira KO'd for series as the Rangers shove Yanks to the brink."

While the Yankees would go on to win Game 5 and force a return to Texas, the series had, indeed, turned on one monumental swing of the bat from Molina in a defining 10–3 victory that was later dubbed as a "Texas pain-saw massacre."

"That was more special than the cycle actually, because it put us ahead," Molina said afterward.

When the heavyset Molina went to the plate needing a triple to complete the cycle, manager Ron Washington casually asked third baseman Michael Young where he thought Molina needed to place the ball inside Fenway Park to leg out a triple.

"Nowhere in this ballpark," Young replied.

But Molina actually received the perfect break when he drilled a Ramon Ramirez fastball to center and it ticked off center fielder Eric Patterson's glove and caromed to the right into the triangle in right-center field near the 420' sign, the very deepest part of the ballpark. That bounce and a wide relay throw to third base allowed Molina, even after stumbling around first, to stroll into third with a stand-up triple.

It was the sixth triple of Molina's 13-year career and his first cycle. Overall, it was the fifth cycle in Rangers history, and Molina became the eighth player and first catcher since 1900 to hit for the cycle with a grand slam. It also made for some great calls on the Rangers' television and radio broadcasts.

Here's the TV call of the eighth-inning triple from the 2010 team of play-by-play announcer Josh Lewin and color commentator Tom Grieve:

Lewin: "There goes Bengie again to center field."

The ball glances off Patterson's glove.

Lewin: "Now, could this be a triple? Come on? Bengie, get going, kiddo. You've got this!"

Grieve: "C'mon, Bengie! Come on, Bengie!"

Lewin: "You've got the cycle, big guy. Get there! Get there!"

Grieve: "Get there!"

Lewin: "He did it!"

Grieve: "Ha, ha, ha, haaaaa!"

Lewin: "Pigs have flown in Boston, Massachusetts."

Now, here's the radio version of the call from Eric Nadel:

"Two balls and one strike to Bengie. Davis on deck and then Andrus. And the pitch.... Swung on. High drive, deep center again! Patterson going back. On the track. At the wall! It's off his glove. It bounces off the wall. Could it be a triple for Bengie? He's digging around second base. He's heading for third base. Here's the relay throw. Bengie is in there, standing up with a triple and a cycle! The impossible has happened at Fenway Park!"

86 The '94 Rangers Finish First, 10 Games Under .500

Coming off an 86-win, second-place finish the previous year, the 1994 season was one of the most anticipated years in Rangers history, as the team moved into a sparkling new ballpark and opened a new era of expanded playoff possibilities with the three-division format.

Rangers fans responded by filling the Ballpark in Arlington at a rate that still had not been equaled through the World Series season of 2010. The front office did its part, acquiring a key veteran and team leader in first baseman Will Clark and infusing the club with youngsters like rookie starting pitcher Rick Helling and rookie outfielder Rusty Greer.

The team, led by heroic performances of American League Comeback Player of the Year Jose Canseco and left-handed pitcher Kenny Rogers, also did its part, as Texas claimed its first-ever American League West Division title.

Sort of.

The Rangers finished in first place in the reconfigured four-team American League West. But you won't find any championship banners inside the ballpark recognizing the feat. The 1994 season ended when Seattle's Randy Johnson struck out Oakland's Ernie Young at 11:45 CDT on August 11. The following day the players began what turned out to be the longest work stoppage in the history of major North American professional sports leagues, a more than seven-month marathon.

It canceled the playoffs and the World Series for the first time in 90 years, and it also cost the Rangers a legitimate chance to make the playoffs for the first time in team history.

Instead, Texas earned a dubious distinction, becoming the first major league team to ever finish in first place despite a losing record (52–62).

Under manager Kevin Kennedy, the Rangers opened the new ballpark on April 1 with an exhibition loss to the New York Mets. They also lost the regular-season home opener to Milwaukee (then an American League team). And they finished the year by losing six straight. The Rangers allowed 697 runs and scored only 613.

Before the strike, the Rangers were just 8–22 against their foes in the weak, weak West. Nevertheless, it was still good enough to hold onto first place, as Texas led Oakland by one game and Seattle by two when the season ended.

It was also entertaining enough to keep the fans' interest. While many fans may have come primarily out of curiosity regarding the new ballpark, they filled it at a remarkable rate.

The 1994 Rangers reached 1 million fans in 27 home games. In 2011, a year after reaching the World Series for the first time, the Rangers surpassed 1 million fans in 28 home dates, the second-best start. From 1972 to 2010, the Rangers had never managed to surpass 3 million fans in total attendance. But they probably would have made it in '94 if not for the strike.

Even without any games in the second half of August and all of September—when a playoff race may have been heating up—the

'94 Rangers drew 2,503,198 fans, the most in team history to that point.

While the team was often more frustrating than fascinating, Texas did have its moments. Rogers threw a perfect game on July 28, and in his first season in Texas, Clark hit .329 to reach the All-Star Game, where he was joined by catcher Ivan Rodriguez.

Dean Palmer and Juan Gonzalez both hit 19 homers, and Canseco, who played in more games than any other Ranger in 1994, blasted 31 homers. One of those traveled 480 feet, which was the record for a homer at the Ballpark in Arlington until Josh Hamilton surpassed it with a 490' shot in 2010.

Texas also featured an interesting pitching staff, led by Rogers and Kevin Brown in the starting rotation. The bullpen included 36-year-old closer Tom Henke, who'd begun his career in Texas in 1982 before becoming a star in Toronto, along with left-handed specialists like 40-year-old Rick Honeycutt and 23-year-old pup Darren Oliver.

But perhaps the best addition to the '94 Rangers came after the strike. On October 14 Texas announced it was replacing Kennedy with former Baltimore manager Johnny Oates. In his second season with the Rangers, Oates led the team to an actual division title. Complete with a winning record.

87 Bullpen Fracas in Oakland Costs Rangers Dearly

The 2004 Rangers began September 4½ games out of first place in the American League West. Texas closed the gap somewhat by the end of the year, finishing three games out. In hindsight, the Rangers' undoing was a result of close losses.

From September 1 to September 29, Texas lost nine games—five of them to division foes—by two runs or less. While they were all tough losses, one was particularly excruciating.

On September 13 at Network Associates Coliseum in Oakland, the Rangers built a 4–2 lead against the first-place Athletics. A win would have moved Texas to four games back of Oakland with 19 left to play.

Regrettably, that didn't happen. The Texas bullpen blew a couple of leads. Then several members of the pen completely blew a gasket.

When the dust finally settled, the A's had scored three runs in the bottom of the eighth and two more in the bottom of the 10th to claim a 7–6 win, stretching their division lead to six. Just as significantly to Texas in the long haul, three Rangers relievers faced suspensions for their involvement in a fracas alongside the visitors' bullpen.

What started out as a verbal confrontation between fans and Rangers relievers escalated into complete chaos when 25-year-old rookie right-hander Frank Francisco hoisted a folding chair into the stands during the ninth inning, striking a 41-year-old woman in the face. Moments earlier, fellow Texas reliever Doug Brocail was being physically restrained by teammates from confronting a heckler.

The bizarre event and its aftermath resulted in a 19-minute delay of the game. Texas' Mark Teixeira scored a go-ahead run in the top of the 10th to give the Rangers a brief 6–5 lead, but Oakland used three Francisco Cordero walks to rally for two game-winning runs in the bottom of the inning.

After the game, Francisco was taken from the stadium to jail, where he was booked and his mug shot was taken. He was released about two hours later on $15,000 bail.

"On behalf of the Texas Rangers, I want to apologize for the conduct of some members of our club last night in Oakland," former owner Tom Hicks said in a press release on September 14. "Their behavior, especially the injury to a fan, was unacceptable. Even in a difficult or abusive environment, players should never be provoked into such actions."

The league obviously agreed. Reliever Carlos Almanzar was originally suspended for five games, although the suspension was later reduced to four. Brocail served a six-game suspension, and Francisco's suspension cost him 15 games, essentially ending his year. The hard-throwing Francisco had emerged as a key member of the bullpen, going 5–1 with a 3.33 ERA in 51⅓ innings during the '04 season.

Losing him for the rest of the season was costly. Who knows how many of those close games throughout the rest of the year could have turned out differently if manager Buck Showalter would have had his full bullpen in the final 15 games?

Francisco's suspension was among the harshest given by the commissioner's office for on-field conduct in decades, trailing only the 30-day suspension given to Cincinnati manager Pete Rose for pushing umpire Dave Pallone in 1988.

"I don't feel good about it, but whatever they say, I have to take it," said Francisco after the details of the suspension were released.

Texas' only consolation was that it wasn't the A's that represented the American League West in the playoffs. Anaheim won the West by one over Oakland and three over the Rangers.

88 If You Can't Beat Guerrero, Sign Him

For most of his six-year tenure with the Los Angeles/Anaheim Angels, Vladimir Guerrero was the ultimate thorn in the Rangers' side, especially when he played at Rangers Ballpark in Arlington.

Guerrero, the 2004 American League MVP, was a good hitter in every major league ballpark, compiling a .321 batting average, 407 home runs, and 1,318 RBIs in his first 14 seasons with the Montreal Expos and Angels. But he was downright spectacular in Arlington, producing Hall of Fame–caliber numbers in North Texas.

Prior to 2010, Guerrero was a .394 career hitter at Rangers Ballpark, with 14 homers and 33 RBIs in 50 games. And in the first 44 games of his career against the Rangers (2004–06, home and away), Guerrero hit safely in every game, the longest stretch by any player against one team since at least 1957.

If Vlad hadn't been so darned jovial, if he hadn't played every game with such passion and hustle, if he hadn't constantly worn a wide grin on his face, and if he hadn't been so stinkin' fun to watch, it would have been easy for Rangers fans to hate Guerrero as he consistently tormented Texas pitching.

But the bottom line regarding the hard-swinging, strong-armed, fun-loving Guerrero was that it was practically impossible not to admire the way he played the game.

So, when the Angels decided not to re-sign the Dominican-born slugger for the 2010 season—choosing instead to go with free agent Hideki Matsui—the Rangers leapt at the opportunity to ink Guerrero to a one-year deal for $5 million plus incentives.

Wise decision. Serving primarily as the designated hitter in the cleanup position, Vlad played a huge role in helping Texas win its first American League pennant.

Reggie Jackson: Thorn in the Rangers' Side

While Texas managed to sign noted Rangers killer Vladimir Guerrero prior to the 2010 season, the team could never reach a deal with Reggie Jackson, who provided many nightmares for the Rangers and their fans.

Jackson, who entered the Baseball Hall of Fame in 1993, blasted 563 homers in his 21-year career. Most of them came against the Rangers.

Or so it seemed.

Jackson actually clubbed 132 home runs before the Rangers ever moved to Arlington in 1972. But once the team arrived in Texas, Jackson went to work. He still holds the record for a Rangers opponent for most home runs in a season (nine against Texas in 1974) and most career homers against the Rangers (45 overall).

And in the old Arlington Stadium—the one that so many Rangers complained about hitting in because the winds turned home run balls into warning-track flyouts—Jackson blasted 24 dingers.

Guerrero, who often seemed to be on the verge of swinging out of his spikes, carried the Rangers' offense throughout much of the early part of the 2010 season. He finished the regular season with a team-best 115 RBIs. He also hit .300 with 29 home runs and 83 runs scored. And in Game 6 of the ALCS against the Yankees, Guerrero produced the game-winning, series-clinching RBI.

With two outs and a runner on third in a 1–1 game in the bottom of the fifth, the Yankees elected to walk eventual ALCS MVP Josh Hamilton, choosing instead to pitch to Guerrero. The veteran made New York pitcher Phil Hughes pay.

Guerrero smoked a 1–0 curveball to left-center field for a two-run double, giving the Rangers a 3–1 lead and paving the way to a four-run inning.

Through the 2010 season, Guerrero had been one of only seven players in major league history with 10 or more seasons of 25-plus homers and 105-plus RBIs. Of the players on that list, he had been the only one who had never played in a World Series.

That changed in October 2010. Unfortunately, Vlad did not have a good World Series, going 1-for-14 with just two RBIs.

That probably played a role in the Rangers' decision not to re-sign him for the 2011 season, as Vlad signed instead with Baltimore. But his one year with the Rangers was certainly memorable for Texas and Guerrero.

"I just want to thank God that I ended up signing in Texas," Guerrero said in Spanish following Game 6 of the ALCS. "I've been in this league [15] years, and I've never felt happier than I do now."

That's saying quite a bit considering the way Vlad often played the game with a perpetual smile.

89 Rangers Have a History of All-Star Success

Until 2010 the Rangers had never enjoyed a postseason series victory. But that didn't mean that Texas had never played a significant role in determining the location of the World Series games.

Beginning in 2003, home-field advantage in the World Series has been determined by the winner of the All-Star Game. That's the same year when Rangers players began a tradition of All-Star Game success. And by playing so well in the Midsummer Classic, the Rangers have often played a major role in influencing the travel plans of the Fall Classic participants.

With two outs in the bottom of the eighth inning of the 2003 All-Star Game at U.S. Cellular Field in Chicago, Texas' Hank Blalock delivered a game-winning, two-run homer off Los Angeles Dodgers closer Eric Gagne, rallying the American League past the National League 7–6. At the time, the Rangers were in last place in the American League West, where they would also finish the season 20 games under .500. But Blalock's unlikely blast eventually provided home-field advantage to the Yankees in the 2003 World Series (won by the Florida Marlins).

"I'm sure whoever reaches the World Series in a Game 7 or something like that will send [Blalock] a 12 pack of something," said Jason Giambi, then with the Yankees.

The National League had built a 5–1 lead in the sixth, but the American League cut the lead to 6–5 in the eighth when Blalock, batting for Troy Glaus, hit a long drive to right field, just right of the outfield sign that stated, "This Time It Counts." Gagne had been successful on 39 straight save chances for Los Angeles. But Blalock joined a list that included Bo Jackson, Javier Lopez, Terry Steinbach, Lee Mazzilli, Johnny Bench, and others to homer in his first All-Star at-bat.

One year later, Texas infielder Alfonso Soriano outdid Blalock, going 2-for-3 and blasting a three-run homer off former Yankees teammate Roger Clemens to propel the American League to a 9–4 win at Houston's Minute Maid Park. For his heroics, Soriano won the Ted Williams Most Valuable Player Award, becoming the second Rangers player to be honored as MVP.

"I am so happy right now," Soriano said afterward. "My first year with the Texas Rangers [after being traded from New York in the Alex Rodriguez deal], being the top vote-getter at the All-Star Game, now the MVP.... It feels so great because no one was thinking about the Texas Rangers before, and now they'll think about them."

Fans continued to think about the Rangers in 2005, as Mark Teixeira's two-run homer in Detroit proved to be the winning margin in the American League's 7–5 victory.

In 2006 Michael Young drilled a two-strike, ninth-inning pitch into the gap in right-center off Trevor Hoffman for a two-run triple at Pittsburgh's PNC Park. That proved to be the game-winning hit in the American League's 3–2 victory. A few minutes later, Young picked up the Ted Williams MVP trophy from Commissioner Bud Selig, along with the keys to a Chevy truck.

"I'm not going to lie," said Young. "This is a pretty big highlight in my baseball career. I think everyone dreams of having a big All-Star Game. Even coming to the All-Star Game is humbling enough, but to be in this situation now, where I have an All-Star Game MVP is pretty exciting. I can't wait to get back to my teammates in Texas now."

The Rangers were absent from the 2007 game, as Young was selected but did not play. Then in 2008 Josh Hamilton stole the national spotlight the night before the All-Star Game at the Home Run Derby at Yankee Stadium. Hamilton blasted a record 28 homers in the first round. Minnesota's Justin Morneau topped a tired Hamilton 5–3 in the final round to win the derby title. But the night belonged to Hamilton, who put on a dazzling power display in "The House That Ruth Built." Yankees fans responded appreciatively, chanting Hamilton's name.

Hamilton hit three shots that exceeded 500', including his longest that was estimated at 518'. Hamilton's first-round homers totaled 12,458', an average of 445' each.

"They should have juiced the ball up. I'd have hit the subway," Hamilton said.

Hamilton skipped the Home Run Derby in '09, but Nelson Cruz represented the Rangers well, making it to the finals in St. Louis, where he also finished second behind Milwaukee's Prince Fielder.

The Rangers sent six players to the 2010 All-Star Game in Anaheim, but the National League broke a 13-game winless streak with a 3–1 victory. That win gave San Francisco home-field advantage against the Rangers in the 2010 World Series.

Five Rangers players attended the 2011 All-Star Game in Arizona, but C.J. Wilson allowed a three-run homer to Milwaukee's

Prince Fielder, powering the National League past the American League 5–1 in the 82nd Midsummer Classic and providing the Senior Circuit with home-field advantage in the World Series. The wild-card Cardinals were the beneficiaries of Fielder's blast.

Prior to '03 the Rangers' success in All-Star Games was far more sporadic, but Texas players did have their moments. Nolan Ryan picked up the victory in 1989 in Anaheim. In San Diego in 1992, Kevin Brown became the first Texas pitcher to ever start an All-Star Game. Brown pitched a scoreless first inning to earn the win, and Ruben Sierra homered in the sixth inning for the American League.

At the Home Run Derby in 1993 Juan Gonzalez was the first player to hit a homer into the facade of the upper deck in left field (473') at Oriole Park at Camden Yards. He beat Ken Griffey Jr. that year for the derby crown.

Texas' John Wetteland picked up a save at Fenway Park in 1999.

The first Texas All-Star Game MVP was Julio Franco in 1990 at Wrigley Field. With the game knotted at 0–0, Sandy Alomar Jr. led off the American League seventh with a single, followed by another single from Lance Parrish. Franco was due up next, but the game was halted for a 68-minute rain delay. When play resumed, Franco lined a double to right-center field off reliever Rob Dibble, scoring the only runs of the game in a 2–0 American League victory.

90 Rafael Palmeiro: The Face of the Rangers' "Steroids Era"

Based on the numbers alone, there's absolutely no doubt that Rafael Palmeiro was one of the greatest players in Rangers history. In 10 seasons in Texas, Palmeiro produced 1,692 hits, 321 home runs, 1,039 RBIs, and a .290 batting average.

Based on numbers alone throughout his 20-year career, Palmeiro also possesses outstanding Hall of Fame credentials: 3,020 hits, 569 homers, and 1,835 RBIs.

But Palmeiro's bronze bust will probably never make it to Cooperstown, as he has become one of the most prominent faces of the steroids era in Major League Baseball.

In March 2005 Palmeiro wagged his finger at Congress while denying that he ever used performance-enhancing drugs. Then he failed a Major League Baseball drug test for the steroid Stanzolol some five months later.

Palmeiro vehemently denies ever using steroids. He says the positive test result can be attributed to a tainted vitamin B-12 shot he received from former Baltimore Orioles teammate Miguel Tejada. Palmeiro says he had taken numerous B-12 shots throughout his career, especially while combating the heat in Texas.

"It wasn't something new to me," he told *USA TODAY*. "I knew what I was getting into. I didn't get it from a doctor. I got it from a teammate. I should have known better. I was careless. It basically ruined everything."

It appears to have ruined his chance at the Hall of Fame. In 2011—Palmeiro's first year of eligibility on the Hall of Fame ballot—Roberto Alomar and former Rangers pitcher Bert Blyleven were elected to Cooperstown by the Baseball Writers Association of

Rafael Palmeiro hit 321 home runs in 10 seasons with the Rangers, but Palmeiro will forever be remembered for failing a steroids test just a few months after testifying in front of Congress in 2005. (Focus on Sport/Getty Images)

America. But Palmeiro was named on only 11 percent of the ballots (64 total), far short of the 75 percent necessary for induction.

"This is one of those dark days in my life," Palmeiro said on the day when the results were announced. "The last five years, ever since that incident, I've felt like they were putting me in a coffin and putting nails in. Today, they were throwing dirt on my coffin. I wasn't quite sure what to expect but not [11 percent]. It's like that one unfortunate incident my last year in baseball erased everything I did."

It doesn't appear that members of the BBWAA are buying the "one unfortunate incident" story from Palmeiro, who was also named in former Sen. George Mitchell's 2007 report on steroids in baseball because of his failed test. And in his 2005 book *Juiced*, Jose Canseco wrote that he introduced the team's players to steroids and that he personally injected Palmeiro with steroids.

Quite frankly, the Rangers have an ugly reputation and quite a history of players who have failed drug tests, admitted to steroid use, or appeared in steroid investigations such as the Mitchell report. According to a February 2009 article in *The Wall Street Journal*, Alex Rodriguez became the 27th former Ranger to be accused of using performance-enhancing drugs at some point in his career. At the time of the article, only the Yankees, with 30 players mentioned, had more accused steroid users than Texas.

According to the article, four former Rangers had confessed to using banned substances either while playing in Texas or at some point during their careers: Ken Caminiti, who died of a drug overdose in 2004; Canseco, who played for the club from 1992 to 1994; Jim Leyritz, who played in Texas in 1997; and A-Rod, who played three seasons in the early 2000s.

Among the other high-profile players to be accused of steroid use in legal documents or other sources are Kevin Brown, Pete Incaviglia, Sammy Sosa, Ivan Rodriguez, Gary Matthews Jr., Palmeiro, and two-time American League MVP Juan Gonzalez, who also debuted on the 2011 Hall of Fame ballot with Palmeiro. Gonzalez—like Palmeiro—didn't come anywhere close to receiving at least 75 percent of the necessary votes for Hall of Fame induction. Gonzalez received 5.2 percent of the votes (30 total votes), while Brown garnered 2.1 percent (12 votes).

91 Most Unfortunate Trade Sends Sosa, Alvarez to Chicago

Toward the end of June 1989, the Rangers, powered by monster offensive seasons from outfielder Ruben Sierra and second baseman Julio Franco and a powerful pitching rotation fronted by aces Nolan Ryan and Kevin Brown, moved to within two games of first place in the American League West.

It wasn't a widespread epidemic, but playoff fever could, indeed, be detected within the suddenly crowded concourses of Arlington Stadium.

"With the off-season moves we made [acquiring Ryan, Franco, starting pitcher Jamie Moyer, and outfielder Rafael Palmeiro], we thought we had a pretty good team when we broke [spring training]," recalled then–general manager Tom Grieve. "That was confirmed as the season went along."

The '89 team jumped out of the gate in extremely impressive fashion, finishing April at 17–5. Even a miserable May (10–17) didn't dampen hopes significantly, as the Rangers heated up again in June, closing the gap on the "Bash Brothers" in Oakland.

As July approached, Grieve hoped to bolster the lineup with a big-hitting veteran at designated hitter, where players like Kevin Reimer, Jeff Stone, and Rick Leach had rotated following Buddy Bell's retirement.

If the Rangers had been able to pull the trigger on a big deal then—at the end of June—it may have made a major impact. Unfortunately, by the time a trade was actually made on July 29, Texas' playoff hopes had dwindled significantly—because of its own undoing (the Rangers fell seven games back on July 28) and the wheeling and dealing that brought Rickey Henderson back to the A's.

Hoping to light a spark for his own team, Grieve made a move, sending starting shortstop Scott Fletcher, who'd become the first Ranger ever to earn more than $1 million a year in 1988, and two prospects to the White Sox for well-known designated hitter Harold Baines, a hard-nosed, productive hitter who had been with Chicago since 1980. The Rangers also acquired Fred Manrique, a middle infielder who could fill Fletcher's vacancy.

If that had been all it took to land Baines, it would have been a good trade for Texas, even though Baines didn't do much in '89 to add to the Rangers' offense. Baines hit .285 in 50 games for the Rangers but managed only three homers and 16 RBIs. Texas went 28–33 after the trade, slipping to fourth in the American League West. The A's ran away with the division and eventually swept the San Francisco Giants in the World Series.

Baines fared better for Texas in 1990, hitting for an almost .300 average before he was dealt to the A's for Joe Bitker and Scott Chiamparino. Scott Fletcher didn't have much success in Chicago after being dealt and bounced from the Brewers to the Red Sox and finally to the Tigers before his career ended in 1995.

But those prospects Texas parted with to obtain Baines haunted the Rangers for many years to come. Wilson Alvarez, the pitcher in the deal, threw a no-hitter in his first start with the Sox in 1991 and was a 15-game winner in '93 and '96.

The young outfielder in the deal was Sammy Sosa, who spent two and a half seasons with the White Sox before being sent to the Cubs in a 1992 deal for George Bell. On the North Side of

Chicago, Sosa became one of the most beloved personalities in the Windy City, where he hit the majority of his 609 career home runs.

Just imagine if the Rangers had never made this trade. They still wouldn't have made the 1989 playoffs, but think about what kind of lift Alvarez and Sosa could have provided the 1996 Rangers, who reached the playoffs but couldn't beat the eventual World Series champion Yankees. In '96 with the Cubs, Sosa hit 40 home runs with 100 RBIs, while Alvarez went 15–10 with a 4.22 ERA on the other side of Chicago.

Rangers Deal Arms for "Mazzilli the Malcontent"

After going 57–48 in the strike-shortened 1981 season, the Rangers reported to training camp in 1982 with high hopes to contend in the American League West. But nine days before the season opener—on April 1—general manager Eddie Robinson orchestrated one of the most haunting trades in franchise history.

If only it had been an April Fool's joke....

Only the Rangers came out looking foolish on this trade, as Robinson gave away two key pitching prospects in the farm system, Ron Darling and Walt Terrell, for an outfielder, Lee Mazzilli, who loathed Texas and complained throughout his entire 58-game career with the Rangers.

Mazzilli was long gone—traded back to his beloved Big Apple, this time with the Yankees—by the time the 1982 Rangers skidded to a 64–98 finish. Meanwhile, the Mets used Darling and Terrell to build a World Series champion in 1986.

"A lot of people refer to the trade that sent Sammy Sosa and Wilson Alvarez to Chicago [in 1989] as the worst in franchise

The 1983 Lose-Lose Honeycutt-for-Stewart Trade

In 1983 Texas left-handed pitcher Rick Honeycutt was nothing short of dazzling. The 29-year-old with pinpoint precision mesmerized American League hitters in the spring and summer, making the All-Star team and compiling a 14–8 record with a league-leading 2.42 ERA.

In 25 starts and 174 $2/3$ innings from the beginning of the season to mid-August, Honeycutt had allowed only 47 earned runs, 37 walks, and just nine home runs. Two years earlier in his debut season with the Rangers, Honeycutt had helped set a club record by pitching the team's fourth consecutive shutout in April en route to an 11–6 record and a 3.31 ERA.

That was a terrific way to start his tenure in Texas after being traded by the Seattle Mariners, along with Larry Cox, Willie Horton, Leon Roberts, and Mario Mendoza, to the Rangers for Richie Zisk, Rich Auerbach, Ken Clay, Jerry Don Gleaton, and Steve Finch.

But after a very disappointing season in 1982, when Honeycutt went 5–17 with a 5.27 ERA, the 1983 season was especially meaningful. And magnificent. With Honeycutt leading the way, the 1983 Rangers led the American League in team ERA (3.31) and fielding percentage (.982). To this day, Honeycutt is still the one and only ERA champion in franchise history.

For his splendor, the Rangers rewarded him—in typical early Rangers fashion—by trading him before the 1983 season came to an end.

On August 19 the Rangers dealt Honeycutt to the Dodgers for reliever Dave Stewart, $200,000, and a player to be named later (Ricky Wright).

Honeycutt was in the option year of his contract in '83 and wanted at least $800,000 for each of the next five seasons. That was more than the Rangers could afford, so they shipped him to Los Angeles for Stewart, a promising 26-year-old flamethrower who was 5–2 with nine saves and a 2.96 ERA at the time of the deal.

Ultimately, both Honeycutt and Stewart would win a World Series together…in Oakland. But the '83 deal was essentially a major dud for both the Rangers and the Dodgers.

Honeycutt won the ERA title in the American League in '83 (though he switched leagues, only his American League starts counted in that compilation), but he was just 2–3 with a 5.77 ERA the rest of the way with the Dodgers. And in two appearances in the 1983 NLCS (won by the Phillies), Honeycutt had a 21.60 ERA. He had solid seasons in 1984 and '86 with the Dodgers, but he was 8–12 in 1985 and only 2–12 in '87 when L.A. shipped him to Oakland, where he found his niche as a reliever over the next six seasons.

Conversely, Stewart came to Texas, where Rangers manager Doug Rader immediately placed him in the starting rotation. He flourished the rest of the year, going 5–2 with a miniscule 2.14 ERA in eight starts for the Rangers.

But in '84 Stewart struggled miserably, going 7–14 with a 4.73 ERA. He had worked on developing a forkball, which the quick-tempered Rader abhorred. Stewart and Rader almost came to blows in the spring of 1985 when Rader demanded that Stewart quit fooling around with the forkball. Stewart was 0–6 in '85 and 12–20 overall with Texas when the Rangers traded him to Philadelphia in September for Rich Surhoff.

The Phillies released him on May 9, 1986, and he was picked by the Oakland A's on May 23, 1986. In Oakland, pitching coach Dave Duncan encouraged Stewart to throw the forkball more often, which helped him to win at least 20 games four straight seasons and to become the MVP of the 1989 World Series—the same Fall Classic where Honeycutt earned his championship ring.

history," Rangers radio announcer Eric Nadel said. "That may be true, but the Lee Mazzilli deal is probably a close second, and it topped the list until the Sosa deal."

Tom Grieve, the organization's assistant farm director in 1982, was in an important personnel meeting in Florida on April 1 with farm director Joe Klein, various scouts, and minor league managers within the Rangers' system when Robinson called Klein with news. The day before, Robinson had traded Al Oliver to Montreal for rookie Dave Hostetler and third baseman Larry Parrish.

That trade generated mixed reviews throughout the organization. But the one that sent the two best young arms in the system to the Mets was unanimously denounced, beginning with Klein, who heard the news and headed straight for a bar to drown his sorrows.

"Joe was so upset that he left the room," Grieve said. "That was the end of the meeting. It was a pivotal moment in our franchise. It was a really bad day."

Grieve immediately suspected the trade would turn out terribly for Texas—and not just because of the loss of top prospects. He had briefly been a teammate of Mazzilli's four years earlier in New York. And he knew that Mazzilli was a dyed-in-the-wool New Yorker who would never be happy playing in Texas.

Grieve was right. The 27-year-old Mazzilli had been used almost exclusively in center field with the Mets, where he hit .303 in 1979 and .280 in 1980. But he'd suffered through a dismal 1981 season, hitting only .228. In fact, Mazzilli had played so poorly that the Mets acquired George Foster during the off-season and planned to use Mazzilli as a fourth outfielder.

The Rangers wanted Mazzilli to hit near the top of the order and start in left field. Instead of embracing the chance to play every day, Mazzilli referred to left as "an idiot's position."

He hit .241 in 58 games with the Rangers, didn't display much power, looked lost in left field, and was such a malcontent in the clubhouse that the Rangers sent him to the Yankees on August 8 in exchange for Bucky Dent.

While the Rangers desperately attempted to salvage something from the trade, the Mets eagerly made plans for the future with their pitching acquisitions. Darling, the Rangers' first-round pick in 1981, reached the big leagues in 1983, posting double-figure win totals for the Mets every year from 1984 through 1989. During that span, he went 86–52 with a 3.40 ERA.

Terrell, who the Rangers had selected in the 33rd round of the 1980 draft, debuted for the Mets late in 1982. He had two solid seasons in New York before being traded to Detroit for third baseman Howard Johnson, one of the primary offensive heroes of the World Series championship team.

"It was one of those trades that seemed to haunt the organization for about a decade or more," former Rangers beat writer Jim Reeves said. "Especially with the success Darling had, the Rangers had to shake their heads regrettably time and time again."

Dave Stewart's Issues off the Field

While Dave Stewart was rather dismal for the 1984 Rangers, he was considered such a standup guy following losses that he was voted as the team's winner of the Harold McKinney Good Guy Award. And Stewart showed up at the Winter Banquet in Arlington to claim his prize...despite the fact that he had recently been arrested in a parked car on a skid-row street in Los Angeles a few days earlier.

Stewart had been caught with a prostitute named "Lucille," who turned out—to Stewart's shock—to be a 27-year-old transvestite named Elson Tyler. Stewart was arrested on suspicion of participating in an act of lewd conduct in a public place, near Sixth and Crocker streets in downtown L.A.

"Mr. Stewart said he was unaware that Tyler was a male until after the arrest," Police Commander William Booth said. "That was his statement, and we have reason to believe him."

The lewd conduct charges were eventually reduced to soliciting, and Stewart was fined $150 and placed on a year's probation. At the Winter Banquet, he apologized to Rangers fans and teammates.

Stewart's first "issues" with the Rangers came in spring training in 1984, when he told a newspaper reporter he had known all along that his Dodgers teammate in the bullpen, Steve Howe, was using cocaine. Stewart admitted to covering for Howe when he was questioned by Tommy Lasorda and other players.

"It's part of growing up, I guess," Stewart told *Sports Illustrated's* Ron Fimrite in 1987. "I was going through a period where one bad thing after another seemed to be happening to me. I've learned a lesson. Now I try to do what's right, knowing that sometimes I'll fall short. Some people might think of me as a hypocrite when I speak against drugs, since I'm the guy who protected Howe, and if I'm talking to a class, they can say, 'Hey, he was the one with the prostitute.' The thing is, I know I'm a sinner. But I do try. I also know you never finish growing."

93 The Fort Worth Strangers: Not Real, but Not Forgotten

In 1979 the Pat Corrales–managed Rangers went 83–79 and finished in third place in the American League West. The Rangers, led by Buddy Bell, Al Oliver, Jim Sundberg, Mickey Rivers, Fergie Jenkins, Bump Wills, Pat Putnam, and others, were a personable, likeable team that finished five games behind the California Angels in the West.

In the grand scheme of things, however, the 1979 Rangers—despite assembling a collection of interesting personalities, all-around good guys, and hustling, hard-working players—were not even the most popular pro baseball team in Tarrant County that year.

That honor would have undeniably gone to the 1979 Fort Worth Strangers, who captured the imagination of the community and the nation en route to winning the American League West by beating the Angels 12–8 on a grand-slam homer by Larrupin' Lou Merkle in the deciding game of the division chase.

What? Never heard of the Strangers?

Don't worry. And don't bother trying to research them on the Internet.

They weren't real. But they were really popular.

"They were fiction. Made up. Figments of my and many imaginations," wrote the late, great Jerry Flemmons in his 1984 book *Plowboys, Cowboys and Slanted Pigs*. "They were not real; they were unreal. Being unreal, the Fort Worth Strangers most of all were not the Texas Rangers. The Fort Worth Strangers were neither a satire on, nor a parody of, the Texas Rangers. Early on, we pledged to separate the teams, resolved to design each Stranger character so he would not in any way resemble a real Texas Ranger player. When

In 1979 the Fort Worth Star-Telegram *ran a series of articles documenting the antics of the fictional Fort Worth Strangers. The* Star-Telegram *even featured photos of the fictional players, including menacing home run hitter Milo Candidi—portrayed by Associated Press writer Mike Cochran.* (Courtesy of the Fort Worth Star-Telegram)

writing strayed too closely to the Texas Rangers, an editor slashed away."

Even though Flemmons, a noted columnist and reporter for 30 years at the *Fort Worth Star-Telegram*, was adamant about distancing the fictional Strangers from the nonfictional Rangers, once the story went national, it was practically impossible to convince the masses that the Strangers were not a parody on the early struggles of the Rangers throughout much of the 1970s.

The idea for the Strangers was hatched during an editors retreat in East Texas in August 1979. When one of those editors approached Flemmons regarding his willingness to write about a fictional baseball team, he was obstinately opposed to the idea.

"No, sorry, I said," Flemmons wrote in *Plowboys, Cowboys and Slanted Pigs.* "September's my vacation. No, got to do some work around the house. Sorry, my back's been acting up lately. No. Never. Absolutely not, it's a terrible idea, and the next morning I sat down at the typewriter and began inventing the Fort Worth Strangers. The Strangers were introduced on Sunday, September 9...with the uncanny kiss of the best of timing and the worst of timing. The worst of timing was that the Texas Rangers were on a losing streak and did not appear to be contenders for the American League West championship. Ranger fans were edgy.

"The best of timing was that September, the dog days of summer, is a dead period in the news business, and life in general. The kids are back in school. Lingering heat is crumpling the spirit. Football has not yet reached its usual feverish, frenetic pitch. And the summer of '79 was not an auspicious time in history. Fuel shortages, long gas lines, high inflation rates, short tempers."

For whatever reason, the fictional and outlandish Strangers struck a chord with many local readers of the *Star-Telegram.* The stories were accompanied by cartoon sketches or actual posed photos of the alleged players, portrayed by members of the *Star-Telegram* staff and other local media members.

Many hardcore baseball fans hated the Strangers. But casual fans and non-sports readers latched onto Flemmons' folksy writing and the wonderfully witty characters on the team: the foul-mouthed Runt Rovinsky; intellectual snob Doc Sisco; Larrupin' Lou, the best shortstop in the league with questionable sexual preferences (remember, this was 1979); menacing home run hitter Milo Candidi (played by the uncle of this book's author, Mike Cochran, of the Associated Press); the incomparable Inca Inca Doo Zepeda; Bones Zygadio; Gloria (Sic Transit) Zepeda Mundi Leonard, the first woman pitcher in professional baseball; and many others.

The Strangers were entirely an invention and project of the *Star-Telegram's* news department. *Star-Telegram* Rangers beat writers Jim Reeves and Bob Lindley had nothing to do with the Strangers. Even the newspaper's publisher, Amon Carter Jr., did not like or approve of the Strangers.

"But for reasons I still cannot understand nor adequately explain," Flemmons wrote, "the Fort Worth Strangers became famous. A fan club was formed by TCU student Skipper Shook.... [Dallas–Fort Worth] radio stations began giving their listeners daily progress reports on the Strangers. Bill Weaver Sporting Goods advertised and began selling T-shirts and hats emblazoned with the Strangers' feisty little logo.

"One customer, apparently serious, asked at Bill Weaver's for directions to the Strangers' luxurious ballpark, Cowtown Stadium, which we fictionally situated on the large parcel of vacant land at South Hulen Drive and the Trinity River, across from the Cullen Davis mansion. The customer...perhaps even drove there expecting to see a modern, multi-use sports facility complete with chocolate nacho–making machines."

By September 17, the *New York Times* printed a long story about the Strangers on the front page of the sports section. The Associated Press, United Press International, and Knight-Ridder news wires followed suit. And on September 18 the Strangers closed out the *CBS Evening News* with Walter Cronkite before an estimated 16 million people.

"From that moment on the Strangers took on a life of their own, were beyond control by me, by any of us," wrote Flemmons, who died in 1999 after a battle with cancer. "They had a life force. And we were compelled to change their destiny.... Because the Strangers became somehow imbued with humanity, it would have been criminal to allow them to lose, so they won the American League West Division by soundly whipping the California Angels in a game recreated and broadcast by WFAA radio for what every-one suspects was a huge audience."

The Strangers were created and crowned in 1979. Then they drifted way into fictional never-never land. But they are often still remembered—at least by those who are old enough to remember them—and revered as the first American League West champions from Tarrant County.

94 Lenny vs. Lucchesi: The Rangers' Worst Confrontation

During the 1977 season, Lenny Randle made national headlines and appeared in *Sports Illustrated* because of the way he hit. Unfortunately for the Rangers, only a handful of the headlines were related to the way Randle connected with his bat, as opposed to his fists.

Randle, originally selected by Washington in the first round of the 1970 June secondary draft, made his debut with the Senators in 1971. He was extremely versatile for the early Rangers, playing seven positions in his first five seasons in Texas. He also hit .302 in 1974.

But as the everyday second baseman in 1976, Randle hit just .224. Even before spring training ended in 1977, manager Frank Lucchesi announced that the Rangers were going with rookie Elliott "Bump" Wills, the son of the legendary Maury Wills, as the starter at second base.

In the previous two seasons, Wills had hit .307 at Double A Pittsfield and .324 while playing for Triple A Sacramento. Nevertheless, the typically mild-mannered Randle could not under-stand why Lucchesi was so quick to promote the rookie over a veteran.

When Randle was asked about how he felt regarding the decision, he threatened to leave the team. Lucchesi fired back his remarks to reporters.

"It's too bad somebody stopped him [from leaving]," Lucchesi said. "I'm tired of these punks saying, 'play me or trade me.' Anyone who makes $80,000 a year and gripes and moans all spring is not going to get a tear out of me."

That obviously stirred Randle's emotions, and on March 28, 1977, as the Rangers were preparing to face the Twins in a spring training game in Orlando's Tinker Field, Randle approached the manager, who was still in street clothes, to discuss the comment. Lucchesi agreed and turned toward the clubhouse, thinking they would go inside where it was more private. It was the last thing he remembered about that morning.

According to Randle, Lucchesi's first words were: "What do you got to say, punk?" Lucchesi later denied making that comment, recalling that he never had a chance to say anything.

Witnesses said the 28-year-old Randle, who was proficient in karate, hit the 49-year-old Lucchesi in the face with a left, a right, and another left. Unconscious before he hit the ground, Lucchesi was helpless as Randle straddled him and continued punching and kicking him.

"The damage was devastating," former Rangers beat writer Jim Reeves wrote for the *Fort Worth Star-Telegram*. "Lucchesi had a concussion, a fractured cheekbone, and shattered ribs. His lip was split, and his eyes were blackened. This wasn't a fight; it was a street mugging. Lucchesi, who had to be rushed to the hospital, never had a chance to defend himself."

Randle's teammate, shortstop Bert Campanaris, eventually moved between them and pushed Randle away. Another teammate, Ken Henderson, had to be restrained when he tried to attack Randle.

Randle then calmly jogged to center field to run wind sprints and shag fly balls. Randle, probably the most popular Ranger among his teammates before the incident, was suspended by the club for 30 days without pay (a loss of $9,000 in salary) and fined $10,000.

While he expressed regret over his actions, Randle never extended an apology.

"All I wanted to do was talk to him," Randle said. "I never thought that it would come to this, but I guess that these things happen in life sometimes."

Lucchesi underwent plastic surgery to repair the damage. He told *The New York Times*: "The plastic surgeon told me that I almost lost my eye, but there's nothing to worry about now."

Randle was subsequently convicted of battery by a judge in Orange County, Florida. He was fined $1,050. Lucchesi filed a civil suit against Randle for a reported $200,000 in damages, but he settled out of court for $25,000.

On April 26 Randle was traded to the New York Mets. And in typical Rangers luck, he had a career season with the Mets in 1977, leading the team in six offensive categories and batting a career-high .304.

95 Pigskins Made Pitching Coach Tom House Memorable

In the grand scheme of things, most pitching coaches are perceived by fans in the same manner that city government officials are typically viewed by local constituents: easy to forget when things are going well, easy to blame when issues arise.

As longtime Rangers beat writer T.R. Sullivan once wrote, "Simple lesson learned about pitching coaches in 20 years of covering baseball: Every pitching coach reaches and improves some pitchers, but misses out on others. They connect with some, fail on others.... Pitching coaches may be the single biggest target of displaced aggression known to man."

The pitching coach is often the first to be fired when a manager is on the hot seat, even though most coaches preach and teach the exact same principles and techniques. That's why most pitching coaches blend into the dugout background; one is indistinguishable from the next.

Perhaps the biggest exception in Rangers history was Tom House, the high-profile pitching coach during the Bobby Valentine era from 1985 to 1992. The bespectacled House earned a doctorate in psychology and earned the "Mad Scientist" and "Dr. Gadget" nicknames from his players for his pioneering techniques and drills.

The one that attracted continual national attention was House's theory that the motions involved in throwing a football could strengthen the muscles in a pitcher's arm while providing a safe method of warming up.

As a result, the Rangers' pregame warm-ups featured a much different flavor than those of other major league teams. "Opposing teams couldn't believe what they were seeing," said the late Rangers TV announcer Mark Holtz, as reported by former beat writer Mike Shropshire. "Neither could the fans when the team was on the road. People realized that Texas was supposed to be a football-crazy state, but this was carrying things too far."

Many opposing players, managers, and coaches mocked House's methods, but some of the Rangers, mainly Nolan Ryan, were his biggest fans. In Ryan's induction ceremony into the Baseball Hall of Fame, he credited House for prolonging his career.

"I was very fortunate to have a pitching coach by the name of Tom House," Ryan said. "Tom is a coach that is always on the cutting edge. And I really enjoyed our association together. He would always come up with new training techniques that we would try and see how they would work into my routine. Because of our friendship and Tom pushing me, I think I got in the best shape of my life during the years I was with the Rangers."

Former Rangers right-handed reliever Greg Harris was also a major proponent of House's techniques. Under House's guidance,

The Scheduling Issues of Edwin Correa

In November 1985 the Rangers sent Dave Schmidt and Wayne Tolleson to the Chicago White Sox for Scott Fletcher, Edwin Correa, and Jose Mota. In hindsight, it was a pretty good deal for the Rangers, as Fletcher spent four years in Texas, playing in 526 games and hitting .280.

But after the first year, it looked much better for the Rangers. In fact, it appeared like an absolute steal.

That's because Correa won 12 games in 1986, establishing a club rookie record with 189 strikeouts. But during the following off-season, Correa, a Seventh Day Adventist, asked the Rangers not to schedule him to pitch between sundown Fridays and sundown Saturdays so that he could "honor the Sabbath" in his own way. The Rangers gave the request diligent consideration and agreed to do their best.

Throughout much of the first half of the 1987 season, Correa was allowed to leave the park at roughly 6:00 PM each Friday, and he didn't return until 6:00 PM Saturday. But in late June 1987, manager Bobby Valentine asked Correa to start the first game of a doubleheader against Minnesota. It began at 5:35 PM, meaning Correa had to be at the park considerably earlier to prepare for his start.

"It's borderline," Correa told former *Fort Worth Star-Telegram* beat writer Jim Reeves. "The sun goes down so late here. Obviously, I would rather pitch the second game. But they told me I had two choices: the first game Saturday or Sunday. And if I pitch Sunday, then I'll have to wait till the next Sunday to pitch again."

Correa bent his beliefs and did what the Rangers asked. He went five innings and allowed six runs in Texas' 11–6 victory. The problem didn't arise again because in July Correa suffered a stress fracture in his shoulder after 15 starts and went on the disabled list. He was 3–5 with a 7.59 ERA in '87. He never pitched in the majors again.

Harris would alternate throwing right-handed and left-handed in the bullpen, as House believed that making pitches with his less dominant arm gave Harris a better idea of the mechanics involved in throwing a variety of pitches. Harris also embraced the football work.

"Throwing the football has the same motion involved with throwing a sinker," he said. "The football keeps your strength up on the follow-through."

Other pitchers on the Rangers staff did not endorse House. As a pitcher with the Braves, Red Sox, and Mariners in the 1970s, House had relied predominantly on his curveball and screwball. That was appropriate, according to some Rangers, as they viewed House as a bit of a screwball.

But the big issue arose when promising young pitchers Jose Guzman and Edwin Correa developed shoulder problems early in their careers. Both youngsters were projected as possible staff aces for many years, but neither completely fulfilled that potential for extended periods of time because of injuries. Speculation arose that House's unusual training techniques may have resulted in the injuries.

"People started getting on House," former Rangers majority owner George W. Bush recalled. "Some called him an eccentric, a radical. The talk was maybe he was not training our people properly. It concerned me. I'm not at all skilled in evaluating Tom House so I went to my friend, Nolan Ryan, and said, 'Does this guy know what he's doing?' He said, 'Absolutely.' He believes in Tom 100 percent. That stopped my inquiry. If Nolan Ryan speaks highly of him, that's good enough for me."

That was good enough for all the Rangers until Valentine was fired. Kevin Kennedy was hired as manager following the 1992 season, and his first move was to hire Claude Osteen to replace House. Meanwhile, House went on to serve as a pitching coach at other major league destinations and eventually at his alma mater,

Southern California. Interestingly, he later abandoned the football-throwing training technique that made him distinguishable among all other pitching coaches.

96 Watch the Movies with Rangers Cameos

The Indians have *Major League* and the numerous (and bad) sequels that followed. The Red Sox have *Fever Pitch, Still We Believe, Game 6,* and *Wait Til This Year,* among others. The Tigers are featured prominently in *For the Love of the Game* and *Tiger Town.*

There's a boy (Gary Coleman) who transforms the San Diego Padres' fortunes in *The Kid From Left Field,* a kid (Thomas Ian Nicholas) who pitches the Cubs to prominence in *Rookie of the Year,* a boy (Luke Edwards) who manages the Twins triumphantly in *Little Big League,* and a pair of orphans (Roger and J.P., played by Joseph Gordon-Levitt and Milton Davis, Jr.) who have the favor of heavenly angels in helping the then–California Angels win the pennant in *Angels in the Outfield.*

And, of course, the Yankees have been featured in numerous movies through the decades, ranging from *Pride of the Yankees* to *61*.* Even the Astros are prominent in the plot of *Night Game,* a 1989 movie where a serial killer strikes only during the Astros' evening games.

Hollywood has not yet jumped on the Rangers bandwagon, although surely Josh Hamilton's story or Matt Bush's comeback journey (hint, hint) would be the equivalent of an Adrian Beltre blast into the left-field bleachers in Arlington: a box-office smash.

At the time of this writing, however, the Rangers have never been the focus or the primary setting of a silver-screen production.

But that doesn't mean the Rangers have never appeared on the big screen.

As a Rangers fan, you should know—and perhaps own—the movies where your team (or the team's stadium) has made at least a cameo appearance.

Let's start with the one you may need the least, the 1997 movie *My Best Friend's Wedding*, starring Julia Roberts, Cameron Diaz, and Dermot Mulroney. Julianne Potter (Roberts) is a 27-year-old New York restaurant critic who receives a call from her longtime friend Michael O'Neil (Mulroney). In college, the two made an agreement that if neither of them were married by the time they turned 28, they'd marry each other.

Four days before Julianne's 28th birthday, Michael tells her he is marrying Kimberly Wallace (Diaz), a Chicago college student whose father owns the White Sox. Roberts travels to the Windy City to break up the marriage, and there is a scene where the Rangers are playing the Sox at Comiskey Park.

From this perspective, however, a much better romantic comedy is *Fever Pitch*, which stars Drew Barrymore and Jimmy Fallon. Fallon's character, a schoolteacher named Ben Wrightman, is the ultimate Red Sox fan, who initially says finding romance is about as likely as his beloved Sox winning the World Series. The movie was originally written with a bittersweet ending, but the Red Sox ended the Curse of the Bambino and won the 2004 World Series. As such, the ending was rewritten. Part of the beauty of the movie is that it includes clips from actual games.

One of those games involves the Rangers. In the movie, the Rangers are portrayed as Boston's 2004 Opening Day opponent, with Stephen King throwing out the ceremonial first pitch. It is also implied that the Red Sox rolled to a win.

Actually, the Rangers opened the '04 season at Oakland, while the Red Sox game was filmed on September 4, 2004. Thanks to a three-run homer by Michael Young and a two-run shot by Rod

Barajas, both off Tim Wakefield, the Rangers built an 8–1 lead and held on for an 8–6 win that snapped Boston's 10-game winning streak. Chris Young picked up the win, Francisco Cordero earned his 42nd save, and King was blamed for snapping the win streak in the *Boston Globe*. Blame the inaccuracies on "Hollywood's creative license."

In the estimation of many movie critics, *Fever Pitch* is a good film, but possibly the best baseball movie of all time also involves a Rangers trivia tidbit.

In 2003 *Sports Illustrated* rated *Bull Durham* as the "Greatest Sports Movie." *Baseball America* also referred to the 1988 film, starring Kevin Costner, Susan Sarandon, and Tim Robbins, as the best baseball movie of all time. The authenticity of the film is first-rate, as director Ron Shelton, who spent five years in the minor leagues, makes sure the baseball players actually resemble players.

Veteran minor league catcher Crash Davis (Costner) is demoted to the Carolina League in Durham to mold raw rookie pitcher Ebby Calvin "Nuke" LaLoosh (Robbins) into a major leaguer. The film is primarily filmed in North Carolina, but near the very end, LaLoosh earns his call-up, and he is interviewed by a female television reporter, reciting the quotes Crash had taught him…at the old Arlington Stadium.

If you attended many games at the old ballpark, you'll instantly recognize the red armchair seats on the second and third decks behind home plate. HSE and WBAP banners are also pictured hanging from the press-box level. And if you look closely on the credits—just above Keith Underwood and Carlton White (the bull mascot that is pegged by LaLoosh early in the movie)—you will see a "thank you" extended to the Texas Rangers.

Without a doubt, the movie that features the Rangers most prominently—and one the whole family can enjoy—is Disney's 2002 film *The Rookie*, based on the true story of Texas-born pitcher Jim Morris (played by Dennis Quaid).

The film documents Morris' remarkable journey from high school coach to major league reliever. Morris, born in Brownwood in 1964, was originally selected 466th in the 1982 amateur baseball draft by the Yankees but did not sign. He was later selected fourth overall in the 1983 draft by the Brewers, but primarily because of arm injuries he was released in 1987, never progressing past Class A. He landed a brief stint with the White Sox organization in 1989 but was again unable to rise past Single A.

Morris eventually became a teacher and baseball coach for Reagan County High in Big Lake, Texas, promising his team he would try out for a major league squad if they won the district title. The Owls did, and Morris tried out for the Devil Rays, delivering 12 consecutive 98 mph pitches. At 35 the Rays signed him, and against the longest of odds, Morris made his major league debut with Tampa on September 18, 1999, in Arlington. He struck out Texas shortstop Royce Clayton on four pitches in his first appearance and made four more appearances later that year. He made 16 major league appearances in 2000 before recurring arm problems ended his career.

The movie touches on Morris' childhood and jumps to when he is a coach. It documents his major league tryout, his family life, his rise through the minor league ranks (with footage shot at Dell Diamond in Round Rock), and his '99 debut in Arlington. The footage in Arlington was shot in 2001, following a Rangers game against Cleveland. Movie directors purposely chose to place actors in the Rays' and Rangers' 2001 uniforms—as opposed to their '99 uniforms—so that they could easily use actual game highlights, particularly with close-up shots of the Rangers, in the movie.

The voice of Rangers public-address announcer Chuck Morgan is also prominent in the movie, but Morgan had a much bigger role than merely announcing as normal. It was his job to encourage fans to stay for extended periods after the game so specific scenes could be shot. For example, there was a scene where Morris was in the bullpen talking to his wife, Lorri. But since that is not feasible in the actual visitors' bullpen at Rangers Ballpark in Arlington, the scene was shot in the home bullpen after the game.

Incidentally, Quaid also came out of the Rangers' bullpen when he entered the game in the movie, a scene shot between the top and bottom of the seventh inning in the actual game between the Rangers and Indians.

But in order for other scenes to look authentic, the directors needed fans in the stands after the game. That's where Morgan factored into the equation.

"It was my job to keep people in their seats after the Cleveland game ended," Morgan recalled. "I did an interview with Dennis Quaid prior to the game, and we aired it on the video board. Quaid talked to the fans about what they were going to see, and what he wanted them to do. We probably had 15,000 to 20,000 people stay for at least a couple hours. When we got down to four or five in the morning, a lot of people had trickled off."

To encourage fans to stay, Morgan arranged for many prizes to be given away.

"They would film a couple scenes, and we would play, *Let's make a Deal* or *Name that Tune*," Morgan said "I'd gone to Disney and told them our ideas. We wanted to offer prizes for staying, and Disney supplied them. We would bring fans down on the field to play these games, and that got a lot of people to stay. Some people left once we ran out of DVD players or other items.

"When the movie came out, it was great to hear your voice, but that night was a lot of fun. It was a long night, and we had a game the next day. That made it tough, but that was a fun night. Playing those games and keeping the people in their seats is what I will always remember about *The Rookie*."

97 Read the Book *Seasons in Hell* by Mike Shropshire

Warning: Unlike Josh Hamilton's book, *Seasons in Hell* does not have an uplifting spiritual message. And this is absolutely not a book to share with less-than-mature audiences.

But for its historical perspective on some of the Rangers' early teams (1973–75)—and its pure adult entertainment value—this book, originally published in 1996, is certainly worth finding at a second-hand bookstore or online.

Mike Shropshire, one of the Rangers' beat writers for the *Fort Worth Star-Telegram* from 1973 to 1975, is an exceptionally gifted humor writer. The entire book is written like the script of an irreverent, candid, and trashy—but very funny—R-rated movie that might star Will Ferrell, Owen Wilson, or Chris Farley.

The greatness of the book involves the behind-the-scenes details and perspectives that only a player, manager, coach, or beat writer could possibly know. Shropshire does an amazing job of portraying just how bad the Rangers were in 1973 and how the amusing and quick-witted manager of the team, Whitey Herzog, dealt with the dismal, talent-deprived roster.

"This team is two players away from being a contender," Herzog told Shropsire during spring training in 1973 while consuming volumes of scotch and soda at the Yard Arm Restaurant, "Sandy Koufax and Babe Ruth."

And prior to that spring training, the manager told Shropshire: "If Rich Billings is the starting catcher again, we're in deep trouble."

When that evaluation was passed on to Billings, he nodded and said, "Whitey has obviously seen me play."

Shropshire also does a fabulous job of detailing the desperation of the Rangers' first owner, Bob Short, in his attempt to put butts in seats at Arlington Stadium.

"Every night was Something Night at the ballpark. Bat Night—they staged about five of those. Ball Night. Cap Night. T-shirt Night. Rangers Keychain Night. Rangers Calendar Night. Yes, even Panty Hose (guaranteed to yield fewer runs than the home team) Night. Still on the drawing board was Insane Relative Night and Law Enforcement Appreciation Night, where Grand Prairie cops would stage a pregame demonstration of interrogation techniques."

Short's most successful ticket-selling promotion of all was the direct "promotion" of David Clyde from high school draft pick straight to the major leagues. Shropshire details Clyde's triumphant debut, the ridiculous expectations placed upon him, and his quick fall from grace. Likewise, Shropshire provides insightful perspective on manager Billy Martin's stunning turnaround in 1974, Jeff Burroughs' disdain for Arlington Stadium, Jim Fregosi's outlandish personality, and so many other characters associated with the early Rangers.

On the other hand, it's pretty easy to understand why Shropshire was ultimately fired by the *Star-Telegram*. He spends way too much time specifying—or gloating about—his excessive drinking and about how he kept a large grocery bag full of premium-grade marijuana under his hotel bed in Pompano Beach, Florida, the dilapidated first spring home of the Rangers.

Shropshire also appears to be preoccupied about the size of pitcher Jim Bibby, who accounted for the first no-hitter in Rangers history. Not in reference to his height or weight, either.

But if you can endure Shropshire's relentless sense of sophomoric humor, *Seasons in Hell* is a very informative and mostly entertaining view regarding the early Rangers. Of course, even the title is a little misleading. The long version of the title is this:

Seasons in Hell: With Billy Martin, Whitely Herzog and 'the Worst Baseball Team in History'—the 1973–1975 Texas Rangers.

The 1974 Rangers were very good, winning 84 games and finishing second in the American League West to an Oakland team that won the World Series. But Shropshire obviously never allowed facts to interfere with a good story or title.

98 Oddibe McDowell Completes the Rangers' First Cycle

During the franchise's first 13 seasons in Texas, several Rangers players came extremely close to hitting for the cycle. Johnny Grubb, for example, produced a four-hit game in 1982 that featured a triple, a home run, and two doubles, but he did not have a single.

Al Oliver and Mickey Rivers also came up a single short of the cycle in the early 1980s. But until the summer of 1985, no Texas player had ever managed to complete the rare feat.

Rookie outfielder Oddibe McDowell changed that with a memorable performance against the Cleveland Indians on July 23, 1985, at Arlington Stadium, showcasing a combination of speed and power that made him the Rangers' first-round draft pick (12th overall) in 1984.

"Oddibe was a really intriguing young talent," recalled former Rangers general manager Tom Grieve. "He had a lot of success in college and was a star on the Olympic team [in 1984], so when he finally came to us, he had some very good experience."

The 5'9", 160-pound McDowell was a two-time All-American at Arizona State, where he'd won the 1984 Golden Spikes Award, presented annually by USA Baseball to the top amateur player in the country. McDowell made an equally impressive impact in the 1984 Olympics, where he was part of a U.S. team that included Will Clark, Mark McGwire, Bobby Witt, B.J. Surhoff, and Barry Larkin. McDowell's two-run homer in the semifinals propelled the Americans to the gold medal round, where they were eventually upset by Japan.

McDowell had been drafted twice in 1981, twice in 1982, and once in 1983 before finally signing with the Rangers in 1984. As a nonroster player invited to spring training in 1985, McDowell hit .360 in 10 Grapefruit League games, but former Rangers manager Doug Rader chose not to bring McDowell to Arlington to start the season. Rader didn't last long with the '85 Rangers, however, and McDowell didn't spend too long in Triple A Oklahoma City, where he hit .400 in 31 games.

Bobby Valentine replaced Rader in mid-May, and Valentine brought McDowell to the big leagues on May 19, installing him as the Rangers' leadoff hitter and center fielder. Although he hit only .239 in 111 games, McDowell finished the 1985 season second on the team with 18 home runs and 25 stolen bases. But Rangers fans remembered him most fondly—and were most excited about his long-term potential for the club—based on what he did on July 23 against the Indians.

McDowell was 4-for-4 with two singles, a double, and a triple entering the eighth inning when he came to the plate against Indians reliever Tom Waddell. Needing a home run to complete the cycle, that's exactly what McDowell delivered.

"I was aware of [the cycle], but I'm not a home run hitter," McDowell said afterward. "I wasn't thinking of hitting a home run. I just wanted to get a hit."

Including the three straight hits he had compiled the previous game, McDowell tied Rico Carty's 1973 club record for eight consecutive hits.

Unfortunately for the Rangers, the rest of McDowell's career in Texas was probably more mediocre than magnificent, and in December 1988 the team dealt him, Jerry Browne, and Pete O'Brien to the Indians for Julio Franco.

But McDowell will forever hold one distinction as a Ranger that can never be matched. He was the only Ranger and was one of just two players, joining Baltimore's Cal Ripken Jr., to ever complete the cycle at the old Arlington Stadium.

99 Scoring the Most Runs in a Game in More Than a Century

Entering the August 22, 2007, doubleheader at Baltimore's Camden Yards, the Rangers offense was in the midst of a particularly anemic stretch. In its previous five games, Texas averaged just two runs per contest and was hitting .190 in those games.

To make matters worse, the team's best hitter, then-shortstop Michael Young, was nursing a sore back, and his health was enough of a concern that the Rangers called up an extra infielder, Travis Metcalf, from their Triple A affiliate in Oklahoma City. But Metcalf certainly wasn't expected to provide an offensive spark. In 18 games at Oklahoma City, he was hitting only .148 with six RBIs in 61 at-bats. And in two earlier stints with the Rangers, he had only six RBIs in 100 at-bats.

Metcalf didn't start the first game, but the Rangers' offensive struggles continued against Baltimore starter Daniel Cabrera, who held a 3–0 lead after the first three innings.

In the top of the fourth, however, Texas' bats finally heated up, igniting a fire that blazed the rest of the night, torching the Orioles and lighting up the scoreboard in record-breaking fashion.

1996 Rangers Rip Orioles with 16-Run Eighth

On April 19, 1996, the Rangers scored four touchdowns against Baltimore but missed two extra points. At least that's what the final score looked like when the four-hour and 15-minute marathon (one minute short of the longest nine-inning game in American League history at that time) came to an end.

Rangers 26, Orioles 7.

"A T-ball score," said Baltimore outfielder Tony Tarasco, as reported by Buster Olney, then of the *Baltimore Sun*.

The game started well for the Rangers and continually improved. Baltimore scored one run off Rangers starter Roger Pavlik in the top of the first, but Texas answered with five runs in the bottom of the frame off Kent Mercker. The Orioles chased Pavlik with five runs in the fourth to tie the score at 6–6, but the Rangers answered with three in the fifth and one more in the seventh to take a 10–7 lead into the eighth inning.

That's when things went crazy.

The Rangers scored 16 runs in the bottom of the eighth—the second-biggest inning in the century at that point—turning a three-run game into a 19-run blowout. It became so absurdly lopsided that infielder Manny Alexander finished on the mound for the Orioles. Alexander recorded the final two outs but gave up five runs in the process. He finished the game with a 67.50 ERA.

All 26 runs were earned, so the Orioles' team ERA jumped from a league-leading 3.00 to 4.53. Meanwhile, the Rangers pounded out 19 hits in 38 official trips to the plate. Many of those plate appearances came in the historic eighth inning, as 19 Rangers batted.

The first three Texas hitters reached base in the eighth off Baltimore reliever Armando Benitez. Jesse Orosco relieved Benitez and didn't fare much better. He retired just one of the nine hitters he faced.

With the bases loaded, Juan Gonzalez doubled off Orosco, and two batters later, Dean Palmer homered to make it 15–7. Rusty Greer, Mark McLemore, and Kevin Elster followed with singles; Darryl Hamilton walked; Dave Valle singled; and Will Clark walked to chase Orosco and make it 17–7.

Alexander then entered the game to pitch and promptly walked Gonzalez, Mickey Tettleton, and Palmer to make it 21–7. Greer hit a sacrifice fly, followed by another walk to McLemore. Elster then delivered a grand slam to make it 26–7. The inning finally ended when Hamilton grounded out in his third plate appearance of the inning. The Orioles issued eight walks in the inning.

"It was funny," said Rangers slugger Juan Gonzalez, who homered and drove in six runs. "A walk, a walk, a base hit, a home run. It was great for us."

Orioles manager Davey Johnson saw it much differently. He was particularly disturbed that Tettleton tagged up on Greer's sacrifice fly and advanced to third with the Rangers already in complete control.

"I've seen it all," Johnson said. "But guys tagging up from second with an 18-run lead. It's ridiculous."

For the Rangers, Palmer homered twice and drove in five runs, while Elster also collected five RBIs in the highest-scoring game by an American League team since Chicago beat Kansas City 29–6 on April 23, 1955.

"It's amazing," said Mercker, who allowed eight runs in 4⅓ innings. "It's a fluke. I bet you anything—anything—that'll never happen again. Ever."

Mercker was wrong. Eleven years later on August 22, 2007, the Rangers surpassed the 26 runs scored by the 1996 squad by scoring 30 runs in the first game of a doubleheader...against the Orioles.

Jarrod Saltalamacchia and Ramon Vazquez each homered twice, Marlon Byrd launched a grand slam in the sixth, and Metcalf, after arriving in Baltimore that afternoon and entering the game in the seventh, drilled a grand slam in the eighth as the Rangers exploded for a 30–3 win.

The 30 runs were the most in Major League Baseball since the nineteenth century and set an American League record. The Boston Red Sox scored 29 runs in 1950 against the St. Louis Browns, and the Chicago White Sox matched that in 1955 against the Kansas City Athletics.

Every Texas starter had at least two hits and scored at least one run. Every starter except Nelson Cruz had an RBI. The 49 total bases on 21 singles, two doubles, and six home runs was also another single-game club record.

In the nightcap, the Rangers gained a sweep and set another American League record for most runs in a doubleheader in a 9–7 victory. The previous American League record for most runs in a twinbill was 36 by the 1937 Detroit Tigers.

Metcalf added four RBIs in the second game, including a game-tying single in the eighth. That gave him eight RBIs in the doubleheader, tying a club record held by Toby Harrah and Bobby Bonds.

"[Metcalf] did a great job," manager Ron Washington told T.R. Sullivan of MLB.com. "He stepped right in and did an awesome job."

Metcalf's grand slam was the first of his career and just his second home run in the big leagues.

"I'm tired," Metcalf said after his historic evening. "It's been a long day. It was amazing. I've never been a part of something like that. It was just a great day all around. It was *amazing*, in capital letters."

In the opener, the Rangers scored five runs in the fourth, nine in the sixth, 10 in the eighth, and six more in the ninth. Saltalamacchia and Vazquez each finished with a career-high seven RBIs, two short of the club record for one game set by Ivan Rodriguez in 1999. Saltalamacchia and David Murphy tied a club record by scoring five runs, done previously by Pete O'Brien, Luis Alicea, and Kevin Mench.

"It was unbelievable," Saltalamacchia said. "That was ridiculous. I've never been in a game like that in my life. We were just seeing the ball and hitting the ball. You can't help but laugh. It's nothing they did. It's not like they made a lot of errors. It was just ridiculous. Everybody is going to remember it."

100 The Chan Ho Park Debacle

Following the conclusion of the 2001 season—a year in which the Rangers finished third in the American League in runs scored (890), first in home runs (246), but dead last in the American League West standings (43 games out of first)—general manager John Hart began tinkering with a pitching staff that had become notorious for yielding high-fives.

Not the kind where teammates slap hands in celebratory fashion. The high-fives—5.71, to be specific—references the Rangers' wretched team ERA in '01, ranking last in baseball...by at least a mile or more. So Hart, the mastermind of the triumphant transformation in Cleveland from 1995 to 2001, began renovating the Rangers pitching staff.

Kind of like a tornado "renovates" a trailer park.

One off-season earlier, Tom Hicks had signed Alex Rodriguez to a 10-year, $252 million contract, which proved to be a disastrous financial drain. Hart's first big move as Rangers general manager, however, proved to be even more deplorable.

At least A-Rod produced big numbers, as promised. Not so with Chan Ho Park, the Korean right-hander whom Hart signed in December 2001 to be the ace of the Rangers staff. Park, then 28, had been perceived as the prized free-agent pitcher on the market. Texas had the inside track on him because Park's agent, Scott Boras, also represented A-Rod.

Lucky Rangers, huh?

Park came to Texas with some impressive credentials. He'd gone 15–11 with a 3.50 ERA for the Los Angeles Dodgers in 2001, leading the team in wins, starts (35), innings pitched (234),

The Early Legend of Pete Incaviglia

After an absolutely astonishing collegiate career at Oklahoma State, Peter Joseph Incaviglia—"Inky," for short—was drafted by the Montreal Expos with the eighth pick of the 1985 amateur draft.

He had just one demand for the Expos: No minor league ball. Not Triple A, not Double A, nothing. Straight to "the Show." Big leagues or bust. The Expos were flabbergasted.

The Rangers were not.

Five months after the Expos drafted him, they shipped Incaviglia to Texas for Jim Anderson and Bob Sebra. Coming off a 99-loss season in 1985, the Rangers were willing to make Incaviglia the 15th player in draft history to debut in the majors without playing minor league ball.

And why not? In three seasons at OSU, Incaviglia blasted 100 home runs in 213 games and generated a career slugging percentage of .915. In his final season at OSU, Incaviglia crushed 48 homers, produced 143 RBIs, and compiled a 1.140 slugging percentage.

He still holds NCAA records for career and single-season home runs. With new bat restrictions implemented by the NCAA in 2011 to reduce the exit speed of the ball, those numbers will likely never be broken. Or even approached.

Incaviglia reported to spring training in 1986 with a Babe Ruth–like image that seemed to be an impossible burden for a youngster to bear. But then his legend grew larger in spring training, as Incaviglia ripped seven homers in the Grapefruit League and smashed one ball that put a hole in the outfield wall at Pompano Beach Park. No joke. It really tore through a piece of the fence.

It should be noted that the wooden fence was rotting, but Incaviglia and the Rangers received some terrific media exposure because of it.

Inky made his major league debut on April 8, 1986, and collected his first hit. Three days later, he hit the first of what would be 30 home runs for the year.

It was a remarkable debut season except for one thing: Incaviglia struck out a league-high 185 times, an average of once every 3.28 trips to the plate. Over the next three seasons, his home run totals dropped each year, but he continued piling up the strikeouts. In five seasons with the Rangers (1986–90), Incaviglia hit 124 homers, drove in 388 runs, and struck out 788 times while compiling a .248 batting average.

In 1991 he signed with the Tigers and also played with the Astros, Phillies, Orioles, and Yankees in his 12 major league seasons. For his career, he averaged 26 homers and 161 strikeouts per 162 games. Cooperstown will not be calling, but in 2007 Incaviglia was elected to the College Baseball Hall of Fame.

strikeouts (218), and opponents' batting average (.216). And his best season came in 2000, when he went 18–10 with a 3.27 ERA.

But even though he'd played his home games at pitcher-friendly Chavez Ravine, Park had been susceptible to the home run ball and had only finished in the top 10 in the National League in ERA once in his six full seasons with L.A. Park had also been nagged by back injuries in his final year as a Dodger. Nevertheless, Hart and the Rangers signed Park to a five-year deal worth $65 million.

To clear payroll, the Rangers opted not to offer a contract to Rick Helling, who'd won 20 games in 1998 and had gone a team-best 12–11 in 2001. Hart also traded left-handed starter Darren Oliver and signed right-handed starter Dave Burba, who'd won 56 games in Cleveland the previous four seasons. In the bullpen, Hart added Todd Van Poppel, John Rocker, and Jay Powell.

He probably couldn't have done more damage with a wrecking ball. None of those moves really worked out, unless it was *for* Helling or Oliver after leaving Arlington. Helling helped the Diamondbacks win the National League West in 2002, and Oliver pitched well for the Red Sox. But of all the bad moves Hart made, the worst was signing Park.

He strained a hamstring during spring training in 2002 and aggravated it in an Opening Day loss to Oakland, sending him to the disabled list for over a month. He was out another three weeks in August because of blisters. In his final eight appearances, he strung together six quality starts, five wins, and a 3.35 ERA. But the short-term success didn't become a long-term trend.

His injuries continued in ensuing years, and the Rangers eventually traded him to San Diego before the trade deadline in 2005. For his Rangers career, Park was 22–23 with a 5.65 ERA and five trips to the disabled list. In return for Park, the Rangers landed first baseman Phil Nevin from the Padres. Nevin hit .182 for the Rangers in 29 games in 2005 and .216 in 46 games in 2006 before being dealt to the Cubs for Jerry Hairston.

Works Cited

Books

Flemmons, Jerry. *Plowboys, Cowboys, and Slanted Pigs.* Fort Worth, TX: TCU Press, 1984.

Hamilton, Josh, and Tim Keown. *Beyond Belief: Finding the Strength to Come Back.* New York: FaithWords, 2010.

Herzog, Whitey, and Kevin Horrigan. *White Rat: The Whitey Herzog Story.* New York: HarperCollins Publishers, 1988.

Jenkins, Fergie, and Lew Freedman. *Fergie: My Life from the Cubs to Cooperstown.* Chicago: Triumph Books, 2009.

Shropshire, Mike. *Seasons in Hell: With Billy Martin, Whitey Herzog, and "the Worst Baseball Team in History," the 1973–1975 Texas Rangers.* Lincoln, NE: University of Nebraska Press, 2005.

Magazines

Anderson, Bruce. "Not Enough Hurrahs for Harrah." *Sports Illustrated,* May 17, 1982.

"Business: Mad Eddie." *Time,* May 26, 1980.

Callahan, Gerry. "Texas Rangers: The Meat of the Order Has Been Beefed Up, but It's Hard to Be Bullish on Texas Pitching." *Sports Illustrated,* March 29, 1999.

Fimrite, Ron. "Deep In the Heart, for a change." *Sports Illustrated,* May 20, 1974.

—— "The A's New Stew Can Do: Dave Stewart, Once Washed-Up, Is Now Awash in Success." *Sports Illustrated,* October 5, 1987.

Gammons, Peter. "He's an Angel Now: California Manager Doug Rader has Overcome His Devilish Reputation and Raised His Ball Club to Heavenly Heights." *Sports Illustrated,* August 7, 1989.

Hannon, Kent. "One Mindless Moment." *Sports Illustrated,* June 6, 1977.

—— "Huffing and Puffing in Texas: Owner Brad Corbett is Kicking and Screaming About the Rangers' Showing." *Sports Illustrated,* August 7, 1978.

Hecht, Henry. "Life with the Gozzlehead: Mickey Rivers Often Seems to Speak No Known Tongue, but His Bat Is Eloquent." *Sports Illustrated*, October 6, 1980.

Keith, Larry. "A Good Old Country Boy: Mike Hargrove Sure Does Like Snuff, and Eats Up Steak and AL Pitching." *Sports Illustrated*, July 28, 1975.

Kurkjian, Tim. "Good As It Gets: Kenny Rogers of the Texas Rangers Joined an Elite Group of Perfect-Game Hurlers." *Sports Illustrated*, August 8, 1994.

—— "Been There, Never Done That: To Appreciate the Current Rangers, One Must Consider Their Former Culture of Losing." *ESPN The Magazine*, October 17, 2010.

Montville, Leigh. "The Great Survivor: In Seven Seasons, Rangers Manager Bobby Valentine Hasn't Even Won His Division. But He Still Has His Job—and That's a Triumph." *Sports Illustrated*, April 6, 1992.

—— "Texas-Sized Trade: The Oakland A's Sent Superstar Jose Canseco to the Rangers in a Deal That Was Both Bold and Bewildering." *Sports Illustrated*, September 14, 1992.

Murphy, Austin. "Rising to the Top of the Game: Ruben Sierra of the Texas Rangers Was a Near MVP in '89—Not Quite Good Enough for 'the Next Clemente.'" *Sports Illustrated*, April 16, 1990.

Nack, William. "Rangers Risin' in a Texas-Sized Flip-Flop, the Rangers Have Vaulted to the Top with Newcomers like Julio Franco and Nolan Ryan." *Sports Illustrated*, May 1, 1989.

Neff, Craig. "Cincy Welcomes a Good Buddy: Traded at Last, Buddy Bell Wound Up with His Father's Old Ball Club." *Sports Illustrated*, July 29, 1985.

Patoski, Joe Nick. "Team Player: How He Ran the Texas Rangers and Became, Finally, a Successful Businessman." *Texas Monthly,* June 1999.

Pearlman, Jeff. "The Texas Rangers' Young GM." *Fast Company Magazine,* July 1, 2008.

Roberts, Selena. "Mr. 252: During His Three Years with the Rangers, Alex Rodriguez Was Synonymous with His $252 Million Contract, and the Pressure Brought Out the Best and the Worst in Him." *Sports Illustrated*, May 11, 2009.

Stephenson, Tom. "Ten Reasons Why the Texas Rangers Will Win the Pennant." *D* magazine, May 1975.

Telander, Rick. "Wild Thing: Mitch Williams, the Cubs' Ace Reliever, Is as Unpredictable as the Movie Character He Idolizes. But Who Cares? It Works." *Sports Illustrated*, August 28, 1989.

Verducci, Tom. "Shopping Daze: Juan Gonzalez Goes to the Tigers, Presaging Other Stunning Deals." *Sports Illustrated*, November 15, 1999.

—— "Can You Say Cliff Hanger?" *Sports Illustrated*, November 01, 2010.

Whitford, David. "Glory Amid Grief: Battered but Unbowed by Family Tragedy, Ferguson Jenkins Looks toward His Induction into the Hall of Fame." *Sports Illustrated*, July 15, 1991.

Wulf, Steve. "You Don't Know Me, Says Al." *Sports Illustrated*, April 21, 1980.

—— "Basebrawl: Nolan Ryan's Pummeling of Robin Ventura Epitomizes a Season Marred by Bench-Clearing Incidents." *Sports Illustrated*, August 16, 1993.

Newspapers

Anderson, Dave. "Pitcher John Burkett Never Expected to End Up with Texas When Trade Rumors Were Flying." *New York Times*, October 3, 1996.

—— "The Mismanaged Career of David Clyde." *The New York Times*, June 22, 2003.

Andro, Anthony and Jeff Wilson. "Former Texas Ranger Jeff Burroughs Makes Appearance in Camp." *Fort Worth Star-Telegram,* March 15, 2011.

Futterman, Matthew. "Why Everything Is Bigger in Texas: Along with A-Rod, Many Former Rangers Are Accused of Using Banned Substances." *The Wall Street Journal,* February 20, 2009.

Giannone, John. "Bombers Take Texas." *New York Daily News,* October 3, 1996.

Johnson, Chuck. "Numbers Tell the Story for Braves' Franco." *USA TODAY,* June 10, 2004.

Madden, Bill. "Burkett Controls Yanks." *New York Daily News,* October 2, 1996.

Madigan, Tim. "Longtime Rangers Fan 'Zonk' Still Keeps the Beat as Ballpark Drummer." *Fort Worth Star-Telegram,* October 16, 2010.

—— "Rangers' Radio Announcer Has Given Every Game His All Since 1979." *Fort Worth Star-Telegram,* October 23, 2010.

McCarron, Anthony. "Where Are They Now? Former Met Jon Matlack Can't Stay Away from the Game." *New York Daily News,* November 29, 2008.

Mosier, Jeff. "New Rangers Sign on Rise as Fan Favorites Claw, Antlers Appear Less Often." *Dallas Morning News,* September 1, 2010.

—— "Texas Rangers Sue Former Owner Tom Hicks Over Parking at Ballpark in Arlington." *Dallas Morning News,* April 13, 2011.

Nightengale, Bob. "The Pitcher Is Perfect, but Greer Gets the Save." *L.A. Times,* July 29, 1994.

—— "Hall of Fame Snub Disappoints Rafael Palmeiro." *USA TODAY,* January 7, 2011.

Olney, Buster. "Rangers Rip O's, 26–7, On 16-Run 8th. *"Baltimore Sun,* April 20, 1996.

Rogers, Phil. "The Cubs' Trade of Rafael Palmeiro to Texas in 1988 Remains Unpopular with Fans, but It Paved the Way for Sammy Sosa." *Chicago Tribune,* June 18, 2002.

—— "Still Obeying His Speed Limit: Ageless Julio Franco Credits Rest, Relaxation for His Longevity." *Chicago Tribune,* March 14, 2007.

Schmuck, Peter. "Rangers Throw It Away in 12th, 5–4." *Baltimore Sun.* October 3, 1996.

Seminara, Dave. "Branded for Life with 'the Mendoza Line.'" *St. Louis Post-Dispatch,* July 6, 2010.

Sherman, Ed and Paul Sullivan. "Rader Enjoying His Second Time Around." *Chicago Sun-Times,* May 14, 1989.

Shlachter, Barry. "Texas Rangers Claw and Antlers Gestures Become Hit Apparel." *Fort Worth Star-Telegram,* October 17, 2010.

Shpigel, Ben. "Jim Kern is Saving Memories: Years after His Career, Quirky Reliever Still Has Stories to Tell." *The Dallas Morning News*, May 22, 2005.

Wilkerson, William. "The Inside Story of Rangers' 'Claw' and 'Antlers.'" *The Dallas Morning News*, October 22, 2010.

Online Resources

Beck, Jason. "Bruising Retort: Tigers Roar in Game 3." MLB.com, October 12, 2011. http://detroit.tigers.mlb.com/mlb/gameday/index. jsp?gid=2011_10_11_texmlb_ detmlb_1&mode=recap_home&c_id=det

Burchett, Scott. "Notes: Hall of a Time for Hough." MLB.com, August 2, 2003. http://texas.rangers.mlb.com/news/article.jsp?ymd=20030802&content_id=458357&vkey=news_tex&fext=.jsp&c_id=tex

Cockcroft, Tristan. "Ranking The Ballparks: The Best Hitters' and Pitchers' Parks Based on Five Years of Data." ESPN.com, *March 18, 2010. http:// sports.espn.go.com/fantasy/baseball/flb/story?page=mlbdk2k10ballparks*

Durrett, Richard. "Jet Stream Has Balls Flying All Over." ESPNDallas.com, April 22, 2011. http://espn.go.com/blog/dallas/texas-rangers/post/_/id/4863436/jet-stream-has-balls-flying-all-over-the-place

—— "'Juan Gone' Lived Up to His Nickname." ESPNDallas.com, July 11, 2011. http://sports.espn.go.com/dallas/mlb/columns/story?columnist=durrett_richard&id=6746977

Goldstein, Richard. "Johnny Oates, 58, Cerebral Catcher and Manager, Dies." *The New York Times*, December 25, 2004. http://query.nytimes.com/gst/fullpage.html?res=9D02E1DB1E30F936A15751C1A9629C8B63

Gonzalez, Alden. "World Series Spotlight Finally Shines On Vlad." MLB.com, October 23, 2010. http://mlb.mlb.com/news/article.jsp?ymd=20101023&content_id=15810854&vkey=news_mlb&c_id=mlb&partnerId=rss_mlb

"Hicks: Gonzalez's Injuries and Early Retirement Suspicious." ESPN.com, June 21, 2007. http://sports.espn.go.com/mlb/news/story?id=2910661

Johns, Greg. "Feldman Carries Heavy Load to Save 'Pen." MLB.com, October 10, 2011. http://mlb.mlb.com/news/article.jsp?ymd=20111010&content_id=25596134&vkey=news_mlb&c_id=mlb

Kaegel, Dick. "Treanor Knows All About Texas Jet Stream." MLB.com, April 23, 2011. http://kansascity.royals.mlb.com/news/article.jsp?ymd=20110423&content_id=18153734&notebook_id=18153736&vkey=notebook_kc&c_id=kc

Kearney, Seasmus. "Roger Moret." The Baseball Biography Project. http://bioproj.sabr.org/ bioproj.cfm?a=v&v=l&bid=1326&pid=9962

McTaggart, Brian. "Pudge Sets Record for Games Caught." MLB.com, June 18, 2009. http://mlb.mlb.com/news/article.jsp?ymd=20090617&content_id=5376890&vkey=news_mlb&c_id=mlb

Morris, Adam J. "#41 -- The 50 Greatest Rangers of All Time." Lone Star Ball, October 22, 2006. http://www.lonestarball.com/2006/10/23/03135/065

—— "#35 -- The Greatest Rangers of All Time." Lone Star Ball, May 23, 2011. http://www.lonestarball.com/2011/5/23/2183315/35-the-greatest-rangers-of-all-time

Newberg, Jamey. "Swapping Stories: The Canseco Trade. Rangers Dealt Sierra, Witt, Russell for A's slugger in 1992." MLB.com, August 23, 2007. http://texas.rangers.mlb.com/news/article.jsp?ymd=20070823&content_id=2165464&vkey=news_tex&fext=.jsp&c_id=tex

Paulling, Daniel. "Harrah, Sierra Set for Rangers HOF Induction." MLB.com, August 1, 2009. http://texas.rangers.mlb.com/news/print.jsp?ymd=20090801&content_id=6183342&vkey=news_tex&fext=.jsp&c_id=tex

"Rangers Fan Favorite Greer Packs in Comeback, Retires." SportsLine.com, February 20, 2005. http://www.cbssports.com/mlb/story/8213368

Reeves, Jim. "Hicks Wasn't All Bad; It Just Seems Like It." ESPNDallas.com, January 29, 2010. http://sports.espn.go.com/dallas/mlb/columns/story?columnist=reeves_jim&id=4867116

Sanchez, Jesse. "Where Have You Gone, Buddy Bell?" MLB.com, August 7, 2002. http://texas.rangers.mlb.com/news/article.jsp?ymd=20020807&content_id=98675&vkey=news_tex&fext=.jsp&c_id=tex

—— "Oates Makes a Return to Texas." MLB.com, August 1, 2003. http://mlb.mlb.com/news/article.jsp?ymd=20030801&content_id=455975&vkey=news_mlb&fext=.jsp&c_id=mlb

—— "Four Elected Into Rangers' HOF." MLB.com, August 2, 2003. http://texas.rangers.mlb.com/news/article.jsp?ymd=20030802&content_id=457799&vkey=news_tex&fext=.jsp&c_id=tex

—— "Notes: Oates Fondly Remembered." MLB.com, August 6, 2005. http://texas.rangers.mlb.com/news/print.jsp?ymd=20050806&content_id=1160181&vkey=news_tex&fext=.jsp&c_id=tex

—— "Fans Spark Move to Stop the Wave in Texas." MLB.com, August 4, 2011. http://texas.rangers.mlb.com/news/article.jsp?ymd=20110804&content_id=22739058&vkey=news_tex&c_id=tex

Schlegel, John. "Mikey Likes It: Napoli, Mom Thrilled by Series." MLB.com, October 18, 2011. http://mlb.mlb.com/news/article.jsp?ymd=20111017&content_id=25695332&vkey=news_mlb&c_id=mlb

Schulman, Henry. "Aurilia Taught Brewers' GM a Lesson." SFGate.com, April 7, 2003. http://articles.sfgate.com/2003-04-07/sports/17488690_1_alou-times-three-rich-aurilia-san-diego

Sullivan, T.R. "Ryan Named Rangers Hometown Hero." MLB.com, September 27, 2006. http://texas.rangers.mlb.com/news/article. jsp?ymd=20060927&content_id=1686153&vkey=news_tex&fext=. jsp&c_id=tex

—— *"Greer Set to Join Rangers Hall of Fame." MLB.com, August 9, 2007. http://texas.rangers.mlb.com/news/article.jsp?ymd=20070809&content_ id=2139413&vkey=news_tex&fext=.jsp&c_id=tex*

—— "Emotional Sierra Enters Rangers Hall." MLB.com, August 2, 2009. http://mlb.mlb.com/news/article.jsp?ymd=20090801&content_ id=6190610&vkey=news_tex&fext=.jsp&c_id=

—— "Pudge Rejoins Rangers for Chance to Win." MLB.com, August 18, 2009. http://texas.rangers.mlb.com/news/article.jsp?ymd=20090818&content_ id=6482172&vkey=news_tex&fext=.jsp&c_id=tex

—— "Blyleven's Stay in Texas Short, Sweet." MLB.com, January 5, 2010. http://texas.rangers.mlb.com/news/article.jsp?ymd=20100105&content_ id=7877526&vkey=news_tex&fext=.jsp&c_id=tex

—— "How 'Bout Them Rangers! Texas Takes Game 3." MLB.com, October 30, 2010. http://mlb.mlb.com/news/article.jsp?ymd=20101030&content_ id=15912270&vkey= recap&c_id=mlb

—— "Feldman Activated; O'Day Optioned to Triple-A." MLB.com, July 14, 2011. http://mlb.mlb.com/news/article.jsp?ymd=20110714&content_ id=21786666&vkey= news_mlb&c_id=mlb

—— "Big-Game Rangers Pull Even in ALDS." MLB.com, October 2, 2011. http://texas.rangers.mlb.com/mlb/gameday/index. jsp?gid=2011_10_01_tbamlb_texmlb_1&mode=recap_home&c_id=tex

—— "Trop Notch: Rangers on Cusp of ALCS Return." MLB.com, October 3, 2011. http://texas.rangers.mlb.com/mlb/gameday/index. jsp?gid=2011_10_03_texmlb_tbamlb_1&mode=recap&c_id=tex

—— "Belt-Trey: Three Homers Power Texas to ALCS." MLB.com, October 5, 2011. http://texas.rangers.mlb.com/mlb/gameday/index. jsp?gid=2011_10_04_texmlb_tbamlb_1&mode=recap_away&c_id=tex

—— "Full Nelson: Cruz Belts Walk-Off Slam in 11th." MLB.com, October 10, 2011. http://texas.rangers.mlb.com/mlb/gameday/index. jsp?gid=2011_10_10_detmlb_texmlb_1&mode=recap_home&c_id=tex

—— "Rangers Strike First but Fizzle in Game 3." MLB.com, October 12, 2011. http://texas.rangers.mlb.com/mlb/gameday/index. jsp?gid=2011_10_11_texmlb_detmlb_1&mode=recap&c_id=tex

—— "Rangers Book Return Trip to World Series." MLB.com, October 16, 2011. http://texas.rangers.mlb.com/mlb/gameday/index. jsp?gid=2011_10_15_detmlb_texmlb_1&mode=recap_home&c_id=tex

—— "Starting Pitchers Expect to Rise to Challenge." MLB.com, October 17, 2011. http://mlb.mlb.com/news/article.jsp?ymd=20111017&content_ id=25694264&vkey=news_mlb&c_id=mlb

Vittas, John. "Shaping the Rangers #6: The Sammy Sosa Trade." LoneStarDugout.com, February 17, 2008. http://rangers.scout. com/2/729837.html

Young, Jeff. "Lenny Randle's Attack on Mgr. Led to Fine, Suspension and Lawsuit." Baseball @ Suite101, March 10, 2011. http://jeff-young. suite101.com/lenny-randles-attack-on-mgr-led-to-fine-suspension-and- lawsuit-a357580

About the Author

Rusty Burson is the Director of Membership and Communications at Miramont Country Club in Bryan, Texas. He is formerly the associate editor of *12th Man Magazine*, where he covered all Texas A&M sports from 1996 to 2014. Burson, a 1990 graduate of Sam Houston State, has authored 17 previous books and is a former sportswriter with the *Galveston Daily News* and *Fort Worth Star-Telegram*. He attended his first Rangers game in 1972, worked at the old Arlington Stadium every summer from the time he could drive until he graduated college, and has made certain that his family members—wife, Vannessa; son, Payton; and daughters Kyleigh and Summer—are fanatical in following the only major league team in Texas to ever win a World Series game.